THOUSAND PEAKS

PERMISSIONS:

Acknowledgement is made to the following for their kind permission to use materials from their publications:

Selections from *Sosan Taesa and his Handbook for Zen Students.* © 1978 Rebecca Bernen. Reprinted by permission of the author.

Selections from Robert E. Buswell Jr., *The Korean Approach to Zen: The Collected Works of Chinul.* © 1983 University of Hawaii Press. Reprinted by permission of the publisher.

Selections from Thomas Hoover, *The Zen Experience.* © 1980 Thomas Hoover. Reprinted by permission of New American Library.

Selections from *Korean Journal,* Vol. 5, 11 and 21. Reprinted by permission of the Korean National Commission for Unesco, Korea.

Selections from Kyung-bo Seo, *A Study of Korean Zen Buddhism Approached through the Chodangjip.* © 1969 Kyung-bo Seo. Reprinted by permission of the author.

Selections from Zen Master Seung Sahn, *Dropping Ashes on the Buddha.* © 1976 Providence Zen Center. Reprinted by permission of Providence Zen Center.

Selections from Zen Master Seung Sahn, *Only Don't Know.* © 1982 Providence Zen Center. Reprinted by permission from Providence Zen Center.

THOUSAND PEAKS

Korean Zen—
Tradition and Teachers

by Mu Soeng Sunim

Parallax Press
Berkeley, California

Printed in the United States of America

Library of Congress Cataloging-in-Publication Data pending
ISBN 0-938077-03-1

Cover photo of Monks Entering the Temple by Lee, Kwan-jo. Reprinted from the book *Search for Nirvana*, published by Seoul International Tourist Publishing Company, with permission of the publisher.

Cover calligraphy by Jakusho Kwong, Roshi.

Cover design by Gay Reineck.

Parallax Press
P.O. Box 7355
Berkeley, California 94707

Contents

Foreword

By Zen Master Seung Sahn

I am very happy to welcome this book on the history of Korean Zen. It is especially valuable because it is the first English-language book to give an in-depth look at the Zen tradition in Korea, and was written by a monk trained in that tradition. Mu Soeng Sunim combines a scholarly treatment of the subject with a genuine, heartfelt appreciation of the tradition, possible only to one who has practiced it daily for a number of years. His book speaks from the heart.

Today, Korean Zen is taking root in the West. Understandably, the branches of this tree in America are different from those in Korea. Sometimes the two seem to contradict each other, but they both emerge from the same trunk, the same roots. In its pure form, Buddhism is not confined to any geographical location or culture. Many people have fixed ideas about what Buddhism is or what it should be, but in fact, every country has its own Buddhism. These ideas present difficulties for some people; others are liberated by them. If we cling to our idea of what American Buddhism is, or what Korean Buddhism is, we become narrow-minded, and the world of duality, of opposites, appears. The true Korean idea is "no idea."

America is a wonderful country. Some people call it a melting pot. When any religion or idea first comes to America, it is thrown into the pot, where it simmers along with all the other religions and ideas that have come before. Soon it is digested and a new style appears..This is true for any religion, philosophy or business idea that comes here—it mixes with what is here already, and something new appears. But the point of American Buddhism is the same as Korean or Japanese or Chinese Buddhism: to let go of our opinion, our condition, our situation. Our American direction is to practice together with other people, become harmonious, find our true human nature and become world peace.

Knowing the history of a tradition is like meeting our ancestors. Many years ago in India, one person appeared and got enlightened. We know him as Shakyamuni Buddha. He is our original root. Then Bodhidharma, the 28th Ancestor, went to China. At that time in China there were many kinds of Buddhism, all scholarly and metaphysical. Bodhidharma brought something vital to that situation: a method for correctly perceiving our mind, that is, Zen meditation. From China the teachings of Zen spread to Korea, Japan and Vietnam. As Mu Soeng Sunim points out in this book, Buddhism suffered intense persecution in Korea for 500 years. But persecution is a strong force, and it caused many dedicated monks to appear. The stories of many great monks and Zen masters who appeared during that time are told here.

Now Zen has come to America and although its form is changing, the roots of a tree don't move. As this book will show you, an important root of Zen is from Korea. If we come face to face with our ancestors, we will have a much wider understanding not only of Korean or Chinese or Japanese Zen, but also the Zen tradition that is evolving now in America. In writing this book, Mu Soeng Sunim has rendered us a great service, bringing us face to face with these ancestors. I hope that everyone will benefit from reading it, that you will become wide and open and harmonious, and that everyone will soon become world peace.

Preface

Korean Zen has been one of the best-kept secrets of the Orient. Until the early 1970's, western knowledge of Zen came almost entirely from Japanese sources—primarily the writings of D.T. Suzuki and, through him, Alan Watts and Christmas Humphreys. Most westerners who wanted to study Zen went to Japan or to the centers in the U.S. and Europe started by Japanese teachers.

The first hint of a *Korean* Zen came in 1972, with the arrival of two *Son* (Korean pronunciation of "Zen") masters, Seung Sahn Soen Sa Nim, who started the Providence Zen Center, in Rhode Island, and Ku Sahn Sunim, the resident master at Songgwang-sa monastery in Korea, who paid a brief visit. When Master Ku Sahn returned home with one student, it marked the first time in its thousand-year history that Songgwang-sa, the premier Zen temple in Korea, opened its doors to a westerner.

Seung Sahn Soen Sa Nim established, in rapid succession, residential Zen Centers in Cambridge, New Haven, New York, Los Angeles, Berkeley, and Toronto; and within 15 years, traveling and teaching throughout North and South America and Europe, he established a network of more than 50 groups stretching from Poland to Brazil, known as the Kwan Um Zen School. In addition centers have been founded by other Korean monks in the West, including the Zen Lotus Society of Samu Sunim in Ann Arbor and Toronto.

Despite this flowering, very little is known in western Zen circles about the Korean tradition. Americans just do not have the same fascination with Korea as they do with China and Japan, even though the U.S. fought a war there 30 years ago and reports concerning Korea's current political situation fill the news daily. For all the hundreds of books on Chinese and Japanese Zen, there are only a handful of books in English on Korean Zen.

Korean Zen, as we shall see, is one of the few living links with the ancient schools of Chinese Ch'an Buddhism, and it is in imminent danger of extinction in Korea's headlong rush for social and economic modernization (i.e. westernization). Because of cultural differences, the forms of Zen which have evolved in

Korea, as well as Vietnam, Japan and elsewhere, have been quite different from one another, and for this reason, each has much to offer as we develop new and unique expressions of Zen here. It is the intention of this volume to narrow the gap in our knowledge of Korea's Zen tradition and teachers and to encourage future scholars to delve more deeply into this timely, important subject.

I have benefited greatly from the pioneering translation efforts of a number of scholars of Korean Buddhism. Dr. Kyung-bo Seo's translation, *A Study of Korean Zen Buddhism Approached through the Chodangjip*, as well as his rendering of the oral tradition of Korean Zen, provided a wealth of information for the writing of this book. Robert E. Buswell Jr.'s *The Korean Approach to Zen: The Collected Works of Chinul* is a model of translation and scholarship that will inspire all future scholars of Korean Buddhism. Becky Bernen's thesis at Harvard, *Sosan Taesa and his Handbook for Zen Students*, provided valuable information about an obscure part of Korean Buddhist history. To all these scholars my deeply-felt thanks and appreciation.

I am much indebted to Nancy Herington who has not only been a generous friend but also critically edited the manuscript. Many thanks also to Sam Rose and Arnold Kotler for their enthusiasm in seeing this book published, and to Paul Weigand and Therese Fitzgerald for long hours typing and proofreading.

Most of all, I am grateful to my teacher, Zen Master Seung Sahn Soen Sa Nim, whose inimitable retelling of Buddhist stories from Korea's oral tradition inspired me to research its historical background. His bringing the Korean Zen tradition to North America has transformed the lives of myself and many others. I am also thankful to many friends at the Ontario Zen Centre, the Providence Zen Center and all the other centers in Kwan Um Zen School who have provided bonds of friendship and practice. Without their support, it would have been difficult to journey alone. All errors of interpretation or presentation in the book are, of course, mine alone.

Mu Soeng
Cumberland, Rhode Island
July 1987

NOTES ON THE TEXT

Although the Korean word for Zen is *Son*, throughout this book I have used *Zen* and *Son* interchangeably in dealing with the Korean tradition. Zen is now an established part of our vocabulary in the West and it seems quite appropriate to use it in place of *Son*.

The Korean word *Sa* means both a temple and a teacher. When used with a temple's name such as Haein-sa it denotes a place of teaching; when used with an individual's name such as Seung Sahn Soen-sa, it means a teacher.

Keeping in the mind the western reader's familiarity with Japanese Zen, I have tried to give both Japanese and Chinese renderings for Korean words whenever possible. In such cases the abbreviations read C=Chinese, J=Japanese, and K=Korean.

A note on the sources: Where original research or translations are available, footnotes are provided at the end of the book. However, many of the stories told here are part of the Korean oral tradition. Corroboration or authentication of such stories is not easily possible. I have discarded some of the improbably wilder stories and have used only those which seem pertinent to the narrative at hand or can contribute to an increased understanding of the tradition.

THOUSAND PEAKS

Sites of Prominent Buddhist Temples in Korea

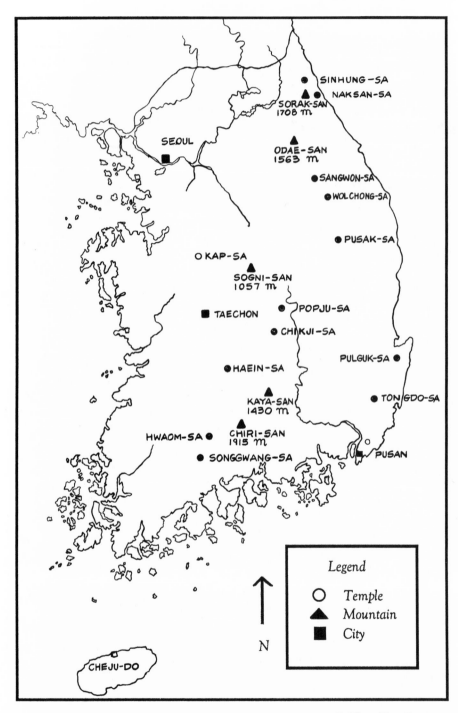

SINHUNG-SA

NAKSAN-SA

SORAK-SAN
1708 m

SEOUL

ODAE-SAN
1563 m

SANGWON-SA

WOLCHONG-SA

PUSAK-SA

O KAP-SA

SOGNI-SAN
1057 m

TAECHON

POPJU-SA

CHIKJI-SA

PULGUK-SA

HAEIN-SA

KAYA-SAN
1430 m

TONGDO-SA

HWAOM-SA

CHIRI-SAN
1915 m

SONGGWANG-SA

PUSAN

Legend

○ Temple

▲ Mountain

■ City

N

CHEJU-DO

P. Bhatt/Sam Rose

CHAPTER ONE

Korean Zen: An Introduction

Korea boasts what is probably the strongest Mahayana Buddhist Church in the world. For a thousand years, from the middle of the fourth century to the beginning of the fifteenth, Buddhism was the state religion, and it left an indelible imprint on Korean culture and thinking. To an even greater extent than in China or Japan, the culture of Korea has been Buddhist throughout most of its history.

Korean Zen (K: Son), too, is distinct from its Chinese and Japanese counterparts and has a unique and rich tradition of its own. Despite five hundred years of persecution under the Confucian-dominated Yi dynasty (1392-1910) and vigorous attempts by the occupying Japanese authorities in this century (1910-1945) to dilute the core of its practice, the orthodox monastic sangha of Korea has not only survived but has managed to preserve the tradition of hard training, total dedication and the rigorous life of the earliest Zen (C: Ch'an) communities in China.

Comparisons with Japanese Zen are inevitable. Korean Zen has a tone and flavor which is quite distinct from the Japanese Zen. It is less formal, even rustic, more spontaneous and closer in form and spirit to the original Ch'an tradition of T'ang dynasty China

(618-907). Where Japanese Zen is given to aesthetic considerations in multitudinous forms, Korean Zen is earthy, natural and unpretentious. Koreans are earthy people, ready and easy to laugh, and these qualities are reflected in their Zen and Buddhist traditions. As we shall see again and again, Zen never assumed a distinct, cultural personality in Korea's popular imagination apart from its Buddhism. In Japan, the reverse was true almost from the very beginning. Patronized by the samurai warriors of Kamakura, it was as far removed from the strongholds of Kyoto and Nara Buddhism as Calvin's version of Christianity was from Rome. Since the samurai needed their own culture in Kyoto's dandified, imperial court, Zen served them as a religion, a military discipline and a fount of the arts all rolled into one.

Large numbers of Korean Zen monks were illiterate. This may partially account for their traditional antipathy toward the sutra-reciting Doctrinal School. The harsh, mountainous environment of their monasteries may have convinced them that their time was better utilized in farming whatever arable land they had rather than reading the sutras! Here again we have the echoes of Ch'an communities of ancient China who were able to survive repeated persecutions against Buddhism largely because they were economically self-reliant farming communities. The famous motto for Zen monks, "A day of no work is a day of no eating," is not without its economic history. Since Korean Zen had to survive in remote mountains amidst harsh conditions and persecution, and since a large number of its monks could not read or write, the Korean Zen tradition has been overwhelmingly oral. No records of formal talks or theses in beautifully-written calligraphy have been preserved from generation to generation. What we have instead is a rich folklore, recounting stories of Zen eccentrics and sages, no doubt embellished and turned as each re-teller's fancy took flight. And that somehow seems quite appropriate. The tradition of Zen is, after all, anecdotal rather than scholarly.

> The anecdote, incidentally, is the perfect Ch'an teaching device, since it forces the listener to find its meaning in his own inner experience. The sermon provided the theoretical basis for an idea,

but the anecdote showed the theory in action and made the listener share in a real experience, if only vicariously.[1]

Subsequent generations of Zen students may sometimes take the stories in *Blue Cliff Record* or *Mumunkwan* a bit too reverently, but for the participants in these stories and their contemporaries, these exchanges were an expression of personal freedom. In a rationalistic, Confucianist culture where all expressions were prescribed and regulated by institutionalized norms and sensibilities, these expressions of freedom were quite intoxicating and liberating. The Zen anecdote, in the form of *kong-an* (J: koan) study, continues to perform that function even today.

Today, large Korean temples combine, within one compound, different Buddhist practices which in other Buddhist countries may be seen as antithetical to each other. In one temple complex, for instance, there may be a sutra-reading hall, a hall for ritual devotional offerings, a hall for ritual chanting, and a meditation hall for Zen practice. Today in Korea, Zen (Son) lives under the same roof with the Doctrinal (Kyo) school. There are almost no large exclusively Zen-oriented temples. In the mountains, one can find very small temples which are devoted exclusively to Zen practice, but these are off-the-beaten-track and are not visited by curiosity-seekers. For centuries, there were fierce rivalries between the Zen and Doctrinal schools in Korea, but a merger between the two in 1935 created the Chogye Order, which has become the repository and administrator of Korea's traditional celibate, monastic sangha. Under its auspices, Korean scholars of Korean Buddhism, though a relatively new breed, are trying to sift through their oral tradition to piece together a reliable history of their Zen and Buddhist traditions.

Despite the strident controversy between the Zen and Doctrinal schools, Korean Buddhism has had a tendency for syncretism and ecumenism from its beginning, largely due to the influence of the monk Won Hyo. As one scholar of Korean Buddhism noted:

> Early on, however, the Koreans, somewhat like the Sung dynasty Chinese Buddhists, found an important role for themselves as

preservers and interpreters of the greater Buddhist tradition. By
treating evenhandedly the vast quantity of earlier material produced by Chinese Buddhists, the Koreans formed what was in
many respects the most ecumenical tradition in Asia. It is this
feature which makes Korean Buddhism so fascinating today, for
the tradition is a repository of many forgotten qualities of ancient Chinese Buddhism. And with the apparent obliteration of
Buddhism from China, it offers us a means of evaluating and, in
certain cases, still experiencing directly some of the finest flower-
ings of Chinese Buddhist culture.[2]

In keeping with this ecumenical tradition, a Korean Zen master
may unhesitatingly recommend a mantra practice to a student,
such as reciting Kwan Seum Bosal (the name of the Bodhisattva of
Compassion), to help the student keep a one-pointed mind. This
seeming contradiction between a "self-power" practice (Zen) and
an "other-power" practice (incantation) is an offshoot of the syncretic trend in Korean Buddhism. Within the context of East
Asian Buddhism, as John Blofeld has pointed out in his numerous
writings, the paths of Pure Land (invoking the name of Amitabha
Buddha or Kuan-yin) and Ch'an (Zen) were considered to be of
equal efficacy by adepts in China.

The daily liturgy in Ch'an temples in China and Zen temples in
Korea is indeed a Pure Land rite. At the same time, it includes a
poem:

> If you wish to thoroughly understand
> All the Buddhas of past, present and future,
> Then you should view the nature of the Universe,
> As being created by the mind alone.[3]

A pure Zen sentiment, if ever there was one. Recommendations
of a mantra practice by a Zen master are by no means universal
within Korean Zen; but overall, name and form do not demand
the same adherence in Korean Zen as they do in Japanese Zen.

It is instructive to note the role of a Zen master in contemporary
Korean Buddhism. Korean Zen is normally not accessible to ordi-

nary Koreans or even to ordinary Buddhists. In Japan, Zen has been, for centuries, integrated with popular culture. Today, Japanese office and factory workers do *zazen* (sitting meditation) en masse in their workplace as part of their work ethos. In Korea, on the other hand, Zen has always been regarded as a mysterious mountain-ascetic practice, in much the same way that yogis are perceived in India. A Zen Master is regarded as a wise man with special powers—part ascetic, part shaman, part counselor. Members of the laity would seek audience with a Zen master not necessarily to gain clarification of basic Buddhist insights but for help with personal problems. Hence, the recommendation of a mantra practice by a Zen master with a view to help the student cut off his or her thinking is a bestowal rather than a contradiction of Zen practice.

Korean Zen has no sub-divisions like the Rinzai and Soto Zen sects of Japan. Traditional Korean Zen has been dominated by the kong-an style of practice (which, in Japan, is identified exclusively with the Lin-chi or Rinzai school), but Koreans insist that their tradition predates Lin-chi and is *Chogye* Zen. Chogye (C: Ts'ao-chi) is the mountain in south China where the sixth patriarch, Hui-neng, had his temple, hence, an insistence that their tradition is derived directly from the sixth patriarch. We shall have a look at these historical details when we come to the history of Korean Zen proper.

The training of a Korean Zen monk or nun is radically different from their Japanese counterparts. After ordination, a novice may choose to pursue sutra studies or do Zen training. All larger monasteries have facilities for sutra studying, a course that usually takes six years and is devoted mainly to studying Mahayana texts. Haein-sa is the premier temple in Korea for sutra studies. The novice may, on the other hand, choose to devote himself to training in Zen and may enter a small Zen temple or a Zen hall in a larger monastery. The recent trend is for monks to pursue Zen training after completing their sutra studies.

Life in a Korean Zen temple for both new and senior monks revolves around sitting two three-month retreats a year, in winter and summer. The Zen meditation hall itself (K: Son Bang; J: Zendo) is a bare floor, covered with varnished, yellow paper and heated from underneath. These floors, known as *ondol*, have been used in Korea for hundreds of years to keep warm during cold seasons. The doors to the meditation hall are traditional paper-screen sliding doors (J: shoji) that allow the sunlight to enter in soft, warm tones. The room is simple and unadorned; the small, unobtrusive altar has a mirror hanging over it to symbolize the pure, original mind. Two rows of cushions run down the length of the hall and the monks sit on these during daytime meditation and sleep on them at night.

During the three-month retreat, variously called *yong maeng jong jin* ("to leap like a tiger while sitting") or *kyol che* ("tight Dharma"), the monks are not allowed to leave the monastery compound and must follow the retreat schedule. The day begins, as it begins every day of the year, at 3:00 in the morning with a monk walking around the compound chanting a *dharani*. In larger temples, the big bell is also sounded 108 times. When the chanting is finished, all the monks are expected to gather in the meditation hall. They bow three times to the altar and start sitting, which continues for the rest of the day. The sitting periods are usually fifty minutes long followed by ten minutes of brisk walking. Depending on the temple, there are one-hour breaks during the day for two or three meals. After the meals, the monks use the remaining time to rest or go for a walk in the surrounding hills.

The meditation hall itself is separate from all other buildings in the compound. Just before the mid-day meal, the monks walk in a single line in their formal robes to the main Buddha hall where the entire community gathers for a service. After the service, they walk in single file to the dining hall for their lunch. The three meals of the day are identical—rice, kimchee (pickled cabbage), soup, and some condiments on a side tray. They day usually ends at 9:00 in the evening; the monks simply put two cushions lengthwise and go to sleep.

The days of the full and the new moon are for ritual head-shaving and bathing. Next morning the retreat participants recite the temple rules, and in the afternoon the Zen master delivers a formal lecture (J: teisho) from a high podium. The Zen master also gives a formal talk at the beginning and at the end of the retreat. These talks are given in the lecture hall and the whole community gathers to listen. Sometimes the Zen master may give informal talks to retreat participants in the meditation hall itself. Other than these formal or informal talks, there is no structured or personal contact between the monks and the Zen master. The monk sits on his cushion in the meditation hall, hour after hour, day after day, and concentrates on his *hwatu* (C: hwa-tou); there is no one patrolling the meditation hall with a long stick (as is the case in Japanese Zen training halls) to wake up those who are sleeping or feeling drowsy, or even to keep a straight sitting posture. As a result, a Korean Zen monk is left to his own devices to deal with drowsiness, boredom or lack of effort. Most monks, when they are feeling sleepy, slip out during the walking meditation and take a cold shower.

While a monk may receive any hwatu from his teacher to work on, most novice monks work on "What is this?" (*Im-oo-ko*). If a monk feels that he has penetrated deeply into his hwatu, he may go over to the master's quarters and present his understanding. Otherwise, there is no need to "check" with the Zen master. The monk is quite independent. In Korean Zen, there are no progressive series of kong-ans to be "passed," nor is there a fixed period of training. If a monk makes a breakthrough in his hwatu practice, he is expected to defeat, or at least hold his own with, his teacher as well as three other Zen masters in "Dharma combat." From these masters he gets *Inka* or a seal of approval. Receiving Inka is an indication that one has completed his "homework." A monk may then get "Transmission" in the lineage from his teacher. Nuns may get Inka from a teacher but are not allowed to get Transmission either from a male teacher or female teacher; hence there are no lineages of nuns in Korea.

The three months of retreat are followed by three months of *hae jae* (or "loose Dharma") during spring and autumn. Most of the monks disperse at the end of the retreat and many travel from temple to temple. Most travel first of all to their own teacher to pay their respects and also to discuss their practice with him. Although the tradition of *unsui* (floating cloud) monks, the wandering monks with no fixed home, is still maintained in Korea, their numbers are not very large. Many monks who travel during hae jae periods may do so to see old friends or to make contact with some other teacher in a different temple. Those who wish may remain at the retreat temple and continue their practice in whatever fashion they choose. Each season a new group forms for another retreat.

As a monk's practice grows, he may place himself under the guidance of a teacher with whom he feels particular affinity and may stay at his teacher's temple for an extended time. Even then it is probable that he will travel to another temple to participate in winter and summer retreats.

Individual retreats, lasting from 100 to 1,000 days, are more common in Korea than in Japan. These retreats are often done in isolated hermitages. Every large temple has a number of hermitages spread out in the hills beyond the main compound. A temple near Seoul has arrangements for six-year retreats. The monk is locked into a small room with a bathroom and a small trap-door in the wall through which food is put two or three times a day. There the monk stays for six years. The retreatant's choice is either to go crazy or become enlightened! Another temple on Mount Chiri has similar facilities for six-year retreats, but its participants do a group retreat and are not allowed to leave the meditation hall where the retreat is being held.

Nuns follow the same rules and the same structure for their three-month retreats as do the monks. There are only a handful of nunneries in Korea where nuns may do Zen retreats during winter and summer months. Also, nuns tend to travel much less during their *hae jae* periods; most stay at their own temple during this time and help with attending to the needs of the parishioners.

In studying Korea's Zen tradition, one is struck again and again by the fact that an overwhelming number of monks entered the temple as young boys, sometimes only seven or eight years old. Teen-aged monks are quite common. Almost all of them were orphans or destitute youngsters who entered the temple as errand-boys, took their vows in their teens and, more often than not, spent the rest of their lives serving one or a number of temples. The temple has thus, traditionally, provided an economic, social and religious system wherein the orphans and the destitute could not only find shelter but also an environment in which to grow spiritually, and make a contribution to the tradition that nurtured them. Perhaps the fledgling Buddhist monastic tradition in the West could learn a few lessons from this model.

Buddhism came to the Korean peninsula as a religion under "state protection." Throughout its history, there has been a symbiotic relationship between Buddhism and the ruling dynasties, characterized by patronage and munificence on the part of the royal house in exchange for ritual prayers for prosperity and longevity. This support for the royal house was demonstrated most noticeably during the Hideyoshi invasions of 1592 and 1598 when a monk's militia provided effective resistance against the invader. This symbiosis continues even today in the form of a Monks' Militia for National Defense (*Hoguk Sungdan*), organized and administered by the Chogye order, the official-administrative arm of Korea's largest Buddhist sect. All monks must serve the military draft through this militia.

Before we go on, a word of caution is in order. In the West, many of us have the impression that Zen in Japan is an independent tradition. Whether or not this is true, it is by no means the case in Korea. To separate the history of Korean Zen from that of Korean Buddhism is an arbitrary act. The two are intertwined. Zen is an organic part of the larger Korean Buddhist history, and we cannot talk of Korea's Zen without reference to its Buddhism.

CHAPTER TWO

Indian Buddhism and Chinese Ch'an

Throughout its long and varied history, Buddhism has shown extraordinary flexibility in adapting to new social environments. It has aptly been called "The Vagrant Lotus;" for its history has been one of transmigration from one culture to another. Unlike Christianity and Islam, both of which sought to dominate and convert indigenous religious beliefs, Buddhism has always accommodated and adapted itself to local beliefs. Consequently, Buddhist cultures in every country into which it has been introduced have been distinct. Chinese Buddhism turned out to be radically different from Indian Buddhism; Korean Buddhism is in sharp contrast to Japanese Buddhism. The same is true of Buddhist cultures in Thailand, Vietnam, Cambodia, Burma, Sri Lanka and Tibet. Each has a unique personality.

Following the death of the Buddha Shakyamuni in 483 B.C., his followers split into two major groups, known as Hinayana (Lesser Vehicle) and Mahayana (Greater Vehicle). The origins of this split remain unclear to this day. There was no open schism, no radical break. There was no Martin Luther nailing his theses on the church door. The process of the split probably took place gradually over two or three centuries. What seems most likely is that there was mild dissent over how to interpret the *Vinaya* or monastic rules which the Buddha had sanctioned during his lifetime. The dissenters wanted these rules to be flexible enough to include the laity which, even during Buddha's lifetime, had become a major component in the emerging new order. These dissenters later came to be known as the *Mahayanists*. If meditation practice and striving for *nirvana* had infused the earlier Hinayana (or Original Buddhism) with its religious vitality, the Mahayana doctrine developed with the Bodhisattva ideal at the core of its belief-system. In any case, after a period of slow decline, orthodox Hinayana moved southward to Sri Lanka, Burma and Thailand. The more flexible Mahayana, which taught that any practical method of reaching salvation was generally acceptable, moved westward to Central Asia and China, and northward to Tibet.

Of all these movements, the transplanting of Mahayana Buddhism from India to China must rank as one of the landmark events in religious history. Buddhism was to undergo a peculiar Chinese transformation in its new homeland and would heavily influence Chinese culture and civilization. After supplanting Taoism as the main belief-system in China, Buddhism entered Korea and Japan. This Chinese Buddhism, constantly modified as it went from country to country, was to have a far-reaching, long-lasting, impact on all the satellite cultures of China—Korea, Japan, Laos, and Vietnam. Mahayana Buddhism's early acceptance of local deities as a means of drawing the masses to Buddhist temples for eventual study of the more orthodox Buddhist practices proved highly congenial to the Chinese, and later to the Koreans and others.

The first contacts between Indian Buddhism and China are lost in the haze of antiquity. The influx began most likely in the first century of the Christian era, probably through merchants and missionaries carrying copies of Buddhist texts and scriptures traveling along the fabled "Silk Road" through Central Asia and northern China. The first recorded Buddhist personage in China is one An Shih-kao (fl. 147-170 A.D.) who was most likely an Indian monk. It is said that he first visited Loyang (then the capital of Han China) in 150 A.D. and undertook the translation of Buddhist texts into Chinese. By 170 A.D., we are told, he had translated 115 volumes of 95 scriptures. What these scriptures were is not known.

Tao-an (312-385) is the first important figure in the evolving native Mahayana tradition in China. He is known to have studied the *Prajña Paramita* sutras and was influenced by the cult of Amitabha Buddha (the Pure Land sect), which had made inroads into Chinese consciousness by that time. His disciple, Hui-yuan (334-416) was a monk and became the founder of the Chinese Pure Land Sect on Lushan Mountain on the Yangtze River and established the first Buddhist community in China. The Pure Land Sect survives to this day with great vigor in all the countries of East and Southeast Asia. Though a monk, Hui-yuan was close to the nobility of the capital and introduced Chinese intellectuals to the sophisticated metaphysical ideas of Mahayana Buddhism.

The translation of Buddhist scriptures into Chinese took a quantum leap with the arrival in 401 A.D. of Kumarajiva (343-413) at Chang-an (the western capital). An Indian, and a follower of Nagarjuna's Middle Way, he established a translation institute at Chang-an. In a brief span of ten years, he produced remarkable results. His brilliant, gifted, and short-lived disciple, Seng-chao (384-414) combined the metaphysical speculations of the Middle Way with the doctrines of Chuang-tzu, Lao-tzu and the Neo-Taoists to produce a remarkable synthesis, which would become the forerunner of the Zen tradition. As Heinrich Dumoulin has written, "The relationship of Seng-chao to Zen is to be found in his orientation toward the immediate and experiential perception of absolute truth, and reveals itself in his preference for the paradox as the means of expressing the inexpressible."[4]

Another of Kumarajiva's outstanding disciples, Tao-sheng (360-434), has been called the "actual founder of Zen" because of his espousal of a new doctrine of instantaneous enlightenment. However, Tao-sheng's doctrine was based not so much on meditational practices (as was the case with mature Ch'an and Zen traditions), but on a radical reinterpretation of the sutras. It encountered vigorous opposition from his contemporaries, most prominent among whom was Hui-kuan (d.443 ?), still another disciple of Kumarajiva from the translation institute. Ironically, Hui-kuan's disciple, Fa-yuan (d.489), shared Tao-sheng's views and explained his interpretation of the doctrine to Emperor Wen-ti in 436 at a public assembly. He became a footnote, albeit a prominent one, in the early period of Chinese Buddhist history.

While Kumarajiva and his disciples were translating the sutras and making Mahayana metaphysical speculations appealing to the Chinese intellectuals, a great meditation master arrived from India. Buddhabhadra (359-429), while not as great a scholar as Kumarajiva, devoted his best energies to meditation. Upon his arrival in China, he lived for some time with Kumarajiva in Chang-an, but when his stay became unwelcome, he moved to Hui-yuan's community on Lushan Mountain, the first Pure Land monastery. Today, Buddhabhadra is best remembered for his translation of the *Avatamsaka Sutra* which became the basic text of the Hua-yen (K: Hwa-om) school. The future development of Chinese Buddhism was to come from the twin sources of the sutra-oriented followers of Kumarajiva and the meditation-oriented followers of Buddhabhadra.

By the time Bodhidharma (ca. 470-532), the legendary founder of the Ch'an sect of Buddhism, arrived in southern China in 520, Mahayana Buddhism was already established as the dominant religion of the Chinese, at least in the areas where the authority of the converted rulers counted. This conversion of the rulers was at the expense of the Taoists who, understandably, hated the rulers for abandoning them. They despised the Buddhists even more. When an emperor like Wu (r. 502-49) converted, he became a fanatic Buddhist.

> Emperor Wu led Buddhist assemblies, wrote learned commentaries on various sutras, and actually donated menial work at temples as a lay devotee. He also arranged to have all the Chinese commentaries on the sutras assembled and catalogued. Concerned about the sanctity of life, he banished meat (and wine) from the imperial table and became so lax about enforcing criminal statutes, particularly

capital punishment, that critics credited his good nature with an increase in corruption and lawlessness. While the Taoists understandably hated him, the Buddhists saw in him a model emperor. Quite simply, Emperor Wu was to southern Chinese Buddhism what Emperor Constantine was to Christianity.[5]

It was in Emperor Wu's court that Bodhidharma appeared shortly after his arrival in China. Whether by invitation or on his own initiative is not known. In perhaps the single most dramatic encounter in the history of Zen Buddhism, the Emperor enumerated to the visiting monk all the good deeds he had done, charities donated, temples built, sutras translated, and so on. Then he asked his guest, "What do you think is the merit of all this?" To this Bodhidharma's replied, "None whatsoever, your majesty." Quite taken aback by the brutal directness of this answer, the Emperor asked a second question, "What is the most important principle of Buddhism?" To this Bodhidharma replied, "Vast emptiness." This answer was, no doubt, equally perplexing to the emperor who, in exasperation, finally asked who exactly was the bearded stranger standing before him. Bodhidharma cheerfully told him he had no idea. Perhaps the encounter was equally unsatisfying to both parties, for we learn that shortly thereafter Bodhidharma crossed the Yangtze River just outside Nanking and headed north.

The legend of Bodhidharma says that he finally stopped at the Shao-lin monastery, near Loyang in northern China. Here he is reputed to have sat meditating in a cave, looking at a gray wall, for nine years. He came to be known to subsequent generations as the *pi-kuan* (or wall-gazing) Brahmin. These, then, are the origins of Ch'an (Zen) meditation. Just sitting and looking at a blank wall. This practice in itself may have been one of the many *dhyana* (literally, "to concentrate or pay attention;" origin of the word ch'an or zen) practices to be found in the India of Bodhidharma's time. But the introduction of it into China at a time when Mahayana Buddhism was exclusively sutra-oriented, and its intellectuals enthralled by metaphysical speculations, was to challenge the very efficacy of the sutra approach.

In a famous stanza attributed to Bodhidharma and now a corner-stone of Zen tradition, the uniqueness of the "wall-gazing" practice is asserted thus:

> A special transmission outside the scriptures;
> Without depending on words and letters;
> Directly pointing to one's mind;
> Understanding one's own nature.

Other legends of Bodhidharma and of his successors and their place in Zen history belong to a proper study of Ch'an tradition and need not detain us here. The next person of interest to us in the history of Chinese Zen is Hui-neng (638-713), the so-called "Sixth Patriarch" since he received his "Dharma Transmission" from Hung-jen (601-674), the Fifth Patriarch in line of succession from Bodhidharma. As a fatherless boy, Hui-neng and his mother sold wood in the marketplace in a small village near Canton to support themselves. One day, the teen-aged boy heard a monk, in the marketplace where he sold his wood, recite a passage from the *Diamond Sutra*: "Let your mind function freely, without abiding anywhere or in anything." Upon hearing these words, Hui-neng was instantly enlightened. Upon inquiry, he found that the monk reciting the sutra was a follower of Hung-jen, the Fifth Patriarch, who had a monastery in northern China.

Shortly thereafter, Hui-neng made his way to Hung-jen's mona-stery. Hung-jen recognized the boy's enlightenment and secretly transmitted to him Bodhidharma's robe and copy of *Lankavatara Sutra* as symbols of the Patriarchate. Hui-neng's stay at Hung-jen's monastery, his participation in a *gatha* contest testifying to his awakened nature, the "transmission," and his subsequent flight south to escape the fury of his rival monks, make for one of the most colorful stories in the Zen tradition. What is important to us here is Hui-neng's doctrine of "sudden enlightenment."

In the *Platform Sutra* (the only Buddhist sutra ever written by a Chinese, part autobiography and part collection of sermons), Hui-neng asserts that a condition of "no-thought" is a necessary pre-lude to enlightenment. The challenge to the fledgling Ch'an tradition, and to Chinese Buddhism in general, was the assertion that meditation was not sufficient or even necessary to arrive at the state of "no-thought." Hui-neng fails to explain how to get to this state, but his doctrine nonetheless marks a watershed moment in the history of Zen. His successors in southern China, founders of the iconoclastic *Hung-chou* school of Zen, adopted him as their "patriarch" and ushered in an era which is now called the "Golden Age of Zen."

With Hui-neng, Chinese Zen entered a new phase. Until his flight from Hung-jen's monastery (after the secret transmission of the patriarchate), the school of Ch'an had been one of the many Buddhist schools in and around Chang-an, the capital of northern China. There it competed with other teachings for favor and patronage by intellectuals at the imperial court. With Hui-neng's establishment of a temple in southern China, near Canton, Ch'an came to be rural, economically self-reliant through farming, anti-intellectual and inconoclastic. The southern Chinese Ch'an was characterized above all, by its disassociation from scholarship and sutra reading, firmly grounded in the experiences of daily life.

The founder of the Hung-chou school, and the creator of what is known today as Rinzai Zen, is the famous Ma-tsu Tao-i (709-788). As towering a figure in Zen history as Bodhidharma or Hui-neng, Ma-tsu (K: Ma-jo) introduced radical and groundbreaking ideas into the Ch'an tradition. He became the inventor of "shock tactics" for jolting novices into a condition of "no-thought" and thus bringing them into enlightenment. He invented such techniques as asking a novice an unanswerable question and, while the person struggled to fathom any sense in the question, delivering an ear-splitting shout in his ear to jolt him into a non-dualistic state of mind. Other tricks included shouting the person's name just as he was about to leave or delivering a sharp blow as the novice pondered an unanswerable question, to bring him back to immediate reality.

Ma-tsu and his successors in the "Golden Age" developed a repertoire of tricks in order to break through conceptual constructs. They redefined "enlightenment" in simple terms to mean understanding (intuitively, not rationally) your own true nature—

who you are and what you are. Towards this end, any gesture or action, or even silence, could be used as a legitimate and effective teaching device. The Hung-chou school came to be identified with the bold tactics and histrionics of its celebrated masters. Ma-tsu and his successors made exuberant, unfettered, and completely spontaneous experiments to bring novices into a state of enlightenment. This was an era of 10,000 experiments on 10,000 mountaintops. The fact that Ma-tsu was ordained at an early age by a Korean monk shows an organic relationship between Korean and Chinese Buddhism almost from the very beginning.

A natural, and perhaps logical, outcome of these experiments of Ma-tsu's school was a repudiation of all the trappings of traditional Buddhism. The masters of Ch'an sought to evoke in this "Golden Age" a secular, natural condition of human mind, expressed in simple, everyday human affairs. Although Ma-tsu and most of his successors were familiar with the major Mahayana sutras, no reference to the sutras is to be found in their exchanges or formal talks. Ch'an, under their tutelage, became experiential, divorced from the metaphysical speculations of earlier northern Chinese Buddhism. If there was one dominant feature of Ch'an during this era, it was a distrust of language. Language gives us concepts and distorts our perception of "reality." The Ch'an teachers of the "Golden Age" sought to demolish all conceptual constructs and habitual modes of thinking in the novice in order to bring him to a non-dualistic perception of things as they are. The line of succession from Ma-tsu to Pai-chang to Huang-po to Lin-chi during this period of Ch'an history is the most celebrated and influential of all the Zen lineages.

Pai-chang Huai-hai (720-814) was the formulator of a monastic system for the newly-emerging Ch'an communities of southern China and is credited with devising rules of conduct and discipline for Zen monks. These rules, with minor variations, continue to form the backbone of monastic conduct in Zen communities of Japan, Korea and all other countries where Zen is practiced. His famous dictum, "A day of no work is a day of no eating," gave the Zen monasteries a work-ethic which, in retrospect, may have saved them from the fury of repeated anti-Buddhist persecutions in China.

Huang-po (d.850?) is best remembered today as the teacher of the famous master Lin-chi (d.866?), yet he was a most thoughtful philosopher in his own right. He struggled mightily with the problem of "transmission." What exactly was this "mind" that was being passed on in a "Mind-to-mind transmission" from patriarch to patriarch? He finally concluded:

> You have heard the expression "transmission of the mind" and so you think there must be something transmitted. You are wrong. Thus Bodhidharma said that when the nature of the mind is realized, it is not possible to express it verbally. Clearly, then, nothing is obtained in the transmission of the mind, or if anything is obtained, it is certainly not knowledge. . .A transmission (of Void) cannot be made through words. A transmission in concrete terms cannot be the Dharma. . .In fact, however, Mind is not Mind and transmission is not really transmission.[6]

The terrible persecution of Buddhism in China in 845 brought to a close the golden, creative age not only of Zen but of Chinese Buddhism as well. Buddhism, which had enjoyed nearly 500 years of unprecedented respect and privilege, was thoroughly destroyed and was never to regain its pre-eminent position in China. Only the Ch'an sect survived. Economically self-reliant, not depending on imperial favors or largesse, iconoclastic, as much a way of life as a religion, and far removed from the politics of the imperial court in northern China, Ch'an had nothing to lose by the burning of the Buddhist scriptures and statues. When Buddhism regained favor under the Sung dynasty (960-1279), Ch'an became practically the imperial court's house religion.

After the persecution of 845, Ch'an became fragmented into five "houses," two of which survive to this day: the Lin-chi (J: Rinzai) and the Ts'ao-tung (J: Soto) schools. Lin-chi (d.866?) is remembered today as the patriarch of the school named after him. His teaching device of unexpectedly shouting "Ho!" (J:Kwatz, K:Katz) has become a byword in Japanese and Korean Zen.

Ma-tsu's other disciples who left their mark on Ch'an history during the golden age were Nan-ch'aun P'u-yuan (K: Nam Cheon) (748-835), founder of a famous monastery and a brilliant, though short-lived lineage. His most famous disciple was Chao-chou T'sung-shen (778-897) (K: Jo-ju), one of the most influential and beloved teachers in Zen history. In all, Ma-tsu is said to have had 800 students in his monastery at the height of his fame and to have given transmission to 139 disciples. Many of them went on to become leaders of Ch'an communities in their own right. Besides the monks Pai-chang and Nan-chuan, his disciples included the famous layman P'ang and, quite possibly, the poet Han-shan.

The informal, spontaneous exchanges between Ch'an teachers and their students during this time became the stuff of legends. These exchanges later came to be known as *kung-an* (J: koan, K: kong-an) or "public cases." In the earlier period of Ch'an history, each exchange was unique; the ones that brought a novice into the experience of enlightenment were avidly noted and recorded by their contemporaries. Later, as the number of students grew and personal contact and instruction with the teacher became limited, the Ch'an masters started using the "old cases" as a time-honored formula, hoping that the process would repeat itself and their own students would be enlightened. There is evidence to suggest that Nan-yuan Hui-yung (d.930), a third-generation descendant of Lin-chi, was the first Ch'an master to use Lin-chi's exchanges and public discourses in the manner of a pedagogical device. Under Ch'an master Ta-hui Tsung-kao (1089-1163), a Lin-chi school patriarch, the use of kung-an entered its most creative and influential period. In one single summer of instruction, Ta-hui is reputed to have brought thirteen of his students into enlightenment.

We thus have the four key elements in Zen practice in place: Bodhidharma's meditation-technique of "wall-gazing"; Hui-neng's doctrine of "sudden enlightenment"; Ma-tsu and his successors; the use of "shock tactics" like shouting and beating; and the development of the kung-an system, most notably under Ta-hui. With this bird's-eye view of the early history of Zen in China, we can now turn our attention to the traditions of Buddhism and Zen as they moved from China to Korea.

CHAPTER THREE

Early Buddhism in Korea

There seems to be agreement among scholars that Buddhism was introduced into the Korean peninsula in 372 A.D. In that year, an official mission from King Fu Chien of the eastern Ch'in dynasty (317-420) arrived in Koguryo, the northernmost of Korea's "Three Kingdoms." The group was led by a priest named Shun-tao (K:Sundo) and carried with it Buddhist images and scriptures.

We know that Buddhist sutras had been translated into Chinese as early as 179 A.D., but the Chinese intellectuals did not, in all likelihood, get a taste of the sophisticated speculations of Mahayana Buddhism until Kumarajiva arrived in Chang-an in 401 A.D. and established his translation institute. Apparently, religious Buddhism had enough impact on Chinese consciousness, even without a scholarly understanding of the sutras to provide them with a comprehensive view of Buddhist orthodoxy, and to encourage them to undertake missionary activities in neighboring countries.

In 384 A.D., twelve years after Shun-tao's mission to Kaguryo, an Indian monk, Marantara, arrived in the neighboring kingdom of Paekche by the southern shipping route and was given an elaborate welcome by the royal court. It was the kingdom of Paekche which, in turn, sent Buddhist statutes and sutras to Japan, 200 years later, where the patronage of Prince Shotoku (r.574-622) helped Buddhism plant itself in that land. The immediate and enthusiastic reception given to the emissaries of Buddhism in both Koguryo and Paekche seems to indicate two trends within Korea: first, Buddhist ideas must have already been disseminated in one form or another for quite some time in these two kingdoms so that when the religious embassies arrived, some understanding of what they were bringing must have already been in place. Secondly, it would seem that a receptive attitude towards importing and adopting Chinese culture was also in place. The first trend is easier to understand through the prism of the second trend. Beginning with prehistoric times and continuing through the tribal culture in the Korean peninsula, the development of a Korean "civilization" was an organic outgrowth of contact with the "higher" civilization of China, just as all the nations of the Far East can trace the growth of their "culture" back to China. In the case of Korea, for long stretches of time, the Chinese empire was less of a military presence than the fountainhead of a "superior" culture flowing down to a "lesser" culture.

The rather sudden acceptance of Buddhism as the official religion of Koguryo and Paekche also underscores the fact that Taoism had never really taken root in Korea, even though a few scattered symbols of Taoist legacy survive to the present day. Chinese civilization had flowed uninterrupted into the Korean peninsula throughout the Three Kingdoms period (37 B.C.-668 A.D.) (Chinese ancestor worship had been commonly accepted for some time) and though its early influence was profound, it merely overlaid and did not supplant the native culture of Korea. The strength of native Korean beliefs can be seen within Buddhism in the pictures of mountain spirits and other symbols from the pre-Buddhist, shamanistic culture, painted on the walls of almost all the Buddhist temples in Korea.

The time when Buddhism was introduced into the Korean peninsula was one of great strife and turmoil. The three kingdoms of Koguryo, Paekche and Silla had to wage frequent wars to subdue local tribes and clans within their territories, and they also fought with each other to establish political supremacy. One of the functions of imported Buddhism was to provide the rulers of these kingdoms with a belief-system that this religion would protect the state and bring good fortune to its rulers. Acting on this premise, the rulers established temples and lavished funds on Buddhist images. Thus, in its earliest phase, the royal houses and not the populace took the main initiatives for the acceptance of Buddhism.

The introduction of Buddhism into the Three Kingdoms set the stage for some revolutionary changes in the outlook and ways of thinking of both rulers and subjects. Buddhist doctrines such as the "Three Seals of Law." the "Four Noble Truths," and the "Chain of Causation and Deliverance" brought the concepts of universal law and egalitarianism to a people who were just moving out of a clan-centered, shamanistic society. In a sense, they moved directly from tribalism to a democratic society. The doctrine upholding individual salvation enhanced peoples' awareness of their personal identity and infused them with the idea that everyone was equal before the Law of the Buddha.

After Buddhism's official recognition in the Three Kingdoms, the Law of the Buddha also became the law of the state. For the common people, the Buddhist faith and its cosmology replaced their tribal myths. For the ruling elite, Buddhism provided a vehicle for national defense by equating the person of the ruler with an incarnation of the Buddha, and a genuine effort was made to run the kingdom in accordance with Buddhist ethics.

With the disintegration of the clans, the masses had already lost their faith in tribal myths. Buddhism, with its profound theology, presented itself to the rulers and the elite of the Three Kingdoms as a superior substitute for the already deteriorating primitive myths. The people of simple faith developed a great reverence for Amita (Amitabha) Buddha and Maitreya Buddha, and for the invocation of blessings. This pragmatic, grace-soliciting form of Buddhism, resulting from Chinese influence, was more readily acceptable to the populace than the ascetic, seemingly nihilistic form of Indian Buddhism. Moreover, the Buddhism that came through China had already taken on a distinctive nationalistic character and was welcomed by the ruling Korean elites as a belief-system that would be compatible with, and sympathetic to, the existing Korean beliefs. That indeed turned out to be the case. Over a period of centuries, Buddhism in Korea has developed a unique Korean flavor, rather than surviving as a mere residue of Chinese or Indian Buddhism.

Overall, Buddhism provided not just a new doctrine and a new consciousness, but a prime moving force in the cultural vanguard during both the Three Kingdoms period and the Unified Silla period (668-935). In bringing the highly developed cultures of China, India and Central Asia, into Korea, Buddhism formed the nucleus of a new culture. This new culture provided the basis for an artistic renaissance in the three kingdoms. By blending elements of their native society with imported arts from China, India and Central Asia, the artists of Koguryo and Paekche (and later Silla) created a unique artistic culture in the Korean peninsula which found its fullest flowering during the Unified Silla period.

Buddhism was officially recognized as the official state religion in the kingdom of Silla in 527 A.D., about 150 years after its acceptance in Koguryo and Paekche and nearly a century after it had been disseminated among the populace in Silla itself. This belated recognition has to do not so much with Silla ignorance as with the conservative nature of Silla society. The geographical location of Silla—in the south, far from the influence of continental Chinese civilization—made it less open to influences from Taoism, Buddhism and Confucianism. For a much longer time than the other kingdoms, Silla continued on the foundation of a clan-centered society. Even when Buddhism was officially adopted as a state religion by King Pophung (r.514-540), it faced vehement opposition from his own courtiers. It has been suggested that the king's decision was based on a conviction that Buddhism would help centralize royal power and promote a civilization based on a government of universal law.

Conversely, the opposition of the courtiers may have had its roots in the resistance by the clans to an expansion of royal authority. Indeed, Buddhism as a doctrine for the "protection of the state" was a powerful attraction during the Three Kingdoms period. Buddhism, of course, was a vehicle for ensuring the well-

being of the individual through prayers, but evidence shows that
its patronage by the royal houses was based more on a faith which
assured the well-being of the state. Implicit was the calculation
that, as the state became more powerful, the ruling house would
have more power for itself.

Based on this conviction, numerous Buddhist temples were
built during the Three Kingdoms period. Paekche's Wanghung-sa
and Silla's Hwangnyong-sa were built on a grand scale. It was an
article of faith among the people of Silla that the nine-story pagoda of Hwangnyong-sa manifested Silla's destiny to conquer nine
other states of East Asia, including China and Japan. There was
also a conviction in Silla that Maitreya Buddha, the Buddha of the
Future, had experienced several reincarnations in Silla in the
form of famous *hwarang* warriors. Buddhist monks in all three
kingdoms exhorted the soldiers to fight bravely in the battle not
only to safeguard not only the Way of the Buddha but to protect
the state as well.

In Silla, King Chinhung (r.540-576), Pophung's successor, pro-
moted Buddhism to an even greater extent. It was during his
reign that the great temple of Hwangnyong-sa and such imposing
temples as Chowon-sa and Silche-sa were built. Chinhung also
created a government-protected Buddhist clergy into which lay
people were permitted to enter. During his reign, Buddhism
permeated the conservative society of Silla.

Chinhung's outstanding contribution to Korean history was the
establishment of hwarang-do.; which functioned as a kind of West
Point Corps to train young men from the nobility for military and
political leadership. It would appear that Chinhung's motives in
establishing the hwarang-do were not narrow or self-seeking;
rather he genuinely wanted to ensure national development and
prosperity through this institution. This paramilitary corps was led
by a *kukson* (leader) who was revered as an incarnation of Maitreya
Buddha. This faith in Maitreya Buddha came to be linked in Silla,
as well as in Koguryo and Paekche, with faith in a "sacred" king.
In some cases, an effort was made to portray the king and the
queen of a kingdom as a reincarnation of King Sudodhana and
Queen Maya, the parents of the historical Shakyamuni Buddha.

Whatever belief there may have been behind the training of the hwarang warriors it turned out that some of ablest leaders of Silla were shaped by the rigorous military discipline and the Buddhist and Confucian ideals of the hwarang or the "flower-knight" system. An echo of the hwarang system may be seen in the training of the samurai elite in medieval Japan where the austere training of Zen provided the discipline and value system for the government's leadership.

It may be surmised that in all the three kingdoms, Buddhism was seen more as an instrument for amassing greater political power and creating social stability than as an enlightened philosophical system. At the same time, because Buddhism had little conflict with the native religions, it was easily internalized, thereby forming a climate into which a new culture could be born. In the course of its 1600-year history in Korea, Buddhism has co-existed with Confucianism providing Korean culture with a unique flavor and leaving an indelible mark on the religious and philosophical thought, as well as on its arts and architecture

During the years 660-668 A.D., T'ang China made military alliances with Silla and helped it destroy the kingdoms of Koguryo and Paekche. In 668, the peninsula was politically unified for the first time and the Unified Silla dynasty (668-935) came into existence. To be sure, T'ang China had its own designs and did not wait long to send expeditions to try to defeat Silla and take over the peninsula for itself. Under a brilliant military and political leadership, however, Silla was able to hand the Chinese a series of stunning defeats. Finally, a truce was arranged by which Silla agreed to pay an annual tribute to China, and in return, China agreed to let Silla's borders remain inviolate. This tributary relationship lastedmore than 1200 years until 1910 when the Korean monarchy was finally abolished by the occupying Japanese. Although never physically occupied by China, Korea retained a vassal relationship to its big neighbor to the north for more than a millenium. All Korean kings and queens, on their ascension to the throne, had to send tribute to the emperor of China, seeking his approval for their rule.

CHAPTER FOUR

Buddhism During the Unified Silla Period

Buddhism became the dominant system of thought in the Korean peninsula during the Unifed Silla period (668-935). Patronized by kings and courtiers and revered by the populace, it permeated every aspect of Silla culture and society. The political unification of the peninsula (in 668) ushered in a golden age of Korean Buddhist scholasticism. Many monks traveled to T'ang China or even to distant India to study the Way of the Buddha. The monk Wonchuk (fl. sixth century) is particularly noteworthy for the major contributions he made to Buddhism in Korea through his sutra translations and other writings during a long sojourn in T'ang China. The monk Hyecho went to India and described his pilgrimage to Buddhist holy places in a well-known account called *Record of a Journey to the Five Indian Kingdoms.*

The many monks who returned to Silla after studying in China brought back with them doctrines and scriptures of the many sects which had proliferated during the early years of the T'ang dynasty. As a result, a diversity of schools arose in Silla, and a number of monks appeared who performed the pioneering, creative work which helped sustain the tradition during later centuries. The early years of the Unified Silla period were also the years when major approaches to the doctrine were developed which became the mainstays of the mature Korean tradition later on. Out of these early years emerged five main schools of Doctrinal Buddhism: Vinaya school (K: Kyeyul Jong), Nirvana school (Yolban Jong), Dharma Nature school (Popsong Jong), Avatamsaka school (Hwaom Jong), and Yogacara school (Popsang Jong). These early schools were to play an important role in the future development of Korean Buddhism.

Of the many monks during the early years of Unified Silla dynasty, three are outstanding. The monks Chajang, Won Hyo, and Uisang were instrumental in firmly establishing Buddhism in Korea. Through their personalities and achievements, they not only won favors from the royal houses but also captured the popular imagination. The three of them are among the most important personages in Korean Buddhist history.

CHAJANG, THE NATIONAL PRECEPTOR

The monk Chajang (608-686) is the St. Paul of Korean Buddhism. While Buddhism had been officially recognized as the state religion of Silla as far back as 535 A.D., it was Chajang who transformed it from a religion of the aristocratic classes into a religion of the masses. Chajang himself was born into an aristocratic family. His father, Murim Kim, was a nobleman of the third rank and a high court official. As he had no son, he and his wife prayed to the Buddha for a son and vowed that if a son was born to them, they would enter him into the priesthood. Chajang's legend says his mother dreamt that a star fell from the heavens and entered her womb. Soon thereafter she conceived and a son was born to her on the day of Buddha's birthday. While his parents were alive, Chajang was married, and probably in his teens, he begot children and fulfilled his obligation to his parents. After their death, Chajang took leave of his wife and children and donated his estate to a temple. No dates are available for this momentous decision, but Chajang was probably in his early twenties at the time.

Chajang went into remote mountains and practiced extreme austerities alone. About this time, an official post became vacant at the royal court and the king wanted to appoint Chajang to that post. Messengers went into the mountains, carrying the king's wishes to Chajang. But he refused to even consider the matter. Displeased, the king sent a message that if Chajang did not comply with his wishes, his head would be chopped off! To this, Chajang's celebrated reply was, "I would rather live for one day keeping Buddha's precepts than live for a hundred years violating them." The king was much moved by Chajang's courage and dedication, and gave official sanction for his pursuit of a hermit's life.

During this period of austerities, according to legend, a heavenly being appeared before Chajang in a vision and asked him what he was looking for. Chajang replied that he wished to help all beings in accordance with the Law of the Buddha. The heavenly being thereupon administered the five precepts to Chajang and told him to help all beings through these precepts. Chajang came down from the mountain, and as he walked through the towns and the villages, he administered these precepts to the local people. Word of this holy man's pilgrimage spread, and people came from all over the region to take the precepts from him. A significant part of Silla's population is said to have embraced Buddhism as a result of Chajang's pilgrimage.

Chajang applied to the royal court for permission to go to T'ang China which, at that time, was the place where all the great Buddhist scholars and teachers lived. The permission was granted in 636 by Queen Sondok (r.632-647) who became the greatest patron of Buddhism in Silla's history. Upon his arrival in T'ang China, Chajang traveled to Wutai-shan Mountain to pay homage to Manjusri,the Bodhisattva of Wisdom, who reputedly lived on that mountain. He meditated before a clay image of Manjusri for seven days and nights. One day he dreamt that Manjusri had stroked his forehead and taught him a mantra in Sanskrit. Believing this dream to be a transmission from Manjusri himself, Chajang left the mountain and traveled to Chang-an, the capital of T'ang China. The emperor received him courteously at the imperial court and invited him to stay at one of the imperial sub-temples.

During his stay at the temple, certain incidents brought him fame and attention. One day a thief broke into the temple and stole all of Chajang's belongings. When he found out that he had stolen from a monk who had come from a faraway land, the thief was so ashamed, he came to seek Chajang's forgiveness. Chajang gave him the five precepts and the thief became his disciple. A blind man came to Chajang, listened to his Dharma speech, and then took the five precepts. Soon afterwards this man recovered his eyesight. When word of these incidents spread, large crowds started coming to the temple to take the five precepts and seek Chajang's blessings. Finding this to be too cumbersome and distracting, Chajang sought the emperor's permission to travel to Buddhist holy places around the country. He traveled to Chung-nan Mountain south of the capital and stayed there for three years.

On Chung-nan Mountain, Chajang had a chance to meet leading Buddhist personages of the era. Among them were Tu Shun (557-640), the founder of the Hua-yen (Avatamsaka) school, and Tao Hsuan (597-667) the founder of the Nan-shan tsung (Vinaya) school. Chajang returned to the T'ang capital after three years. A legend about Chajang says that when he passed the Pond of Universal Harmony on his way to the capital, a heavenly being appeared before him in a vision and told him that his country was extremely vulnerable to invasions by neighboring kingdoms because it was ruled by a woman. The heavenly being advised Chajang to return to his country and build a nine-story pagoda for its protection and prosperity. Queen Sondok was ruling in Silla at that time and Silla had indeed been invaded by Koguryo in 638, and by Paekche in 642 when it lost 40 walled towns. Later in 642, Silla was invaded again by the combined armies of Paekche and Koguryo and lost an important strategic position.

Chajang narrated his vision to the T'ang emperor who agreed, in view of the then friendly diplomatic relations between T'ang and Silla, that Chajang should return home posthaste. He lavished many gifts on Chajang, including bales of silk and brocade and Buddhist images and scriptures. Chajang returned to Silla in 643 after a seven-year stay in China and was enthusiastically received by Queen Sondok and her court. He relayed his vision to the

Queen who immediately authorized the construction of a nine-story pagoda at Hwangnyong-sa temple. Upon completetion, this eighty-meter high, nine-story wooden pagoda towered over the capital city and was one of the architectural wonders of ancient Silla. Chajang was installed as the second Abbot of Hwangnyong-sa temple and was made the National Preceptor. He was also appointed as the overseer of the clergy and was assigned the task of formulating disciplinary rules for monks and for conduct in the monasteries.

Chajang was at the height of his fame and political influence. First, he was able to work his way into the goodwill of the T'ang emperor and now he occupied a position of unparalleled political and spiritual influence at the court of Queen Sondok. Chajang fully availed himself of his influential position and it is said that under his exhortation eight or nine out of every ten households in Silla took five precepts.

His formalization of disciplinary rules for the monastic community brought him many applicants aspiring to become monks. In order to accommodate these increased numbers, Chajang established the Tongdo-sa temple near the Silla capital. Tongdo-sa continues to exist to this day and is one of Korea's three most important temples as well as its largest. From the Ordination Platform at Tongdo-sa, Chajang preached sermons to multitudes on the meaning of Buddhist precepts. There he also received new applicants into ordination. Thus he became the founder of the Vinaya school of Buddhism in Korea.

Chajang's political position made it inevitable that he be drawn into Silla's wars with her neighbors. Under his guidance, Silla Buddhism developed prayers and rituals for the safety and victory of her soldiers and country which were incorporated into regular temple practices. We have already noted the symbolic significance in popular imagination of the nine-story pagoda at Hwangnyong-sa temple. Religion became a handmaiden to politics in ancient Silla, and Chajang was partly responsible for this collusion.

As Chajang's influence grew at the court, he proposed that the Silla court adopt T'ang court dress and manners because of their elegance and dignity. His proposal was accepted and, in 649, the

T'ang dress was formally adopted by Silla royalty. Chajang thus became an instrument of an accelerated process of sinicization of Silla culture. Overall, a pattern of "state Buddhism" was born through Chajang's efforts, a pattern in which religion existed to serve the "needs" of the state. This pattern was to have a far-reaching influence on the future course of Korean Buddhism.

The last years of Chajang's life were not happy ones. He seems to have realized at some point that he had become so enmeshed in the politics of state and religion that he had completely lost touch with the austere practices of his youth. He developed a longing to see Manjusri once more in person before he died. He gave up all his official responsibilities and went to Odae Mountain. While in China, he had been told in one of his visions that he would be able to meet Manjusri on this mountain. There are several stories about how he went from one place to another on the mountain in his quest, but the vision never materialized. He died a lonely and painful death on Odae Mountain.

WON HYO, THE UNBRIDLED MONK

If Chajang is the St. Paul of Korean Buddhism, Won Hyo (617-686) is its St. Augustine. Won Hyo gave shape to the form and content of Korean Buddhism during its golden age and remains the dominant personality of the entire Korean Buddhist tradition. He is probably the greatest scholar Korean Buddhism has produced, and is one of the most influential thinkers in Korean history as well.

Won Hyo was born in 617 in the town of Zainmyon in Kyongsang province in Silla. One legend has it that Won Hyo's mother, while pregnant with him, was passing by a sala tree when she suddenly felt birth pangs. Without having time to reach home, she gave birth to Won Hyo right there: A five-colored cloud is said to have appeared in the sky. This story underscores the legend that Sakyamuni Buddha died under a pair of sala trees in northern India. The mythmaker's aim clearly is to connect Won Hyo with Sakyamuni Buddha and glorify him as the greatest Buddhist born in Silla.

Won Hyo was born nearly a hundred years after Buddhism was formally recognized as the state religion in Silla. The later half of Queen Sondok's reign (r.632-647) saw the beginning of a period of national reconstruction which lasted well into the Unified Silla period. Buddhism was becoming more and more a "national protective cult." An apocryphal Chinese Buddhist scripture, the *Scripture for Wise Royalty and National Protection*, was frequently preached. In 645, the monk Chajang, soon to be Silla's High Priest, had returned from his studies in China and had been instrumental in the construction of a nine-story pagoda at Hwangnyong-sa temple in order to invoke the aid of the spirits to bring neighboring countries to their knees, "to open wide heaven and earth and unify the three kingdoms."

Civil war marked the period of Won Hyo's birth and childhood. T'ang China had launched unsuccessful attacks on Koguryo in 598 and 612, as well as in 645 and 647. Silla was invaded by Koguryo in 638, and by Paekche in 642. Both Koguryo and Paekche combined their forces and attacked Silla again in 642. Then T'ang China allied with Silla and attacked Paekche. By 660, Paekche had been destroyed. The joint forces of T'ang and Silla reduced Koguryo in 668. Silla was finally able to bring the whole peninsula under its hegemony. Later, Silla was able to thwart T'ang China's larger ambition of bringing the peninsula under its own direct control. A unified country finally existed and the era of Unified Silla period (668-935 A.D.) was ushered in.

A legend asserts that, as a young man, Won Hyo took part in these bloody civil wars and saw many of his friends slaughtered and homes destroyed. Most sources agree, however, that he became a monk at the age of twenty. One story says that he remodeled his home as a temple which he named Chogye-sa; another says that he shaved his head and went into the mountains to live as a monk. It is not clear under which teachers he studied, if any. Some say his teacher was the monk Nangji on Yongch'wi mountain; others say he was a disciple of priest Popchang at Hwangnyong-sa. Still another story has it that he learned the *Nirvana Sutra* from Podok, a Koguryo monk in exile in Silla.

A major event in the history of contemporary Buddhism at this point was the return, from India to China, of the scholar Hsuan-Tsang (602-662) after seventeen years of Buddhist studies in India. His return was a turning point in the efforts to translate Buddhist scriptures and Buddhist learning into Chinese. Monks from all over China, as well as Korea, flocked to study under the renowned scholar. In 650, when he was thirty-three years old, Won Hyo set out on a journey to T'ang China in the company of his close friend, the monk Uisang who later became the National Teacher in Silla. This was five years after the return to China of Hsuan-Tsang and, like many other Korean monks of the period, both Won Hyo and Uisang were inspired to study under the great Buddhist scholar.

Won Hyo and Uisang took the overland route, traveling north through the kingdoms of Paekche and Koguryo. Their journey was smooth until they were mistaken for spies near the Chinese border and barely escaped capture. They turned back, although it is not clear why. This attempted journey to China is important however because from it comes one of the most famous stories in the Korean Buddhist tradition concerning Won Hyo's enlightenment.

> One evening as [Won Hyo] was crossing the desert, he stopped at a small patch of green, where there were a few trees and some water, and went to sleep. Toward midnight he awoke, thirsty—it was pitch-dark. He groped along on all fours, searching for water. At last his hand touched a cup on the ground. He picked it up and drank. Ah, how delicious! Then he bowed deeply, in gratitude, to Buddha for the gift of water. The next morning, Won Hyo woke up and saw beside him what he had taken for a cup [during the night]. It was a shattered skull, blood-caked and with shreds of flesh still stuck to the cheek-bones. Strange insects crawled or floated on the surface of the filthy rainwater inside it. Won Hyo looked at the skull and felt a great wave of nausea. He opened his mouth. As soon as the vomit poured out, his mind opened and he understood. Last night, since he hadn't seen and hadn't thought, the water was delicious. This morning, seeing and thinking had made him vomit. Ah, he said to himself, thinking makes good and bad, life

and death. And without thinking there is no universe, no Buddha, no Dharma. All is one, and this one is empty. There was no need now to find a master. Won Hyo already understood life and death. What more was there to learn? So he turned and started back across the desert to Korea.[7]

After his return to Silla, Won Hyo's activities became more and more unorthodox. A story from this period of his life, probably apocryphal, sheds light on his transformation from an ordinary monk to an unorthodox personality:

There was a very famous monk in Silla—a little old man, with a wisp of a beard and skin like a crumpled paper bag. Barefoot and in tattered clothes, he walked through the town ringing his bell. "Dae-an, dae-an, dae-an (it means Great Peace), dae-an don't think, dae-an like this, dae-an rest mind, dae-an, dae-an." Won Hyo heard of him and one day hiked to the mountain cave where the monk lived. From a distance he could hear the sound of extraordinarily lovely chanting echoing through the valleys. But when he arrived at the cave, he found the Master sitting beside a dead fawn, weeping. Won Hyo was dumbfounded. How could an enlightened being be either happy or sad, since in the state of Nirvana there is nothing to be happy or sad about, and no one to be happy or sad? He stood speechless for a while, and then asked the Master why he was weeping.

The Master explained. He had come upon the fawn after its mother had been killed by hunters. It was very hungry. So he had gone into town and begged for milk. Since he knew that no one would give milk for an animal, he said it was for his son. "A monk with a son? What a dirty old man!" people thought. But someone gave him a little milk. He had continued this way for a month, begging enough to keep the animal alive. Then the scandal became too great, and no one would help. He had been wandering for three days now, in search of milk. At last he had found some, but when he had returned to his cave, his fawn was already dead. "You don't understand," said the Master. "My mind and the fawn's mind are the same. It was very hungry. I want milk. I want milk. Now it is dead. Its mind is my mind. That's why I am weeping. I want milk." Won Hyo began to understand how great a Bodhisattva the master was. When all creatures were happy, he was happy. When all creatures were sad, he was sad. Won Hyo said to him, "Please teach me." The Master said, "All right. Come along with me."

They went to the red-light district of the town. The Master took Won Hyo's arm and walked up to the door of a geisha-house. "Dae-an, dae-an," he rang. A beautiful woman opened the door. The Master said, "Today I've brought the great monk Won Hyo to visit you." "Oh! Won Hyo!" she cried out. Won Hyo blushed. The woman blushed, and her eyes grew large. She led them upstairs, in great happiness, fear and exhilaration that the famous, handsome monk had come to her. As she prepared meat and wine for her visitors, the Master said to Won Hyo, "For twenty years you have kept company with kings and princes and monks. It's not good for a monk to live in heaven all the time. He must also visit hell and save the people there, who are wallowing in their desires. Hell too is like this. So tonight you will ride this wine straight to hell."

"But I've never broken a single precept before," Won Hyo protested.

"Have a good trip," said the Master.

He then turned to the woman and said sternly, "Don't you know that it's a sin to give wine to a monk? Aren't you afraid of going to hell?"

"No," the woman said, "Won Hyo will come and save me." "A very good answer!" said the Master.

Son Won Hyo stayed the night, and broke more than one precept. The next morning he took off his elegant robes and went dancing through the streets, barefoot and in tatters. "Dae-an, dae-an! The whole universe is like this! What are you?"[8]

He named his trousers *No Obstacle* and wore them as he wandered around villages and hamlets, singing and dancing. Even while living the life of a hippie monk, Won Hyo was writing extensive commentaries on the sutras, and in spite of his lifestyle, he was the trusted adviser to the king of Silla, and preceptor to the noblest and most powerful families. He lived in different temples in and around the capital and was completely accessible to the common people who listened to his spontaneous talks.

One day Won Hyo wandered the streets of the capital, chanting a mysterious song, "Who dares lend me an axe without a handle? I'll hew down the pillars supporting the heaven." No one in the streets knew what he meant. But when King Mu yol heard of the song, he interpreted it to mean that Won Hyo was anxious for a noble woman and a bright son. The king invited him to Yosok Palace and arranged for him to meet with his widowed sister, Princess Kwa. Won Hyo and Kwa fell in love. The result of their liasion was the child Sol Ch'ong who became one of the greatest Confucian scholars of ancient Silla period. Sol Ch'ong's annotations of the Confucian scriptures remained the standard reference work for many centuries in Korea.

It is not clear whether, after his liasion with Princess Kwa, Won Hyo gave up his robes or continued to live the life of a hippie monk. There are suggestions that he formally stopped calling himself a monk. Won Hyo's re-entry and life in the secular world was at once complex and brilliant. Some of his most notable activities took place after he left the priesthood. His activities during this period were filled with prodigious scholarly output and a lifestyle that was shocking to both his religious and secular contemporaries. He never presumed to be a renunciate monk, rather he called himself *Sosong kosa*, or "small layman."

This "small layman" had no scruples about eating and sleeping in the houses of the nobles or the lowly. He didn't conform to the accepted social code, didn't care about his language, and had no hesitation about visiting drinking houses or brothels. He played the zither at temples, and drummed on an empty gourd while singing, "Only a man with no worries and fears can go straight and overcome life and death and transmigration."[9] This was a phrase borrowed from the *Avatamsaka (Hwa-om) Sutra* on which he had made extensive commentaries. He often went to mountains and streams to meditate. At the same time, he was involved in the military activities going on around him. It is said that he interpreted for General Kim Yu-shin a letter of military secrets from the T'ang General Soo Ting-fang.

Won Hyo died in 686 at the age of 70. Chajang, the National Preceptor and Won Hyo's older contemporary died in the same year. Won Hyo's body was laid in state at the Punhwang-sa temple by his son, Sol Ch'ong.

Won Hyo is said to have been the author of some 240 works on Buddhism. Of these, 20 works in 25 volumes are still extant. He made extensive commentaries on the doctrines and scriptures of all the different schools of Buddhism which were competing for religious supremacy at the time. In the process he became the first Korean thinker to make an attempt at harmonizing these various doctrines. The remarkable thing about his commentaries is that, rather than being pedantic, he expostulated his own creative views in treating the sutras.

> His commentaries on the major sutras were not intended simply to explicate terms and theories according to the dogma of a particular sect; rather his approach was to demonstrate the relationship between these texts and the whole of Buddhism by examining them from the standpoint of an ideal, the "One Mind" which vivified each of them. He also wrote outlines of the ideologies of the major Buddhist sects, again explaining them in ways which would lead to fraternal harmony, not sectarian controversy. In his treatise, *Ten Approaches to the Reconciliation of Doctrinal Controversy* (Sim-nun hwajaeng non), he proclaimed that his intent was to harmonize the differences between the various schools of canonical Buddhist thought and to explore avenues which would lead to an all-inclusive vision of those sects.
>
> Simultaneous with this philosophical development, Won Hyo preached and lived a popular form of Buddhism which had direct bearing on the everyday lives of ordinary followers. Won Hyo was the first major Buddhist thinker to attempt, from the standpoint of the scholastic doctrine, a harmonization of the tenets of the major sects of Chinese Buddhist philosophy; his attempts inspired all future efforts of Korean thinkers...[10]

Won Hyo is formally credited with being the founder of the Popsong (Dharma-nature) school, one of the five major schools of

Buddhism in Silla at the time. The Popsong school was an unique sect, based on syncreticism rather than sectarianism.

What mattered most to Won Hyo was not the interpretation of words or demonstration of wide learning, but understanding the essential spirit of the scriptures. To him, Buddhism was no longer Indian or Chinese. It was his own, the everyday religion of a Silla subject. There was no time, Won Hyo felt, for the people of 7th-century Silla, trying to consolidate political power in a remote corner of the peninsula and to breathe vitality into a new religion, to be occupied with the leisurely interpretation of phrases. It was painful for him to see, a hundred years after the transplantation of Buddhism into his native country, "the ascendancy of empty words clad in dignity and prestige."[11]

During his lifetime, Won Hyo dominated the intellectual and religious arenas both within and outside Korea. His scholarly reputation was secured by his theory of "One Mind and Two Doors" in the work *Kishinnon* (Awakening of Faith). Clearly dissatisfied with trends current among contemporary Buddhist scholars in Silla, he wrote in the introductory notes to *Kishinnon*:

> Only a few of those who presume to interpret the deep meaning of this theory understand all the essential points. Most of them are busy preserving what they have learned; [they] quote phrases, not prepared to explore the main core openly and freely. Without attaining to the intentions of the theoretician, they stray near the tributaries, although the source is nearby; or let go of the trunk, holding only onto the leaves; or sew the sleeves with cloth cut from the collar.[12]

Won Hyo authored many works on *Kishinnon* but only two are extant: *Taesung Kishinnon So* (Treatise on the Awakening of Faith), and *Taesung Kishinnon Pyolki* (Special Commentary on the Awakening of Faith). The two works, according to scholars, are inseparable, the former containing his main theories on the awakening of faith, and the latter containing his revised annotations. Together, the two works are known as *Kishinnon Haedong Sogi*.

Most noteworthy among Won Hyo's brilliant intellectual

achievements after his re-entry into the secular world was a series of lectures on the *Kumgang Sammaegyong Sutra* at the Hwang-nyong-sa temple. According to one story, the king of Silla invited all the leading scholars of the day, including Won Hyo, to the royal palace for a series of lectures on Buddhism. The other monks, offended by Won Hyo's carefree and unorthodox lifestyle, prevailed upon the king not to invite him to the gathering. The king agreed, but in a private audience he urged Won Hyo to give a public lecture on the *Kumgang Sammaegyong Sutra*. According to this story, the king had fallen ill after withdrawing his invitation to Won Hyo and, as his illness lingered, he believed he would not recover unless Won Hyo gave a public talk on the sutra. Within a very short time, Won Hyo completed a five-volume annotation on the Sutra. However, jealous monks stole the manuscript. In three days, Won Hyo had restored the first three volumes of his commentaries and lectured on them at the Hwangnyong-sa temple before an assembly of the king, ranking court officials, monks and lay people. This three-volume annotation is still extant. After the lecture, Won Hyo declared, "When they needed a hundred rafters some time ago, they omitted me. In the morning they needed one large beam. I was the only person possessing the function."[13]

This spectacular display of learning provided a legitimacy to Won Hyo's life-style of "no obstacle." The Buddhist world of Won Hyo's time was extremely formal, organizational and hierarchical, tied as it was into its role of a "state religion." Won Hyo was the first Korean monk to operate outside the mainstream, and he was able to get away with it because of his outstanding scholarly merits. The three volumes of *Kumgang Sammaegyong Sutra*, considered to be one of Won Hyo's major works, was introduced into China, where it was received as a great treatise.

In addition, Won Hyo's mastery of the *Avatamsaka Sutra* was so profound that at times he is identified as the founder of the Hwaom (C: Hua-yen) school in Korea. "....in fact, Won Hyo can be considered an important vaunt-courier in the Chinese Hua-yen school."[14] Not content with writing basic texts for the Popsong and Hwaom schools, he wrote commentaries on the *Prajña*

(Wisdom) Sutra, Lotus Sutra, Nirvana Sutra, Amitabha Sutra and *Diamond Sutra.* These were the major sutras in vogue during his lifetime. Without taking any single sutra or treatise as the sole source of his faith, Won Hyo created a unique synthesis of Buddhist thought through the texts of his Popsong school. He argued the necessity of viewing Buddhist doctrine in its totality, or at a higher level of abstraction, in which all contradictions and disputes, could be harmonized and integrated. In his work, *Sinmun Hwajaeng Non* (Treatise on the Harmonization of Disputes among the Ten Schools), he expounded this theory of synthesis. This may explain why in a later age he was given the posthumous title of *Hwajong* (Harmonius Quiescence) or *The National Mentor.*

Won Hyo, it will be noted, was an older contemporary of Hui Neng (638-713), the Sixth Patriarch of Ch'an Buddhism in China, and it is fair to assume that during his lifetime he was personally not aware of the revolutionary insight introduced into the Ch'an tradition by Hui-neng. But he seems to have arrived at the same insight, although his explanation of it was much more scholarly than Hui-neng's. Won Hyo's unorthodox lifestyle may have been one manifestation of his insight into truth. Won Hyo was not a Zen master in a chronological or institutional sense but succeeding generations of Korean Zen monks and lay people have revered him as a great teacher. The following selection of aphorisms from his *Beginner's Mind* speak directly to practitioners of Zen:

> All Buddhas dwell in the Palace of Extinction because they have cut off desire and undergone difficult practice. Sentient beings in innumerable world-systems are subject to ceaseless rounds of rebirth within the "burning house" because they do not cut off desire and craving.
>
> All men know how to satisfy their hunger with food, but few know enough to learn Dharma as a cure for their ignorance.
>
> Wisdom and practice are like two wheels of a cart. Benefitting others, and also benefitting oneself, [they] are like the two wings of a bird.
>
> It is hardly worthwhile to support an empty body devoid of ac-

tual practice. This impermanent, transitory life cannot be maintained forever, however much you may love it. If you wish to attain great virtue, you must be able to withstand great suffering. If you wish to sit on the lion's seat, you must abandon forever desire and pleasure.

The four elements soon disassociate; they cannot be long maintained.

As evening draws near, you regreat that you did not practice early in the morning. The worldly pleasure which you enjoy now becomes suffering in the future. Why then are you attached to this pleasure? One moment of patience becomes lasting pleasure. Why then do you not practice?

Words of admonition can be endless, yet craving is not extinguished. By saying, "next time, next time," attachment is not cut off. The things that keep us busy are interminable, so why not simply throw away all worldly affairs? Plans also have no limit, so why not just cut off the thinking mind?

Moment succeeds moment, and thus day and night are soon past. One day succeeds the next; months slip away. Month follows month, soon next year is here. Years pass rapidly, and you find yourself at death's door. A broken vehicle cannot run; an old man cannot practice.[15]

Won Hyo's great significance lies in his role as a harmonizer and the founder of a syncretic trend in Korean Buddhism. It is a measure of his great contribution that this syncretic trend has continued to dominate the entire historical development of Korean Buddhism despite the persistent controversy between the Zen and the Doctrinal schools. During his lifetime, Won Hyo's efforts to reconcile conflicts within the religious domain paralleled the inherent conflicts in the authoritarian structure of the Silla society. In his personality, Won Hyo combined a major religious intellect and a talent for popularizing Buddhism. His life-style and scholarly output led not to popularization but to a spirit of harmony, a spirit which is his major legacy to Korean Buddhism. Even today this spirit continues to have an immeasurable impact on Buddhist monks and thinkers in Korea.

UISANG, THE TEMPLE-BUILDER

The third personage in the great trinity of ancient Silla monks is Uisang (625-702). Very little is known about Uisang's family or childhood, except that his father's name was Kim Han-sin. We also know that he was a close personal friend of Won Hyo with whom he attempted to travel to T'ang China.

According to *Samguk Yusa*, the collection of legends from the three ancient kingdoms of Korea, Uisang's second attempt to visit T'ang China was undertaken in the year 660. Receiving permission from the Silla court, he had joined the party of a T'ang envoy who was returning home. At Yangchow, he was cordially received by the military governor of the province. From there he traveled inland to Chung-nan mountain, south of Chang-an, the capital of T'ang China. This mountain was the pre-eminent place for Buddhist studies in China, and it was here that Chajang had earlier studied with some of the greatest Chinese monks of the period. On this mountain, Uisang visited Chih-yen (602-688), the second patriarch of the Hua-yen school. The day before Uisang's visit, Chih-yen had a dream in which he saw a great tree growing in Haedong (Silla) whose boughs and leaves covered the whole of Shenchow (land of Gods, i.e. China). At the top of the tree there was a phoenix nest and Chih-yen climbed up to look into the nest. His eyes were dazzled by the sight of Manpo jewels (said to have been emitted from the throat of a King-dragon). When Uisang knocked on his door next day, Chih-yen received him with a special ceremony and said, "In a dream last night, I saw the signs of your coming." They discussed the doctrines of the *Avatamsaka sutra* and Chih-yen was greatly impressed by Uisang's understanding of the subtleties of the sutra, even though Uisang had had no scholarly training of this sutra.

During his stay at Chih-yen's monastery, Uisang developed a special rapport with Fa-tsang (643-712), the third patriarch and the effective systematizer of the doctrines of the Hua-yen school in China. Fa-tsang had great respect for Uisang's insights into the *Avatamsaka sutra* and continued to correspond with him after Uisang's return to Silla.

One of the most endearing, and enduring, legends in Korean folk literature is associated with Uisang. According to this story, while in his teens, Uisang fell in love with a beautiful girl named Myo Hwa ("Delicate Flower"). However, before Uisang and Myo Hwa could announce their engagement, a search party acting on behalf of the king of Silla saw Myo Hwa and selected her as one of the virgins to be sent as a tributary gift for the T'ang emperor of China. Uisang and Myo Hwa were disconsolate but nothing could be done. After Myo Hwa was taken away from the village, Uisang vowed never to marry and became a monk.

During her journey to China, Myo Hwa considered her situation and decided that it was far better to end her life than be a concubine in the Chinese imperial household. While the party was traveling through the treacherous cliffs in Manchuria, she deliberately flung herself into a swollen river. The party leader, rather than risking a search in the treacherous waters, decided to assume that she had drowned and so did not make an extensive search. A nearby fisherman, however, had seen Myo Hwa fall into the river, and after the party had left the area, was able to fish her out of the waters. He cared for her during her recovery and adopted her as his own daughter.

Many years passed. One day Myo Hwa heard that two monks had arrived in her port of a town from Silla. She could not resist going out to see these monks. One can only imagine her joy and surprise when she saw that one of the monks was none other than Uisang. (This was presumably Uisang's second attempt to go to T'ang China. The first overland attempt with Won Hyo was aborted. This time Uisang was traveling by the sea route.) Now Myo Hwa wanted to return to Silla with her childhood sweetheart. But, as Uisang explained, his situation had changed. As a monk, he could not marry her. He had obligations to the Way of the Buddha and to the king of Silla who had sponsored his travel to China. His commitment now was to make Buddhism strong and popular in Silla. Uisang promised, however, that he would stop to see Myo Hwa on his way back from China.

Uisang's studies in China took ten years. During his return journey, he came to Myo Hwa's house to make the promised visit but she was not home. As his ship was about to leave the harbor, Uisang left a note for her saying he could not wait and that he was sorry to have missed her. While he was boarding the ship, Myo Hwa returned home and saw the note. All these years, Myo Hwa had been weaving a robe for her childhood sweetheart. Now she grabbed his robe and ran to the pier. By the time she reached there, the ship was already pulling away. Seeing Uisang sail out of her life, never to return, Myo Hwa decided that she did not want to live any longer. She put on the robe and jumped into the sea. As she hit the water, the robe spread out like wings and Myo Hwa turned into a dragon that followed Uisang's ship back to Silla.

Upon his return to Silla, Uisang dedicated himself to the task of building a temple in the Taebak mountains. From there he intended to disseminate the teachings of the *Avatamsaka Sutra* (*Hwa-om Sutra*) which he had studied extensively in China. He selected a propitious site according to the principles of geomancy (an old Chinese system which sought to determine the "energy" of a place relative to its elevation and contours, and its proximity to running water). But there was a problem. The area, especially a large cave, was being used by bandits as a base of operations. Myo Hwa, now in the form of a dragon, levitated a huge boulder to the roof of the cave where the thieves had their den. Frightened by this supernatural phenomenon, the thieves fled the area and Uisang was able to build his temple. The temple, Pusok-sa, takes its name from this particular incident, and Myo Hwa's "floating rock" can be seen even today to the left of the main hall. A shrine on the premises is dedicated to the memory of this legendary dragon-girl. There is also a portrait of Myo Hwa in the temple, the original of which is said to be in Japan.

Myo Hwa's legend says that after the temple was built, the dragon-girl crawled under the main hall to serve as an eternal protectress of the temple. The head of the dragon was under the altar while the tail was near the stone lantern outside the hall. A few years ago, researchers from Dong-guk University, the Buddhist university in Seoul, came to Pusok-sa and dug up the area in front of the main hall. They uncovered a large rock which had resemblance to a dragon's tail and dragon scales could even be distinguished on the stone! Whether this lends credence to Myo Hwa's legend or not must be left to each individual.

Uisang returned to Silla in 670; Pusok-sa was established in 676 as his head-temple where he regularly held discourses on the doctrines of the *Avatamsaka Sutra*. During his stay in China, Uisang had written, in 661, his major work, the *Chart of the Avatamsaka One-Vehicle Dharmadhatu*, and presented it to Chih-yen as the quintessnce of his understanding of the doctrine. This Chart (or Mandala) is the only extant work of Uisang's scholarship, and is one of the seminal works of extant Buddhist literature from the Silla period. All the subsequent systematizers of Korean Buddhism relied heavily upon Uisang's schematic chart of the *Avatamsaka Sutra* and quoted copiously from it. Through the efforts of Uisang and his disciples, Hwaom (Avatamsaka) theory became the cutting edge of all future doctrinal developments in Korean Buddhism. For this reason also, it placed the Hwaom school in the vanguard of a direct confrontation with the inconoclastic Zen schools.

During his lifetime, Uisang was a prodigious builder of temples. In addition to Pusok-sa, he was instrumental in the construction or expansion of a number of major temples such as Hwaom-sa, Popju-sa, Haein-sa, Naksan-sa. These temples continue to flourish and are among the dozen or so most important temples in Korea today.

As the founder of Hwa-om school of Buddhism in Korea, Uisang left a more visible imprint on history than Chajang or Won Hyo. Just as it had done in China, the Hwaom school became the most important Doctrinal school in Korea and was in the forefront of the struggle for supremacy between the Zen (Son) and the Doctrinal (Kyo) schools. This struggle has dominated the evolution of Korean Buddhism since Uisang's time.

Before we move on to the introduction of Zen into the Korean peninsula, we need to note one other sect of Silla Buddhism if only because it continues to be a major feature of Korean Buddhism even today—the Pure Land sect was, and is, is a faith for the masses, a faith which even the unlettered could understand.

This faith professed that by chanting *Namu Amita Bul* (the invocation Amitabha, the Sun Buddha), the devotee will be re-born in the "Pure Land" (Sanskrit: Sukhavati) of the "Western Paradise" where Amitabha Buddha dwelt. In this faith, no study of abtruse doctrines is required. All that is needed is a simple, un-conditional faith. In both China and Korea (and later in Japan), when monks from the aristocracy and elite educational institutes were competing for mastery over various Buddhist sutras, Pure Land Buddhism held out a hope to those whose day-to-day lives were filled with suffering, with no relief in sight. The Pure Land doctrine finds no comfort in earthly existence, "a sea of torment." It is much more desirable, then, to be reborn into the paradise of the next world. As Pure Land Buddhism became more and more popular in Korea, thousands left their homes to enter novitiates in the mountain temples. This popularity of Pure Land in Silla was in no small measure a reaction of the common people to the gross inequities in Silla society under elitist, authoritarian rule.

Again, Pure Land had to be thankful for its popularity to Won Hyo, that renaissance man of Silla Buddhism. The man who helped establish the Popsong (Dharma-nature) school and the Hwaom (Avatamsaka school), who made scholarly commentaries and annotations to such diverse sutras as the Prajña, Lotus, Nir-vana, Amitabha, and the Diamond sutras, was also a great evange-list. It is said that after his liaison with a Silla princess, Won Hyo traveled as an itinerant monk in repentance through towns and hamlets in every part of the country. During these travels, Won Hyo taught the Pure Land creed, emphasizing that all men and women can be reborn in paradise. His own understanding of the Pure Land faith is well expressed in his work, *Yusim Allak To* (The Way of Bringing Troubled Minds to Rest) thus: "The deeper meaning of the Pure Land is that it always has been for everyone, not just for the Bodhisattva."

Won Hyo, Chajang, and Uisang, then, were in the vanguard of eminent monks who helped turn the Unified Silla period into the golden age of Korean Buddhism. During this period (668-935), Buddhism inspired fine arts, poetry, and music as never before. Consequently, the Buddhist Church became rich and powerful and, as the dictum goes, power corrupts. Buddhism in Silla was no exception, and it entered a period of decadence during the middle years of the Silla dynasty. Then, partly as a result of this stagnation, and partly due to the efforts of some brilliant monks, Zen came into its own.

CHAPTER FIVE

The Nine Mountain Schools of Korean Zen

It must be remembered that even before Bodhidharma came to China, and all through the time when Hui-neng was establishing his school of "Sudden Enlightenment" (the period of the sixth and seventh centuries), Korean monks had been traveling to China. China was the great fount of Buddhist learning, and these Korean monks were intimately involved with the developing tradition of Ch'an either as disciples of great masters or, in some cases, as leaders themselves. According to tradition, Zen is said to have been brought to Korea during the reign of Queen Sondok (632-647) by the monk Pomnang (fl.632-646). Very little is known about Pomnang. Due to the conditions of civil war, and the hope which "state Buddhism" held out during those years, Zen was only vaguely understood and not broadly accepted. As noted earlier, Buddhism during these years was dominated by personalities like Chajang, Won Hyo, and Uisang. It is entirely possible that Pomnang did not have a commanding enough personality to cut a wide swath through the Buddhist establishment of the day.

Two hundred years later, starting with the founding of Porim-sa temple on Kaji Mountain by the monk Toui (d.825), Zen caught on and led to the establishment of the so-called "Nine Mountain

Schools" of Korean Zen. Of these nine schools, seven were founded by disciples of the first-generation successors of Ma-tsu (K:Ma Jo) (709-788), the founder of the inconoclastic Hung-chou school. Thus, even before the teachings of the Lin-chi (J: Rinzai) school became the dominant wing of Chinese Ch'an, these so-called "sudden enlightenment" teachings had been firmly established in Korea. These teachings continued to dominate Korean Zen throughout its history.

The great popularity of Zen in the beginning of the ninth century in contrast to its lackadaisical reception in the seventh century, can be explained by the warm response it received from the gentry families in the countryside. In fact, many founders of the Nine Mountain Schools came from the local aristocracy. This was a radical departure from the trend of "state Buddhism." Zen soon developed as a "religion" of the local gentry, partly in opposition to the Sutra-reading schools of the capital which were patronized by the aristocracy and the intellectuals.

Here we have parallels with the pre-Hui-neng Buddhism of northern China of the fifth through ninth centuries, and Nara Buddhism in Japan during the pre-Samurai period of the seventh through twelfth centuries. Just as Hui-neng established his iconoclastic "school" of Zen as an anti-intellectual, farm-based, self-reliant sect, so did Zen in Korea come into its own at the beginning of the ninth century. The individualistic element in Zen provided an ideological basis for an assertion of "independence" by the local gentry from the ruling aristocratic culture and structure in the capital. Given this background of political and economic conflict between the capital's aristocracy and the local aristocracy, it is not surprising that soon the new schools of Zen were at loggerheads with the older, more established schools of Doctrinal persuasion.

The monk Toui (d.825), generally regarded as the founder of Zen (Son) Buddhism in Korea, was the first to rush headlong into the Zen/Doctrinal controversy, as we shall see.

1 - *TOUI AND THE KAJI MOUNTAIN SCHOOL*

Toui's (d.825) birthdate is not recorded. A native of Silla, he went to T'ang China in 784 and returned in 818 after a stay of 34 years. A legend associated with Toui's life states that before he was born, his father saw a white rainbow in his room. His mother also dreamt of sitting on a couch with a monk, and, on waking up, found her room filled with the smell of incense. Half a month later, the mother conceived and the child was born after 39 months(!) in the womb. On the morning when the child was to be delivered, a strange monk appeared at the parents' door and advised them to bury the placenta of the child on a certain hill beside the river. The parents did as they were told. A big deer came to guard the place and remained all through the night. Because of all these omens, the child was ordained a monk at an early age and given the name Myong Jok.

Toui was born at a time when Buddhist culture in Silla had already passed its zenith and was entering a period of decline. Toui's lifetime also happens to coincide with the golden age of Zen (Ch'an) Buddhism in T'ang China (roughly the eighth and the ninth centuries). During his stay in China, Toui studied under the renowned master, Hsi-tang Chih-tsang (735-814). Along with Nan Chuan (748-835) and Pai-chang (720-814), Hsi-tang was one of the ablest of the 139 dharma heirs of the great patriarch Ma-tsu (709-788).

Toui received "transmission" from Hsi-tang Chih-tsang. His insight was also recognized by Pai-chang who is said to have praised him by saying, "It seems the orthodox (core of) Ch'an tradition of the Ma-tsu sect will soon leave China and cross the sea to Silla." This was a tribute as well to the vigorous training of a number of Korean monks in the Ch'an monasteries of T'ang China.

Toui's stay in China was an exhilirating time for the Chinese and Korean practitioners of Zen. Earlier, we touched briefly upon how Ma-tsu and his disciples, taking their cue from Hui-neng, reshaped Chinese Buddhism. The notion of "sudden enlightenment" coupled with the shock tactics used in Ma-tsu's "school" made Buddhism free from conventional traditions, and identification as Buddhists. This was a time when, on lonely mountaintops, teachers of sudden enlightenment were experimenting with new ways to transmit wordless insight to their students. The "Zen" they developed was most closely related to everyday life-experience. It stressed simple life, intellectual freedom and independence, more than worldly recognition. Their "Buddhism" was free from scholarship and logic.

There were a number of Korean monks in T'ang China studying simultaneously with Toui. These monks later returned to Silla and established their own schools and temples. The monks Hongch'ok (fl. 810-828) and Hyech'ol (785-861) were fellow-students of Toui under Hsi-tang Chih-tsang. Upon their return to Silla, they became founders, respectively, of the Silsang and Tongni mountain schools. As we shall see later on, seven out of nine founders of the mountain schools of Zen in Korea went to T'ang China for their studies and there they received "transmission" from their Chinese teachers. These nine mountain schools differed from each other, then, not on any ideological or doctrinal grounds but simply in terms of the personalities of their founders or the effective systematizers of their lineage.

The return of these monks from China ushered in an era of unprecedented creative activity within Zen (Son) Buddhism in Korea. It was not an accident that all the nine mountain schools were established within a period of one hundred years after Toui's return from China (between 828 and 931). The economic and political support was there. Following the tradition of T'ang China, these founder-monks also established their temples in the mountain—hence the name "Mountain Schools." These mountain-temples continue to be a unique and distinguished feature of Korean Zen to this day.

Upon Toui's return from China, his preaching of the doctrine of "sudden enlightenment" was greeted with open hostility as Zen was seen as an evil doctrine by the Buddhist establishment of the day. Up to this time, Korean Buddhism had been completely sutra-oriented. As we have noted earlier, Uisang's Hwa-om school had become the most prosperous and influential of all the doctrinal schools. Hwa-om (Avatamsaka) doctrine exercised the greatest influence on the scholastic orientation of Silla Buddhism. Uisang's major work, the *Chart of the Avatamsaka One-Vehicle Dharma-dhatu*, written in 661, had been the major reference point in Silla Buddhist literature for 150 years.

Toui became the first Zen Master to openly challenge the supremacy, indeed even the validity, of the Doctrinal schools. In the next hundred years, the distinction between the Zen (Son) and Doctrinal (Kyo) schools came to be more sharply drawn in Korea than it had ever been in China. In the initial phase of the Son/Kyo controvery, the monks Toui and Mu yom (799-888) were most visible. In his attempt to propagate the superiority of the wordless insight of Zen, Toui brushed aside the concept of *Dharmadhatu*, the basic underpinning of the Hwa-om doctrine. (Dharmadhatu, according to *Avatamsaka Sutra*, is the underlying Law of the Universe and is the reality of both being and non-being. Its causality is interpenetrative and overall, not merely successive.) Toui, in turn, countered with the radical concept of "emptiness." Furthermore, Toui claimed, the long and arduous method of gradual cultivation through faith, understanding, practice and realization (as had been been advocated by the Hwa-om and other Doctrinal schools) is rendered unnecessary if one follows the direct method of non-thought and non-cultivation. No wonder Toui had difficulties with the Buddhist establishment of the day!

An exchange between Toui and a Hwa-om scholar, no doubt recorded by a zealous Zen student, has come down to us:

> Chih-yuan: What other Dharmadhatu is there in addition to the four Dharmadhatus (as outlined in the *Avatamsaka Sutra*)? And is there a so-called Patriarch's Son (Zen) in addition to this doctrine of the four Dharmadhatus?

> Toui (raising his fist): In this fist, there is no so-called Dharma-dhatu. All beings are like snow on a hot oven. And such things as the preachings of the 53 wise masters (as recorded in the *Avatamsaka Sutra*) are nothing but foam on water. Wisdom or Bodhi is but a rock compared to this gold (of emptiness). This is

the reason why Ch'an master Kuei-t'sung Chih-ch'ang only raised his fist when asked, "What is shown in the Tripitaka?"

Chih-yuan: Then what is the purpose of believing, understanding, practicing and realizing, and what can these achieve?

Toui: Son (Zen) is to make one believe, understand, practice and realize the principle without thought, without cultivation. The preaching of the Patriarchs cannot be understood by men. What matters is the direct pointing to the True Nature of your mind. Therefore, in addition to the five divisions of the teachings (a Hwa-om classification of the Buddhist teachings) there is Inka (Mind-to-Mind Transmission from teacher to student). Worshipping Buddhist statues is nothing but resorting to an expedient (*Upaya*) for those who cannot understand the True Nature. However many sutras you have finished reading over the many years, I think you will not understand the way of Mind-to-Mind Transmission.

Chih-yuan (bowing): I have been hearing only the Buddhist teaching, and I did not get a glimpse of the mind of the Buddha.[16]

Despite all his efforts, however, Toui found it difficult to convince his countrymen of the efficacy of the immediate approach to truth without scholarly knowledge, or of "enlightenment" without practice. After repeated attempts to teach what he had learned in China, and not succeeding much, Toui retired from public life. He went to Chin-jung temple in the Sorak-san Mountains, where he lived a secluded life, managing to transmit his Dharma-lineage to Uksung Yumku (?-844) who, in turn, passed it on to Pojo Chejung (803-880).

The monk Chejung became one of the effective systematizers of Zen Buddhism in ninth-century Silla. He went to China in 836 and returned in 840, convinced that there was nothing in Chinese Zen that was not contained in Toui's teachings. At the request of Silla King Honan (r.857-861), Chejung built Porim-sa temple in the year 859 on Kaji Mountain. There he formally began to revere Toui as the founder of the Kaji sect. Chejung is said to have had as many as 800 students, foremost amongst whom was Sungak Hyang-mi (863-917) who won national renown as a teacher of Zen. Both Chejung and Hyang-mi helped Zen become popular in the Silla of their time. Of course, Zen monks from other schools also came to the forefront to usher in an age of intense activity for their sect.

2 - MU YOM AND THE ONGJU MOUNTAIN SCHOOL

Zen Master Mu yom (799-888) was, along with Toui, the most visible partisan in the Son/Kyo controvery. Mu yom was of royal descent, an eighth-generation son of a Silla king. His secular name was Kim and he was born in Kyongju, the capital of Silla. His grandfather, Chuch'on, was a prime minister of Silla as had been his great-grandfather and great-great-grandfather.

Like Toui, Mu yom has a legend associated with his birth. It is said that before his conception, his mother had a dream in which she was given a lotus flower by a heavenly being. In another dream, she was taught the Ten Buddhist Precepts by a heavenly being. These dreams convinced her that her as yet unborn son was destined to be a Buddhist monk. Accordingly, Mu yom was ordained when he was twelve years old, and he went to live at Osaek-sok temple in the Sorak Mountains after his ordination. He went to China in 821 and became a disciple of Ch'an master Ma-ku Po Che (no dates available) who was a Dharma heir of the Patriarch Ma-tsu. Ma-ku told Mu yom, "When I was with the master Ma-tsu he told me prophetically, 'One day you will meet someone from the Eastern Land (i.e. Silla) who is worth watching, and you will make the clean water of a ditch flow to the sea. Then your virtue will not be shallow.' My master Ma-tsu's voice is still ringing in my ears. It is very nice to meet you. I am glad to sanction you now. The way of Ch'an is now going to go to the Eastern Land."[17]

Mu yom returned to Silla in 845 after a stay of 24 years. In 847 he established the Songju temple on Songju Mountain. By this time Toui had been dead more than 20 years, but when Mu yom, with his royal connections and family background, adopted the same confrontational approach, he was taken more seriously than Toui had been. In his teaching, Mu yom made an even sharper distinction between the Son and the Kyo approaches than Toui had. He classified the doctrines (or sutras) as the "tongued realm," and the Son (Zen) approach as the "tongueless realm". For Mu yom, the "tongued realm" was only an expedient (*upaya*) or a vehicle adapted to the capacities of (generally inferior) people. The direct mind-to-mind transmission of the Son patriarchs was the true way. Even the best of words and speeches, according to him, retain traces of dualistic thought and are therefore impure. Since the special transmission of Zen is not dependent on words or speech, it does not carry any trace of purity or defilement. The scholastic teachings are only a partial and provisional explanation of truth; Zen is the truth itself. Furthermore, since there are no words or speech in Zen, it is without teachers or disciples.

> Someone once asked Mu yom, "If there is no teacher and no disciple in Zen, how was it possible that the light of the Dharma was not extinguished throughout 28 generations in India and the six patriarchs in China?" Mu yom replied, "The lineage is only kept for the sake of expediency; it does not express the true way of Zen transmission!"
>
> Again he was asked, "Are there two 'states' under one patriarch?"
>
> "Yes, there are," said Mu Yom. "Thus my teacher, Yang-shan Hui-chi (814-890) said that 'No tongue in two mouths is the essence of our school.'"
>
> Question: "What is the meaning of 2 states under one patriarch?"
>
> Mu yom: "Since in orthodox Zen the seeker does not seek Dharma, a teacher does not transmit [it]. This is what a 'tongueless state' means. However, when you address those who seek Dharma you talk with expedient words. This is what 'tongued state' means."[18]

It is easy to see why Mu yom's insistence that "in the mind-to-mind transmission of Zen there is no teacher or disciple" would have sounded radical to the Buddhist world of his time, caught up as it was in rituals and outer forms. Nonetheless, two of Silla's kings, Kyongmun (r.861-875) and Hongang (r.875-886) appointed Mu yom as a "National Teacher" at their court. Mu yom died in 888 at the age of ninety and was given the posthumous title of "Great Master Tae-nan-hye" (Great Bright Wisdom). The name of the pagoda where his relics were buried was called, "Halo of White Moon."

By the time of Mu yom's death, the Zen sect was fully ascendant within the Korean Buddhist world and enjoyed equal, if not more, power and prestige with the Doctrinal schools at the royal court. Mu yom's personality had much to contribute towards this ascendancy. He left behind more than 200 disciples, ablest among whom was Taegyong Yum (d.929) who had great influence at the court of King Hyogong (r.898-913). Taegyong Yum studied in China for many years under the master Yunchu Tao-ying (d.902) and returned to Silla in 909. He settled at Pori-ap temple and attracted nearly 500 students. One of Mu yom's famous disciples was the monk Pop kyong (dates unknown) who went to China and received transmission from master Chi-feng T'ao-chien (dates unknown). Pop kyong returned to Silla and settled at Chong-to temple where he had more than 300 students.

3 - HYECHOL AND THE TONGNI MOUNTAIN SCHOOL

Zen Master Hyechol (785-861) left home at the age of 15 and became a monk at Pusok-sa, the temple established by Uisang. As the head temple of the Hwa om sect, Hyechol studied the *Avatamsaka Sutra* for a number of years. He went to China in 814 and studied Zen under Master Hsi-tang Chih-tsang. Among Hyechol's fellow students at Hsi-tang's monastery were the monks Toui and Hongjik who, upon their return to Silla, established temples on Kaji mountain and Silsang mountain, respectively.

Hyechol arrived in China early in the same year that his teacher died. But Hyechol's practice/enlightenment was so impressive that Hsi-tang was able to give him transmission before his death.

One of the stories associated with Hyechol says that the ship on which he sailed from Silla to China also carried a large number of convicts. When the ship reached its destination at the Chinese port, Hyechol was mistaken for a convict and put up for trial! During his interrogation he said he was a monk. Other than volunteering this information, he refused to say anything else in his defense. The interrogator did not believe his story and threw him in a prison along with all the others who were found guilty of various crimes. In the prison, Hyechol just sat in *samadhi* and did not complain about the wrong done him. The local magistrate, after reviewing the case, decided to decapitate thirty of the convicts as a warning to all other miscreants. One by one, they went to meet the executioner's sword. Hyechol's turn for decapitation was approaching but he was still immersed in deep samadhi. Seeing this odd behavior, the magistrate had doubts about Hyechol being a criminal. He made further enquiries into his case and decided that this man was indeed a monk. So Hyechol was set free and allowed to continue his monastic journey. The story goes on to say that he did not show any particular delight or emotion in being saved from death just as he had not shown any reproach at being in prison or at the prospect of impending death.

Upon his return to Silla in 839, Hyechol built the Tae-an temple on Tongni Mountain and attracted hundreds of students. He was invited by the Silla king Munsong (r.839-857) to be a monk at the royal court. He accepted this position only for a short time as a courtsey to the king but then returned to his mountain abode. Among Hyechol's students were the Zen masters Toson (827-898) and Yo Taesa (dates unknown). Toson is one of the most influential monks in Korean Buddhist history. He imported techniques of geomancy (a system of divination based on yin-yang energy, having its roots in *I Ching* and other Chinese methods of divination) from China. In time, geomancy transcended the confines of the Buddhist world in Korea and became an integral part of Korean society and Korean world view. Toson thus became an instrument in changing the landscape of the Korean mind. Toson was close to General Wang Kon who later founded the Koryo dynasty (937-1392) and ruled as King Taejo (r.918-943). Toson helped him in selecting a capital-site for the new dynasty and also advised him in all manners of divination. In appreciation, he was made the "National Teacher" and Buddhism continued to flourish as the house religion of the new dynasty just as it had during the Silla dynasty. During his reign, King Taejo ordered the building of some 3,800 temples. But that's getting ahead of the story of the Tongni Mountain School.

The only recorded teaching of Zen Master Hyechol is found engraved on his student Toson's memorial stone. This teaching seems to have been addressed to Toson at some point.

> Originally there is no such thing as Buddha. But by necessity, a name was given to it. And originally there is no such thing as "Mind." To attain enlightenment is to realize the "One Thing." For the sake of illustration, it is said that the "One Thing" is empty. But it is not really empty. Mind of no-mind is the true mind; wisdom of no-wisdom is the true wisdom.[19]

4 - HONGJIK AND THE SILSANG MOUNTAIN SCHOOL

Not much information is available about Zen Master Hongjik except that he entered China in 810 and studied under Ch'an master Hsi-tang Chih-tsang at the same time that fellow Korean monks, Toui and Hyechol, were studying under the Chinese master Hsi-tang. Hongjik received transmission from Hsi-tang and returned to Silla in 826. In 828 he established Silsang temple on Chiri Mountain. It is said that at the height of his fame he had more than a thousand disciples. The most outstanding among his disciples was the monk Suchol (d.893). The name of his pagoda was "Crystallized Quiet." There is a mention of Hongjik's Zen on the memorial stone of another Zen Master (Tohon of the Hui yan mountain school) which says:

> As for [Hongjik's] Zen spirit, he practiced it without any trace of practice, attained enlightenment without any of enlightenment. In

his daily meditation he was always quiet like a "great mountain," and when he moved it was as if all the echoes of the mountains were roaring.[20]

The records of Silsang Mountain School, although they lack information about its founder's life and activities, claim that although Hongjik returned to Silla later than Toui (who had returned in 818) he was the first Zen Master to establish a traditional Zen monastery and offer instructions in Zen practice.

5 - HYON UK AND THE PONGNI MOUNTAIN SCHOOL

Zen Master Hyon Uk (787-869) was ordained as a Buddhist monk in 808 at the age of 21. No records are available about his family or his childhood. He went to China in 824 for his Zen studies and returned to Silla in 837. On his return journey, he joined the party of Kim Ui-chong, a Silla prince who was returning home after paying tribute at the T'ang imperial court.

The records of the Pongni Mountain School indicate that after his return to Silla, Hyon uk stayed at the Silsang temple on Chiri Mountain. The reasons for his stay at this temple are not very clear. We have already noted that Silsang temple was established by Zen Master Hongjik in 828 and was, presumably, carrying on his teaching. It is quite possible that by the time of Hyon Uk's return to Silla in 837, Hongjik had died and there was no fully trained successor to take charge of Silla's only Zen monastery. In keeping with this situation, it is quite possible that the Silla king may have asked Hyon Uk to take up residence at Silsang temple. This line of reasoning becomes more acceptable when we note that four kings of Silla, Minae (r.838-839), Sinmu (r.838), Munsong (r.839-857), and Honan (r.857-861) accepted Hyon Uk as their teacher and invited him frequently to the royal palace for discourses on the sutras as well on the teachings of Zen. King Kyongmun (r.861-875) is also said to have been very solicitious of Hyong Uk's well-being.

According to the records of the Pongni Mountain School, at

the end of a three-month summer retreat, Hyon Uk announced to his disciples that he was going to depart from this world within that year (869). True to his prediction, he passed away on November 15, 869.

A recorded saying of Hyon Uk tells that once someone asked him, "What is Son (Zen) and what is Tao?" Hyon-Uk replied, "That which has a name is not the great Tao. That which is right or wrong is not Son. If you want to know the meaning, it is like stopping a child's crying with yellow paper."[21]

The Pongni Mountain School was officially established in the year 897 on Pongni Mountain by the monk Chingyong Simhui (854-923), the most prominent among the 500 or so disciples of Hyon Uk. Chingyong was born into the royal Kim family and became a monk at the age of 19. With the help of future King Hyogong (r.898-913), he established the Pongnim temple and attracted hundreds of students. His disciple, Zen Master Chanyu Togwang (869-958) made Pongni Mountain School the most prominent of the Korean Zen schools of the time. Chanyu had left home at the age of 13 and sought to be initiated as a monk under Yungje, a disciple of master Chingyong Simhui. Yungje reportedly told him:

> You will be a great dragon some day. You are very welcome to stay here but my teacher Chingyong Simhui is a great master. He is a Buddha living in this world. He stays at the Pongnim temple. You must go there and follow him as your teacher.[22]

Chanyu Togwang followed the advice and went to Pongnim-sa where he was initiated as a monk. He went to China in the year 892 and returned in 921. His stay at Pongnim-sa attracted thousands of monks and lay believers. King Taejo (Wang Kon), the first king of the Koryo dynasty had a high regard for him. The third king of the Koryo dynasty, Chongjong, made him a "National Teacher." He died in August 958 and was given the posthumous title of "Chungjin Taesa" (The Great Illustrious Teacher).

6 - POMIL AND THE SAGUL MOUNTAIN SCHOOL

The monk Pomil (810-889) was the son of Kim Sul-won, once a Governor of Myongju province. The older Kim is celebrated in folk tales as being a wise and compassionate ruler. Pomil's mother also came from one of the noble families. A legend associated with Pomil's life says that before he was conceived his mother dreamt that she was holding the sun in her hands. It also says that Pomil was born with a tuft of hair on his head and jewel portruding from his forehead!

At the age of 15, Pomil sought his parents' permission to ordain as a monk. They are said to have consented by saying, "You did good deeds in your former life, so we cannot make you give up your resolution. May you attain Buddhahood so that you can save us." After a few years of sutra studies, Pomil went to China in the year 831 to study Ch'an (Zen). There he came across Ch'an Master Yen-kuan Chi-an (750-842). Yen-kuan asked him, "Where did you come from?" Pomil replied, "I came from the Eastern Land (Silla)." The master asked again, "Did you come by sea or land?" Pomil said, "I never set foot on sea or land." "Then how could you have come?" To this, Pomil's reply was, "The sun and the moon can go freely eastward or westward. What could stand in their way?" Master Yen-kuan was very impressed by his reply and accepted him as a disciple.

Sometime later, Pomil asked Yen-kuan, "What is the meaning of attaining Buddhahood?" The master said, "The Tao (The Way) is not that which can be sought by cultivation or learning. You should not befoul your own True Mind and should not have any idea of Buddha or Buddhahood. To have constantly the One Mind, that is Tao." On hearing these words, Pomil was suddenly enlightened. He stayed with Yen-kuan for six years and served his master diligently.

During his later years of wandering in China, Pomil met another Ch'an master Yueh-shan (751-834) who asked him, "Where have you come from?" "I left Kiangsi to come here," replied Pomil. "What did you come here for?" "To see you." "How could you have come here? There is no way between here and there." To this

Pomil replied, "If you are going to mount one more step upward, then I shall not be able to look at your face." On hearing this, Yueh-shan exclaimed, "Wonderful, wonderful! Clean wind blowing from outside makes man's desire cool off. You have the true determination of the wandering monk, to have come so far to visit this country."

Another exchange between Pomil and Yueh-shan has come down to us. From its content, it seems this exchange must have taken place at the very first meeting between the two.

> Yueh-shan asked Pomil, "Where do you come from?" "I come from the temple of master Yen-kuan." "What kind of Ch'an did he teach you?" "He said the constant mind is Ch'an."
>
> "What a stale teaching it is! Good, evil, joy, anger, grief, pleasure, everything is Zen. Why should only the constant mind be Zen?"
>
> Pomil asked, "What then is Zen?"
>
> Yueh-shan raised his hand and pointed to the sky and the earth.
>
> Pomil said, "You have only hands, you have no mouth. If you had no hands, how could you answer me?"
>
> "What do you mean?"
>
> "I had asked about the Zen with the mouth, not with the hands."
>
> "Then I will answer you with the mouth. I want you to speak without moving your throat, tongue, teeth and lips."
>
> "That's the very thing I have been wanting to ask you. Why don't you try it yourself first?"
>
> Yueh-shan tapped Pomil on the back and said, "Indeed, you are a wise man from the Eastern Land."

Pomil stayed for a few months at Yueh-shan's temple and helped out with the farm work. One day, as he put down his hoe and was taking a rest, Yueh-shan asked him, "Is it hard work?" Pomil said, "No. Because I don't need to raise the hoe high, it is not such hard work." When Pomil said this, Yueh-shan threw his staff at him. Pomil caught the staff expertly and hit Yueh-shan. Yueh-shan's attendant who was standing nearby got very angry at this behavior. He said to his master, "Are you going to let this crazy monk get away without punishment?" Yueh-shan hit the at-

tendant without saying a single word. The attendant was surprised and confused. Seeing this exchange, Pomil burst into
laughter. Yueh-shan praised Pomil by saying, "Today I have seen a
monk-like monk."[23]

During his wanderings in China, Pomil found himself caught in
the midst of the terrible *Hui-cheng* persecutions of Buddhism (842-
845). The roots of this persecution go back to the resentment felt
by Confucians and Taoists at the material prosperity as well as the
economic and (indirect) political power of the Buddhist temples.
In 819, a Confucian bureaucrat named Han Yu had issued a document in which he criticized many aspects of Buddhism. Buddhism, he said, was un-Chinese. One of his chief complaints
was that Buddha had not been Chinese; hence, in his view, Buddhism had no legitimacy! His exhortations were: "Restore its
people (Buddhist believers) to human living! Burn its books! And
convert its buildings to human dwellings!"[24]

Emperor Wu-tsang (r.841-46), influenced by the Taoists at his
court, started taking strict measures against Buddhists immediately
after his ascension. He appointed prominent Taoists like Chao
Kuei-chen and Liu Hsun-ching to high positions at his court.
Other Taoists like Teng Yuan-chao slandered Buddhism and put
pressures on the court to supress it.

Then an incident took place which added fuel to the imperial
court's smouldering resentment. It is not known whether the incident actually took place or was a trumped-up charge. Nevertheless, it was alleged that a Buddhist monk had a liasion with
a court lady and made her pregnant. Normally, in such a case, only
the guilty monk would have been punished but Emperor Wu-
tsang, in August 845, issued an edict that had the effect of ultimately destroying traditional Buddhism and urbanized Ch'an in
northern China. Within a period of two years, by the emperor's
orders, 4600 large temples and monasteries, and over 40,000
smaller temples were destroyed. An estimated 260,000 monks and
nuns were evicted and forced back into secular life. Nearly
150,000 temple attendants (or "slaves," as the enemies of Buddhism
called them) were "freed." Many Buddhist pagodas and statues
were destroyed and countless sutras burnt. Temple bells were

melted down and made into farming tools and furniture. The state reclaimed several million acres of property that had belonged to these temples and monasteries. The result of this persecution was the destruction of all the great Buddhist establishments of the day, including all the bigger temples in Chang-an and Loyang (the Eastern and Western capitals of T'ang China.) All that was left were two temples and thirty monks in each of these two cities.

One ironic effect of this persecution was that the only Buddhist sect left with any strength was the rural southern Ch'an. The southern Ch'an (Hui-neng's school) had always relied on economic self-sufficiency by farming the land around the monasteries and living a very frugal and simple monastic life. Through this life-style, southern Ch'an had the respect of local officials and when the persecution came, they were able to rescue the monasteries in their area from some of its harsher measures. When Ch'an became popular again in Sung China (960-1279), it was southern Ch'an that became the house religion just as northern Ch'an had been in T'ang China.

During these times of chaos and turbulence, Pomil hid on Sang Mountain and continued to cultivate his Zen practice. By necessity, he had to survive on fruits from the trees in the mountains and water from the streams. His body became emaciated and it was very difficult for him even to walk around since he was so weak with hunger and undernourishment. He survived like this for six months. Then he had a dream in which a strange man appeared and told him, "You may go now." With great difficulty, he made his way out of his mountain hideout and traveled to Shao-chou (in south China) to pay homage before the pagoda of the Sixth Patriarch. A legend from this time has it that, while he was praying at the Sixth Patriarch's pagoda, a fragrant cloud arose around the pagoda and a white crane came to sit on the roof and started singing. Seeing this, everyone was surprised and thought that surely a great saint had come to visit the pagoda.

In August 846, Pomil returned to Silla after a stay of 15 years in China. He stayed on Mount Paekdal until January 851 when the governor of Myongju province (the same province where his father had once been governor) invited him to establish a temple on Sagul-san Mountain. The name of his temple was Kulsan-sa and Pomil stayed there for nearly forty years until his death. During all these years, he did not leave the mountain even once. Three successive Silla kings invited him to become a teacher at the royal court but Pomil refused to leave his mountain habitat.

> Someone once asked him, "What is the intention of the Patriarchs?" Pomil replied, "It has not been lost for six generations." Someone else asked, "What is it that a (novice) monk should strive for?" Pomil said, "You should not follow the steps of the Buddha, nor should you try to enlighten yourself by dint of man."[25]

One day in April 889, Pomil announced to his students, "I am going to go to another world. I am leaving you now. Don't be sentimental. Only cultivate well your mind and try not to befoul the essential meaning of Buddhism." A few days later, on the first of May, he lay down and died.

His disciple, Nangwon Kaechong (834-930), became a famous Zen master and lived to be 96 years old. Nangwon left home at the age of 20 and studied sutras at Hwaom temple. Then for three years he practiced austerities on the Kum Mountain. An old man, who met him in the mountains, advised him to go to Kulsan-sa temple and told him there he would meet a saint. Nangwaon made his way to Kulsan-sa. Upon seeing him, Pomil is said to have remarked, "Why are you so late in coming? I have been waiting for you for a long time." After Pomil's death, Nangwon spent some time as Abbot of the Pohyon temple and then was appointed a monk at the court of King Kyongae (r.924-927).

Another of Pomil's famous disciples was the monk Nanggong Haengjok (833-918). Initially, he studied the *Avatamsaka Sutra* at Haein-sa temple and stayed at Wu-tai Shin Mountain. There he studied with and received Inka from Shi-shuang Ch'ing-chu (no dates available). He returned to Silla in 884. He became Abbot of Kunja-sa temple and was appointed a monk at the royal court by King Hyogong (r.898-913). His disciples numbered more than 500 and the name of his pagoda was "White Moon Nestling in the Clouds."

7 - TOYUN AND THE SAJASAN MOUNTAIN SCHOOL

There is only scant information about the early years of Toyun (797-868), the founder of the Sajasan Mountain School. There are hints that he came from a noble family and became a monk at the age of eighteen. He seems to have ordained at the Kwisin temple where he studied the *Avatamsaka Sutra* for a long time. Not wholly satisfied with the *Doctrine of Perfectness and Completeness* (the main doctrine of *Avatamsaka Sutra*), he took up the life of a wandering monk, wearing rags and carrying a bowl. In popular Zen parlance, the cloud was his blanket and the stream his pillow.

In 825, Toyun went to China and became a disciple of Nan-chuan Piu-yuan (748-835), the most brilliant student of the great patriarch Ma-tsu (709-788). One of the most charismatic teachers in Zen history, Nan-chuan is also famous for being the teacher of Chao-chou, another luminary in Zen history. Toyun received Inka from Nan-chuan, and, in 847, after his teacher's death, he returned to Silla. He built a small temple called Hungyong-sa in the Diamond Mountains and stayed there for the rest of his life. He died on the 18th day of the fourth month in 868.

Toyun's disciple, Chunghyo Cholchung (826-900), greatly expanded the Hungyong temple, making it into one of the foremost Zen training centers in the country. Chunghyo entered the temple of a certain monk Chinjon (dates unknown) at the age of seven and was ordained a monk at 19. At the temple, he studied the *Avatamsaka Sutra*. After his teacher's death, Chunghyo Cholchung met the monk Sogun (dates unknown) who not only became his chief disciple but helped him move the temple to Saja Mountain. Thus Toyun's school came to be known as the Saja Mountain School. Toyun's lineage became established through Chunghyo and Sogun. Chunghyo was greatly respected by kings Hongang (r.875-886) and Chonga (r.886-888). However, he refused an invitation from Queen Chinsong, (r.888-898) to become a monk at the royal court. His records suggest that he died in 900 at the age of 74 while seated in a cross-legged meditation posture.

The founding patriarchs of the seven mountain schools of Zen in Korea which we have discussed so far all went to China for their training and all received transmission from masters who were first-generation successors of Ma-tsu. The tradition they brought back to Korea was that of Zen in its "golden age," at its creative and innovative best.

All the seeds for the eventual establishment of these seven schools were planted within 30 years following the return of Zen Master Toui from China in 818. However, the process of actually starting "schools" was more lengthy. In most cases, the school was not established until an able disciple or grand-disciple founded a mountain temple and formally recognized his teacher as the patriarch of the school. There is no evidence that any of these founding patriarchs intended to start "schools." Their concerns seemed to be limited to teaching Zen and passing on the teaching to a worthy successor.

The founders of other two mountain schools of Korean Zen did not belong to the lineage of Ma-tsu's iconoclastic Hung-chou school of southern Ch'an .

8 - TOHON AND THE HUIYAN MOUNTAIN SCHOOL

Strictly speaking, the monk Pomnang (fl.632-646) was the first "Patriarch" of all Korean Zen, as he was the first person to bring the teachings of Ch'an to Korea. Little is known about his life except that he went to China and studied under the fourth patriarch of Ch'an school, Tao-hsin (580-651). Thus Pomnang precedes even Hui-neng (638-713), the sixth patriarch who is commonly regarded as the founder of Chinese Zen. Pomnang's training, therefore, must have been in the tradition of Bodhidharma rather than in the "sudden enlightenment" tradition of Hui-neng. This is important because the Korean Zen tradition insists that its origin is from Hui-neng rather than from Lin-chi (d.866), the great-great-great-grand disciple of Hui-neng whose system of kung-an teaching came to dominate Korean Zen and in whose line of succession some major Korean Zen masters received their transmission. Therefore, when Pomnang brought the teachings of Ch'an to Korean in the middle of the seventh century, he was introducing a tradition and methodology that was still in the process of experimentation and maturation.

For a number of reasons (not the least being the fact that the Korean Buddhism of his time was completely taken up with seeking favors and protection from the numerous Buddhist deities), Pomnang's teaching of Ch'an did not get much attention in Silla. During the period when Pomnang was active was also the period of Queen Sondok's reign (632-646), probably the greatest royal patron of Buddhism in Korea's history. This was a time as well when Buddhism itself was experimenting with new forms and expression. To add to all these elements, a civil war was going on and it stood to reason that any sect whose practices purported to pray for the success and prosperity of the state in its struggle against the neighboring states would have a better chance of acceptance than the inner-directed teachings of Ch'an. It was also a time of towering Buddhist personalities like Won Hyo, Chajang and Uisang, and it is quite probable that Pomnang did not have a commanding enough personality to compete with the Buddhist giants of his day.

In any case, Pomnang transmitted his teachings to monk Sinhaeng (d.779). Sinhaeng also traveled to China and studied Ch'an there. His successor was the monk Chunbom who in turn was succeeded in the Dharma by Hyeun (no dates available for either of them). Hyeun's successor was the monk Tohon (824-882) who founded the Huiyang Mountain School in 879, laying the claim to his being the oldest Son (Zen) lineage in Korea.

Tohon was born in Kyongju, the Silla capital. He lost his father when he was nine years old. At the age of nineteen, he became a monk at Pusok-sa temple. Instead of going to China, as was the fashion with the Korean monks of his time, he pursued his Zen training under Zen Master Hyeun, the third-generation successor of Pomnang. (The name of Hyeun's temple is not known.) Tohon was invited to be a monk at the royal court of King Kyongmun (r.861-875) but he declined the invitation. Instead, he became the abbot of Allak temple on Hyongye Mountain. In 879, with the help of his disciple Shimchung (no dates available), he founded the Pongnam temple on Huiyang Mountain. In this endeavor, they were supported by King Kyongmun's successor King Hongang (r.875-886). Not long after the founding of his temple, Tohon died in 882 at the age of 59.

Tohon's grand-disciple, Chongjin, was a famous Zen master. He went to China in 900 for his Zen studies and stayed there for 24 years. Upon his return to Silla, he was patronized by King Taejo, the first king of the new Koryo dynasty.

9 - IOM AND THE SUMI MOUNTAIN SCHOOL

The last of the nine mountain schools of Korean Zen shares a distinction with the Huiyan-san school in not belonging to great patriarch Ma-tsu's lineage. Instead, the Sumi Mountain School belongs to the lineage of Chinese master Ch'ing-yuan Hsing-ssu (d.740) which eventually evolved into the T'sao-tung school of Ch'an and the Soto school of Japanese Zen.

Iom (870-936), the founder of the school, was born in Kyongju, the capital of Silla and became a monk at the age of 16 at Kaya-ap temple. In 896, he joined a party of a T'ang envoy returning home and traveled to China for his Zen studies. He became a student of Yun-chu Tao-ying (dates unknown), a disciple of master Tung-shan Liang-chieh (807-869) the founder of the Ts'ao-tung (Soto) school. It is recorded that on seeing him for the first time, Yun-chu asked Iom, "Since parting not long ago, why do we meet again so soon?" Iom replied, "What do you mean ' meet again' since I have never been separated from you?" On hearing this, Yun-chu accepted him as his disciple and Iom stayed with him for six years. He finally received Inka from Yun-chu who said, "Because Zen does not depart from a man, he can spread Zen. The spirit of my teacher lies on me and you rather than on anyone else. Now my spirit of Zen goes to the Eastern Land (Silla) with you."[26]

After leaving Yun-chu's temple, Iom made a pilgrimage to all the famous Zen training centers in China and met many famous Zen teachers of the time. He returned to Silla in 911 and stayed at

Sunggwang temple which the governor of Naju province had built for him.

At the invitation of King Taejo, the first king of the new Koryo dynasty, Iom became a monk at the royal court. In 936, King Taejo built the Kwang-jo temple on Sumi Mountain for Iom and it became the center of his school. Hundreds of students gathered to study under him. After four years at the temple, Iom knew that his time in this world was up. He went to Kaesong, the capital of Koryo, to say farewell to his friend the king. But Taejo was away at the time on a war-mission and could not be found. Iom passed away at Oryong temple in Kaesong in 936 while waiting for the king's return.

The ninth century, then, was a period of extraordinary activity and influence by Korean monks returning from China after studying Ch'an and establishing their mountain temples in Silla. They found patrons in the local gentry and at the royal court. All this prosperity of Son schools, inevitably, came at the expense of the Hwaom school. The ninth and tenth centuries were, as a result, a time of increasingly strident controversy between the Zen and the Doctrinal schools. Wang Kong, known posthumously as King Taejo, (r. 918-943) the founder of the Koryo dynasty (935-1392), was a great patron of Zen monks and invited them to the royal court as resident monks. But after Taejo's death, Zen did not get the same enthusiastic support from his successors. We shall investigate the reasons for this lack of enthusiasm when we take a look at the situation of Buddhism during the early years of the Koryo dynasty.

It was not long after the intense activity surrounding the founding of these nine mountain schools that Zen began to lose much of its vitality. This was partly due to the continuing conflict with the Doctrinal schools and partly from the lack of support from the royal court. In addition, in the tenth century, Fa-ye Zen, with its dual emphasis on Ch'an meditation and recitation of Amitabha Buddha's name (the *yombul* practice performed by believers of the Pure Land sect), was introduced into Korea. In China this yombul (C. nien-fu) practice helped cause the gradual disappearance of Ch'an, and in Korea the Zen followers also dwindled in number and spiritual vigor with its introduction.

CHAPTER SIX

Koryo Buddhism

The declining years of the Silla dynasty and the early years of the Koryo dynasty (936-1392) were marked, as we have noted, by intense activity on the part of the Son (Zen) monks of the nine mountain schools. Wang Kong, the founder of the Koryo dynasty who assumed power under the name of King Taejo (r.918-943), was a devout Buddhist and was personally friendly with many Son monks. He appointed many of them to high official positions at his court. During his reign, Taejo ordered the building of some 3,800 temples, and just before his death, he promulgated ten admonitions to guide his successors, based on his belief that the prosperity of the kingdom was derived from the protective powers of the Buddhas. One admonition says, "We must build temples for both Son and Kyo (Doctrinal) schools and appoint abbots to them, so that they may perform the proper ceremonies and themselves cultivate the Way."[27]

Given Taejo's endorsement, under his successors Buddhist temples received land allotments and tax-exemptions from the state. The monks were exempted from corvee (conscripted labor for public construction projects), a consideration that no doubt led to significant increases in their numbers. Many members of the aristocracy, even royal princes, became monks. (These were usually the younger sons in the family who would normally not share power within the family hierarchy.) The entry of upper classes into the ranks of the monks naturally attracted more donations of land-holdings to the temple both from the aristocracy and the royal family. Since the land was tax-exempt, the Buddhist temples came to wield immense economic power, not unlike the Roman Catholic Church in our own time. The temples controlled vast tracts of tax-exempt paddy and forest lands, presided over an army of serfs and possessed a fortune in precious metals cast as Buddhist icons and artifacts. The new capital of Kaesong itself became a thriving Buddhist metropolis. In rural areas the monasteries built up granaries and, in times of shortage, loaned grain at high interest rates. The temples also became centers of commerce, as had happened in China, engaging in the making of wine, noodles and tea, and the raising of livestock.

A system of examination for the Buddhist clergy, along the lines of a civil service examination, was instituted. This "monk examination" was divided into two parts—one for the Son monks and one for the monks of the Doctrinal schools. A talented and conscientious student could work his way up to appointment as a royal teacher (*Wangsa*) or a National Teacher (*Kuksa*), thus placing himself near the sources of secular and political power.

Inevitably, all the economic and political power contributed to a gradual decline of Buddhism during the middle years of the Koryo dynasty. The ranks of the monks became filled with men pursuing wealth and status, and avoiding the hardships of peasant life and the dangers of military duty. The growing corruption in the sangha and the perversity of motives of so many new monks brought a backlash from the authorities. Beginning in 1059, during King Munjong's reign (1046-1083), a series of measures was adopted to regulate the Buddhist sangha. The first of these decreed that only one son in three in a family could be ordained, and then only after the age of 15. Later, serfs and indigent persons were altogether prohibited from being ordained. Children of monks, born before ordination, could not take part in civil service examinations. The monks were forbidden to lodge in villages overnight. These measures continued to be in force during the rest of the Koryo dynasty. Later, during the Confucianist-dominated Yi dynasty (1392-1910) even more restrictive measures were adopted. Despite all these measures, Buddhism continued to exert great influence on the political, economic and spiritual life of the Koryo kingdom. And the hostility between the Son and Kyo schools continued unabated.

One of the great achievements of Koryo Buddhism, indeed of all Korean Buddhism, was the carving, on woodblocks, of the entire Buddhist Canon, the *Tripitaka*, as rendered in Chinese translation. This mammoth task was begun in the early years of the twelfth century during the reign of King Hyonjong (r.1009-1031) and was not completed until 1087. The carving of the *Tripitaka* was originally undertaken as a kind of prayer for the nation's safety against the invasions from the north. Beyond that, the carving must have also been motivated by a desire to systematize the doctrines of all the Buddhist schools. The authorities must have hoped that such a written body of Buddhist scriptures would help in resolving the conflicts between the Son and the Kyo schools. Unfortunately these woodblocks were destroyed during the Mongol invasions of the 13th century, and a new set had to be carved. It was against the background of this first carving of the *Tripitaka* that the monk Uichon established his Directorate of Buddhist Scriptures.

Uichon (1055-1101) is a seminal figure in Korean Buddhist history. He was the first person to attempt a reconciliation between the two contending schools of Son and Kyo. Known posthumously as the "National Teacher Taegak," Uichon was the fourth son of King Munjong (r.1046-1083) and one of the greatest scholars in Korea's Buddhist history. Uichon combined in himself a scholarly mastery of both Buddhist scriptures and classical Chinese literature. Against his father's wishes, Uichon traveled surreptitiously to Sung China in 1085 at the age of 30. He stayed in China for 14 months and studied with well-known teachers of the Hua-yen, Tien-tai, Vinaya, Pure Land and Ch'an sects. It is interesting to note that with the terrible "Hui-chang persecutions" of Buddhism in China (845-846), Korea was left with the only flourishing Mahayana church in that part of the world. However, the monks and the scholars in Korea still looked for inspiration to Buddhist China partly because Chinese was the language into which all the Buddhist scriptures had been translated and, until the carving of the *Tripitaka Koreana*, China was the place to go to study Buddhist scriptures first hand. It seems that during the persecutions, most of the Chinese monks and scholars went underground with their precious translations of the sutras. When the Sung dynasty (960-1279) again began to patronize Buddhism, these translations became available once more. Uichon's mission seems to have been to secure these translations. It is said that he brought back with him 1,010 texts in 4,740 fascicles, and that they were then carved on wooden blocks and was added as a supplement to the *Tripitaka*. This collection as well as the first edition of the *Tripitaka* itself were burned during the Mongol invasion of 1231-1232.

Upon his return from China with a vast scholarly hoard and royal connections, Uichon tried to reconcile the disupte between the Son and the Kyo schools. He revived and expanded the dormant Ch'ontae school and attempted to merge both Son and Kyo in it. Ch'ontae was the Korean transplant of the Chinese *Tien-tai* (J: Tendai) school, which used the *Lotus Sutra* as the basic tenet of its doctrines. In earlier centuries, many Korean monks had studied in China in the Tien-tai tradition and brought its teachings back to Korea. Uichon himself attributed the origins of the Ch'ontae studies in Korea to the monk Won Hyo who had written an outline of the sect called *Pophwa Chongyo*. Faced with tough competition from the flourishing Son and Kyo schools, the Ch'ontae had never become an independent or major school. Now Uichon sought to revitalize its teachings and establish it as an autonomous school for the first time. He is thus considered the real founder of the Ch'ontae school in Korea.

According to Uichon's analysis of the dispute, both Son and Kyo had lost sight of the fact that meditation was originally an integral part of all the Buddhist schools, including those oriented towards scriptural study. However, both the Son and Kyo schools had polarized themselves into extreme positions—the Doctrinal schools emphasizing theoretical studies at the expense of meditation, the Son school abandoning scriptural studies entirely in favor of meditation. Uichon criticized both these positions:

> The Dharma is devoid of words or appearances; but it is not separate from words and appearances. If you abandon words you are subject to distorted views and defilements; if you grasp at words, you are deluded as to the truth... Students of the scriptures often abandon their inner work and pursue externals; Son adepts prefer to ignore worldly activity and simply look inward. Both positions are biases which are bound at two extremes. They are like fighting over whether a rabbit's horns are long or short, or arguing whether flowers in the sky are profuse or scarce.[28]

Uichon therefore advocated both study and meditation as complimentary—the internal and the external pursuits in balance. He was more critical of the Son school than of the Doctrinal schools, probably due to the traditional Tien-tai antipathy towards Ch'an in China. Uichon pointed out that the original approach of Son was based on perfecting meditation while relying on the instructions in the sutras and other scriptural teachings. Bodhidharma was reputed to have transmitted the *Lankavatara Sutra* along with his robe and bowl to his successor. Hui-neng, the Sixth Patriarch, taught both the *Diamond Sutra* and the *Prajñaparamita Sutra*. The history of Ch'an in China showed that sutras indeed had a place within the framework of Ch'an approach. But Son in Korea, according to Uichon, had tended to place a very narrow interpretation on the alleged Bodhidharma dictum, "without words and speech" and had become intensely anti-scriptural. According to Uichon, such an attitude bordered on heresy.

Uichon had the support of the royal court in his efforts to establish an ecumenical Ch'ontae school. But he died at the early age of 46 and the experiment was brought to a halt. Without his leadership, the Ch'ontae school became just another contending school. His pronounced anti-Son bias led not to the spirit of harmony which he had hoped for, but to an increased insularity of the Son Schools. It was left to Pojo Chinul (1158-1210), the

founder of the native Zen tradition in Korea to improve upon Uichon's experiment and learn from his mistakes.

One inadvertent effect of Uichon's efforts was to give the lan-
guishing Son sect a renewed sense of self-awareness and cohe-
siveness. This came about on two fronts: first, Uichon gathered
around him a number of talented monks from all the nine mountain schools of Zen to help him advance the cause of his Ch'ontae
school. Secondly, he excluded Son texts from his compilation of
the *Supplement to the Tripitaka*. These anti-Son activities galva-
nized the Son sect into a renewed vigor.

That vigor did not last very long however. Two factors which
had been operational for more than a century continued to haunt
the Son sect. In the middle of the ninth century, Zen Master
Toson (827-898) had imported techniques of geomancy from China. Geomancy is said to have wielded enormous influence over
Taejo, the founder of the Koryo dynasty, and later kings. But this
very influence became the nemesis of the Son sect as its monks
became involved in building projects and ceremonies rather than
devote themselves to meditation. A second factor to haunt the
Son sect was the "monk examination" system. We will talk more
about this later on, but here we only need note that it forced
young monks to devote many years of study for the rigorous tests.
That effort was antithetical to the basic interests of the meditation-
oriented Son sect.

Going from the particular problems of the Son sect to the general condition of Buddhism in the early years of the Koryo dynasty,
we need to take note of two "revolts" that were to undermine the
position and influence of Buddhism. The first was the revolt of
the professional soldier. As was common throughout Asia and
Europe in medieval times, the professional soldier was a free-
lancer. He was supposed to have his livelihood assured through
governmental grants of land in exchange for his services during
wartime. During times of peace, he and his family could live on
the land and use it for an economic base. But at this time in Korean history, more and more land was being donated to Buddhist
temples. In some cases, land which had been granted to soldiers
was taken away from them. Many peasants who might otherwise

have been drafted into the military became monks, thus making themselves exempt from military service. To make matters worse, professional soldiers were not only mobilized for wartime service but many were drafted into corvee labor during peacetime as well. Eventually the professional soldiers came to be looked down upon as little more than menial laborers. Added to these resentments were the debauchery of the royal court of King Uijong (r.1146-1170) and the indiscriminate humiliation of the military at the hands of civil officials. In one recorded incident, the beard of a general of the Royal Guards was set afire by a civil official as a prank, and the official went unpunished.

In 1170, when the military escort to King Uijong arrested the king and removed him from the throne, a revolt broke out. This coup introduced a highly volatile period of Korean history in which there were repeated power struggles and counter-coups, and widespread serf and peasant uprisings. The king's authority existed in name only. All the important positions in government were filled by military men. Less reliance was placed on the Chinese model of government, which had been in vogue since the early years of the Silla dynasty, and more emphasis was placed on indigenous political and economic models. For example, private ownership (as opposed to the king's ownership) increased, and land became concentrated in the hands of relatively few powerful families whose estates were worked by tenant and slave labor.

Soon the military rulers had to contend with Mongol invasions from the north. Starting in 1231, the Mongols launched no fewer than six major invasions of Korea within a period of 30 years. The subsequent establishment of the Yuan dynasty (1271-1368) in China by the Mongols meant that for nearly two centuries the Mongols were a large presence in the internal and external affairs of Korea. One direct impact of the Mongol invasions on Buddhism was the burning of the first edition of *Tripitaka Koreana* during the invasion of 1231-32.

The royal court fled to Kanghwa Island, just off the Korean coast. There it proceeded to re-create for itself life as it had been on the mainland before the invasion, i.e. a life of debauchery and profligacy. On Kanghwa Island, a second edition of the *Tripitaka,* carved on wooden blocks as a national prayer against the Mongol invaders, was completed in 1251. The 81,258 wooden blocks, each 9 1/2" wide, 29" long and 2 1/2" thick, are engraved with scriptures on both sides. On average, there are 22 lines on each side and 14 characters in each line. The wood for the blocks is said to have been imported from China, even though Korea was at war with northern China. It was kept submerged in salt water for three years and then in fresh water for another three years. The wood was then buried underground for three years and then dried in open air for three additional years. The actual engraving took 16 years. Today this *Tripitaka* is the oldest and best preserved of all Chinese translations of the entire Buddhist canon. It is housed at Haein-sa temple, and remains Korea's most important Buddhist treasure.

The other "revolt," that of the bureaucrat, was more pernicious from a Buddhist point of view. Since the beginning of its history, Korea had been fed by Chinese culture like an underground stream feeding a well. It was, therefore, inevitable that Confucianism, the system of thought on which the Chinese world view was based, would some day make its appearance in Korea. This it did, not long after the political unification of the peninsula in 668 A.D. under the Silla dynasty. A National Confucian College was established in 682, and, in 717 portraits of Confucius, the "Ten philosphers" and the 72 "worthies" were brought from T'ang China and installed there. The college was renamed as the National Confucian University in 750. In 788 a state examination system for the selection of government officials was initiated. The curriculum at the Confucian University included, naturally, studies in Confucian *Analects* and other Chinese classical texts on rites, history and literature.

The men who championed the cause of emerging Confucianism were middle and lower-level government bureaucrats, the literati who normally could not hope to rise in bureaucratic ranks beyond a certain point no matter what their abilities. The top echelons of the government positions were reserved for members of the traditional *bone-rank* (kolp'um) aristocracy. Not accidentally, the aristocracy had sought to legitimize itself through the use of

Buddhist doctrines and institutions. We have seen earlier how in the hwarang (flower-knight) training system, the leader of the unit was viewed as an incarnation of Maitreya Buddha. Now the lower-level bureaucrats, not born of the bone-rank privileges, argued that Korean society needed to have a set of moral standards applicable to the world of human affairs. Understandably, they were critical of the ambivalent view of man and his mundane existence fostered by the Buddhist world view of life on this earth and hereafter. Sol Ch'ong, son of the famous monk Won Hyo and the foremost Confucian scholar of his day, presented a letter of admonition to the throne known as *P'ung Wang So* (Parables for the King) in which he urged the monarchs to renounce pleasure-seeking and observe strict moral standards. Ch'oe Chi-won (869-903), one of the greatest figures in Korean literary history, became the first Korean to pass the highest Confucian examination held in Peking in 896. He urged the royal court in Silla to appoint men of talent to all government posts on the basis of an examination system similar to the one being used in T'ang China. When his advice was not heeded, he went into self-imposed exile in the mountains where, incidentally, he wrote his best literary works.

From the middle years of the Silla dynasty to the middle years of the Koryo dynasty, Confucianism was a subterranean movement, burrowing itself, ever so slowly and deeply, into the ranks of government officials and their world-view. Over a period of time even the aristocracy and Korean kings came to view Confucianism as vital to the moral training of its political leaders. It became a doctrine by which not only the governing of the state but the ordering of family relationships came to be dictated. Koryo Confucians by no means rejected Buddhism—they regarded it as a doctrine for achieving spiritual tranquility and other-worldly salvation, and they felt that Buddhism could coexist side by side with Confucianism. During this period there were indeed officials who were well-versed both in Buddhism and Confucianism. Complete political rejection of Buddhism came during the Yi dynasty (1392-1910), a rejection that continued until the 1980's, when Buddhists came to realize that if they did not assert themselves politically they were in danger of being phased out of national religious life.

CHAPTER SEVEN

Chinul and the Re-founding of Korean Zen

Pojo Chinul (1158-1210) is to Korean Zen what Hui-neng, the Sixth Patriarch, is to Chinese Zen, and St. Thomas Aquinas to Catholicism. The founder of a native Zen tradition in Korea, Chinul's writings have become the standard frame of reference for all future generations of Korean monks and Buddhist scholars.

As we have seen, the times in which Chinul lived were extremely volatile, not only for Buddhism, but for the political landscape as well. The constant threat of invasions from the north hung over the peninsula from the 11th to the 13th centuries. The Khitan invasions in 993, 1010 and 1018 had thrown into disarray the balance of power at the royal court and had a left a demoralized leadership at the helm. A series of military revolts from 1126 to 1136, and in 1170, 1196 and 1258 combined with the Mongol invasions from 1231 to 1259 helped to erode all semblance of royal authority. Private families in the aristocracy accumulated enough power to rival, and sometimes even eclipse, the power of the king himself.

It was in these unsettled times that Chinul was born in 1158 to a family of the gentry class. As a child, he was quite sickly and his worried father prayed to Buddha that if his son regained his health the boy would be ordained as a monk. This kind of peti-

tioning was not unusual in the Korea of that time. Soon afterwards,
Chinul's illness disappeared and, in keeping with his father's
vow, the boy's head was shaved at the age of seven. When he was
fifteen he received his Buddhist precepts. His preceptor was Zen
Master Chonghwi of Kulsan-sa temple on Sagul-san Mountain,
one of the nine mountain schools of Zen.

It seems that during his years at Kulsan-sa, Chinul did most of
his learning in Buddhist scriptures by himself. In his later writings, he never mentioned the name of a formal instructor during
these years of his life. He used the scriptural instructions to perfect his formal Zen meditation. Using the scriptures in aid of Zen
meditation was a most unusual step for a Zen student of his time,
since there was a bitter sectarian rift between the Son (Zen) and
the Doctrinal schools. For Chinul, however, this period of study
and meditation turned out to be a lifelong effort for accommodation and harmonization of the two approached.

In 1182, Chinul passed the royal examination for Son monks,
held in the capital city of Kaesong. During his stay in the capital,
it seems he was completely disgusted by the jostling for power
and possessions by the resident monks of the city. When Chinul
made his disgust known to some fellow monks who had gathered
for the purpose of entering the examination, he struck a respon-
sive chord. Together, ten of them decided to gather at some future date to form a retreat community dedicated to the development of samadhi and prajña. Years later, Chinul described this
"compact":

> One day I made a pact with more than ten fellow meditators
> which said, "After the close of this convocation we will renounce
> fame and profit and remain in seclusion in the mountain forests.
> We will form a community designed to foster constant training in
> *samadhi* and *prajña.* Through worship of the Buddha, recitation of
> sutras, and even through common work, we will each discharge the
> duties to which we are assigned and nourish the self-nature in all
> situations. We vow to pass our whole lives free of entanglements
> and to follow the higher pursuits of accomplished and true men.
> Would this not be wonderful?

All those present who heard these words agreed with what was said and vowed, "On another day we will consummate this agreement, live in seclusion in the forest, and be bound together as a community which should be named for *samadhi* and *prajña*.[29]

When this community did not take shape readily, Chinul decided to go traveling. He traveled far, down to the southwest corner of the peninsula and settled there at Chongwon-sa temple in Ch'angpyong province. There seems to have been a reason for choosing this location. This region was the only one to have maritime connection with the Chinese coastal regions. Thus, by moving to this corner of the peninsula, Chinul may have hoped to gain some first-hand information about Buddhism in Sung China. As far as we known he never actually attempted to go to China.

During his stay at Chongwon-sa, while reading the *Platform Sutra.*, Chinul had an awakening:

> By chance one day in the study hall as he was looking through the *Platform Sutra of the Sixth Patriarch,* he came across a passage which said, "The self-nature of suchness gives rise to thoughts. But even though the six sense-faculties see, hear, sense, and know, it is not tainted by the myriad of images. The true nature is constantly free and self-reliant." Astonished, he was overjoyed at gaining what he had never experienced before and, getting up, he walked around the hall, reflecting on the passage while continuing to recite it. His heart was satisfied. From that time on, his mind was averse to fame and profit; he desired only to dwell in seclusion in the mountain ravines. Bearing hardship joyfully, he aspired to the path; he was obsessed with this quest.[30]

This experience laid the foundation of Chinul's approach of "sudden enlightenment/gradual cultivation" to all Buddhist spiritual practices. His contention that an initial awakening to the Mind-Nature had to be supported by the simultaneous cultivation of samadhi and prajña became the basis of all his future writings and greatly helped in the harmonization process between Son and Kyo approaches.

In 1185, he took up traveling again. Then in the autumn of that year, he once again settled down at Pomun-sa temple on Haga mountain in the southeastern region. His three-year-stay at Pomun-sa was a period of intense training during which he used the kong-an (J: koan) "Mind is Buddha." He also diligently studied Li T'ung-hsuan's *Commentary on the Hua-yen Sutra.* He had his second awakening when he came across a passage in *Avatamsaka (Hua-yen) Sutra,*

> I came upon the simile about "one dust note containing thousands of volumes of sutras" in the "Appearance of the Tathagatas" chapter of the *Avatamsaka Sutra.* Later (in the same passage) the summation said:
> "The wisdom of the Tathagatas is just like this: it is complete in the bodies of all sentient beings. It is merely all these ordinary, foolish people who are not aware of it and do not recognize it."
> I put the sutra volume on my head (in reverence) and, unwittingly began to weep.[31]

This experience confirmed Chinul's basic insight: "What the World-Honored One said with his mouth are the teachings (sutras). What the Patriarchs transmitted with their mind is Son (Zen). The mouth of the Buddha and the minds of the patriarchs can certainly not be contradictory..."

While at Pomun-sa, Chinul received an invitation from one of the monks who had been a signatory to the *Compact of the Samadhi and Prajña Community* to come join him at Kojo-sa temple and begin a formal retreat. Although reluctant to move again, Chinul decided to travel to Kojo-sa with a fellow meditator. Invitations were sent out to all the original signators of the *Compact* but owing to death, sickness or worldly pursuits, only three or four, out of more than ten, came.

The retreat began in 1190. In commemoration of the occasion, Chinul wrote his first major work, *Encouragement to Practice.* In it he laid down the events and motivations leading up to the establishment of the Samadhi and Prajña Community as well as the style of practice which he and his colleagues intended to follow.

It also contained an explicit criticism of corruption in the contemporary Buddhist sangha.

The community was open to all lay people as well as monks, as
long as they were willing to renounce secular concerns and dwell
in seclusion with the purpose of cultivating samadhi and prajña.
Chinul exhorted fellow meditators thus:

> I humbly hope that men of high moral standards who have grown
> tired of wordly affairs—regardless of whether they are adherents of
> Son, the scholastic sects, Confucianism, or Taoism will abandon
> the dusty domain of this world, soar high above all things, and de-
> vote themselves earnestly to the path of inner cultivation which is
> commensurate with this aim. Then, although they might have had
> no role in the formation of this project, I have allowed them to
> add their names at the end of the compact of this community.[32]

By 1197, seven years after its founding, the community at Kojo-sa
had become quite well-known and had attracted a large number of
practitioners. Although Chinul hadn't intended to be the teacher
of a community, many students gathered around him. Kojo-sa was
too small for the burgeoning community, and Chinul began to look
for a larger place. He found the remains of a small temple,
Kilsang-sa, on Songgwang Mountain. Although the area of the
temple was not big enough, "the site was outstanding and the land
fertile; the springs were sweet and the forests abundant. It was
truly a place which would be appropriate for cultivating the mind,
nourishing the nature, gathering an assembly, and making merit."[33]
In the spring of 1197, the community moved to the new site and
work began on the restoration and reconstruction of the
monastery. In later centuries, these new quarters of the Samadhi
and Prajña Community at Kilsang-sa were renamed Songgwang-sa
after the name of of the mountain. Since Chinul's time, Songgwang-sa has continued to be the main Zen temple in Korea.

While traveling from Kojo-sa to the new site at Kilsang-sa,
Chinul and his party crossed Chiri Mountain. They decided to
do an intensive retreat at Sangmuju-am, a small and isolated her-

mitage near the top of the mountain. Here Chinul had his third awakening:

> I went to live on Mount Chiri and found [a passage in the] *Records of the Son Master Ta-hui P'u-chueh* which said, "Son does not consist in quietude; it does not consist in bustle. It does not involve the activities of the daily life; it does not involve logical discrimination. Nevertheless, it is of first importance not to investigate [Son] while rejecting quietude or bustle, the activities of daily life, or logical discrimination. If your eyes suddenly open, then [Son] is something which exists inside your very own home." I understood this passage. Naturally, nothing blocked my chest again and I never again dwelt with an enemy. From then on I was at peace.[34]

Ch'an master Ta-hui (1089-1163) was a 17th-generation successor of Lin-chi I-hsuan (d.867), the founder of the Lin-chi school. At a time when the school had become outmoded and was in danger of phasing out, Ta-hui had infused it with a new vigor by popularizing the hwadu (C: hua-t'ou) method of kong-an (C: kung-an) practice. Chinul was the first Korean Zen teacher to be influenced by Ta-hui's approach. His adoption of the hwadu method brought him ever closer to recent developments in Chinese Zen. It is possible that Chinul may have first heard of Ta-hui when residing at Ch'ongwon-sa in in the southeast and may even have persuaded some merchants to bring him a copy of Ta-hui's *Records* from China. In any case, Ta-hui's approach and the "short-cut" it represented had a profound influence on Chinul's thinking.

Chinul stayed at Sangmuju-am for three years, from 1197 to 1200. When he finally arrived at Kilsang-sa the site was still under construction. The reconstruction turned out to be a massive project which took nine years for its completion and was not finished until 1205. All members of the community (monastics) as well as Buddhist lay believers from surrounding areas participated in the reconstruction. It is said that when hard labor was needed, Chinul himself joined the rank of workers on the project. To mark the occasion of the completion of the temple, King Uijong (r.1204-1211), who had always held Chinul in high esteem, issued a

proclamation on November 13, 1205, calling for 120 days of cele-
bration. Chinul wrote a small manual of training rules to be followed by members of the community called *Admonitions to Beginning Students*. Over the years, *Admonitions* came to be adopted as
the standard of conduct for all monks and residents of Zen
monasteries in Korea.

King Uijong also ordered a change in the name of the mountain
on which the temple was located, from Songgwang-sa to Chogye-
sa, Chogye Mountain being the site in south China where Hui-
neng, the Sixth Patriarch, had his temple. The name of the temple itself was changed from Kilsang-sa to Suson-sa The King also
sent Chinul a special embroidered robe as a mark of his respect.

Chinul died in 1210 at the age of 52. Earlier in that year he had
given a series of lectures for more than ten days in memory of his
mother. Then he told his listeners, "Before long I will not be able
to lecture on the Dharma. Strive for yourself to attain the truth."
On the morning of April 22, 1210, he asked his attendant, "What
day is today?" When told the day,

> The master then washed and rinsed his mouth and, donning his
> ceremonial dharma robe, said, "These eyes are not the eyes of my
> ancestors; this nose is not the nose of my ancestors. This mouth is
> not the mouth born of my mother; this tongue is not the tongue
> born of my mother."
>
> He then ordered the monastery drum beaten to summon the
> monks of the community and carrying his staff with six rings, he
> walked toward the dharma hall. There he lit incense, ascended the
> platform, and proceeded to perform all the usual formalities. He
> then struck his staff and, after mentioning the circumstances sur-
> rounding the questions and answers exchanged in his room the
> previous evening, said, "The miraculous efficaciousness of the Son
> dharma is inconceivable. Today I have come here because I want
> to explain it fully to all of you in this assembly. If you ask me clear,
> unattached questions, this old man will give you clear, unattached
> answers." He looked to the right and left and, rubbing his chest
> with his hands, said, "The life of this mountain monk is now en-

tirely in all of your hands. You are free to drag me aside or pull me down. Let anyone who has bones and tendons come forward."

He then stretched his legs and, sitting on the seat, gave answers to the different questions put to him. His words were precise and the meaning detailed; his elocution was unimpaired. These details are recorded in the *Death Record* (Imjong Ki). Finally a monk asked, "I am not clear whether the past manifestation of illness by Vimalakirti of Vaishali and today's sickness of Chogye's Moguja are the same or different." The master replied, "You've only learned similarity and difference!" Then, picking up his staff, he struck it several times and said, "A thousand things and ten thousand objects are all right here." Finally, supported by his staff, he remained sitting immobile and quietly passed away.[35]

It is said that seven days after death his complexion was still the same as while living. His hair and whiskers grew as usual even while his disicples burned incense and made offerings. When his body was cremated, his bones issued forth five colors. About thirty big *sariras* (crystals said to remain after a saint's body has been cremated) and many more small ones were collected and enshrined in a pagoda to the north of the temple. The king conferred on him the posthumous title of National Master Puril Pojo ("Buddha-Sun Shining Universally"). His pagoda was named Kampo t'ap ("Sweet-Dew Reliquary").

In 1208, two years before his death, Chinul formally appointed his student Hyeshim (1178-1234) to be his Dharma successor. Under Hyeshim's leadership, Suson-sa blossomed even more into a center for the cultivation of samdhi and prajña. The temple came to wield an immense influence on the direction of Korean Zen. It was Hyeshim who compiled more than 1,700 kong-an of the Korean Son tradition into one single volume, a seminal work which continues to be integral to the practice of Zen in Korea. Chinul and Hyeshim provided a dynamic and authentic leadership not only for their community but for Korean Zen in general. One direct result of their leadership was the outstanding teachers that were nurtured at Songgwang-sa. No fewer than 15 of Chinul's successors (from 1210-1428) became National Teachers.

CHINUL'S SECRETS ON CULTIVATING THE MIND

Secrets on Cultivating the Mind is an outline of basic Son practices, written by Chinul between 1203 and 1205. A seminal text of the Son school, it presents simple yet cogent descriptions of two important elements of Chinul's thought—sudden awakening/gradual cultivation and the simultaneous practice of samadhi and prajña. Although *Secrets* was lost in Korea after the destruction wrought by the Mongol invasions two decades after Chinul's death, it was preserved in the Northern Ming edition of the *Tripitaka*, produced in the early 15th century. Reintroduced into Korea around that time, it was translated in 1467 into the Korean vernacular language using the newly invented *han'gul* alphabet. It remains one of the most popular Son texts in Korea today.

The triple world is blazing in defilement as if it were a house on fire. How can you bear to tarry here and complacently undergo such long suffering? If you wish to avoid wandering in *samsara* there is no better way than to seek Buddhahood. If you want to become a Buddha, understand that Buddha is the mind. How can you search for the mind in the far distance? It is not outside the body. The physical body is a phantom, for it is subject to birth and death; the true mind is like space, for it neither ends nor changes. Therefore it is said, "These hundred bones will crumble and return to fire and wind. But One Thing is eternally numinous and covers heaven and earth."

It is tragic. People have been deluded for so long. They do not recognize that their own minds are the true Buddhas. They do not recognize that their own natures are the true dharma. They want to search for the dharma, yet they still look far away for the holy ones. They want to search for the Buddha, yet they will will not observe their own minds. If they aspire to the path of Buddhahood while obstinately holding to their feeling that the Buddha is outside the mind or the dharma is outside the nature, then, even though they pass through kalpas as numerous as dust motes, burning their bodies, charring their arms, crushing their bones and expos-

* Special thanks to the University of Hawaii Press for permission to reprint Robert Buswell's translation.

ing their marrow, or else write sutras with their own blood, never lying down to sleep, eating only one offering a day at the hour of the Hare (5 to 7 a.m.), or even studying through the entire *Tripitaka* and cultivating all sorts or ascetic practices, it is like trying to make rice by boiling sand— it will only add to their tribulation. If they would only understand their own minds, then, without searching, approaches to dharma as numerous as the sands of the Ganges and uncountable sublime meanings would all be understood. As the World Honored One said, "I see that all sentient beings everywhere are endowed with a tathagata's wisdom and virtue." He also said, "All the illusory guises in which sentient beings appear take shape in the sublime mind of the *tathagata's* complete enlightenment." Consequently, you should know that outside this mind there is no Buddhahood which can be attained. All the Buddhas of the past were merely persons who understood their minds. All the sages and saints of the present are likewise merely persons who have cultivated their minds. All future meditators should rely on this dharma as well.

I hope that you who cultivate the path will never search outside. The nature of the mind is unstained; it is originally whole and complete in itself. If you will only leave behind false conditioning, you will be "such" like the Buddha.

Question: If you say that the Buddha-nature exists in the body right now, then, since it is in the body, it is not separate from us ordinary men. So why can we not see this Buddha-nature right now? Please explain this further to enlighten us on this point.

Chinul: It is in your body, but you do not see it. Ultimately, what is that thing which during the twelve periods of the day knows hunger and thirst, cold and heat, anger and joy? This physical body is a synthesis of four conditions: earth, water, fire, and wind. Since matter is passive and insentient, how can it see, hear, sense, and know? That which is able to see, hear, sense, and know is perforce your Buddha-nature. For this reason, Lin-chi said, "The four great elements do not know how to expound dharma or listen to dharma. Empty space does not know how to expound dharma or listen to dharma. It is only that formless thing before eyes, clear and bright of itself, which knows how to expound dharma or listen to dharma." This "formless thing" is the dharma-seal of all Buddhas; it is your original mind. Since this Buddha- nature exists in your body right now, why do you vainly search for it outside?

Question: You talked about seeing the nature. But when there is true seeing of the nature, the person becomes an enlightened saint and should be able to perform magic and miracles—he would be different from other people. How is it, then, that among those who cultivate the mind nowadays, not one can display these spiritual powers and transformation bodies?

Chinul: You should not utter absurdities lightly; to be unable to differentiate the perverse from the noble is to be deluded and confused. Nowadays, you people who are training on the path chat about truth with your mouth, but in your minds you you only shrink from it and end up falling into the error of underestimating yourselves by thinking that you do not share in the Buddha-nature. This is all that you are doubting. You train on the path but do not know the proper sequence of practice. This is called wrong view; it is not called cultivation. You are not only deceiving yourselves; you are deceiving others too. How can you not be on your guard against this?

Now, there are many approaches to the path, but essentially they are included in the twofold approach of sudden awakening and gradual cultivation. Although sudden awakening/sudden cultivation has been advocated, this is the entrance for people of the highest faculties. If you were to probe their pasts, you would see that their cultivation has been based for many lives on the insights gained in a previous awakening. Now, in this life, after gradual permeation, these people hear the dharma and awaken; in one instant their practice is brought to a sudden conclusion. But if we try to explain this according to the facts, then sudden awakening/sudden cultivation is also the result of an initial awakening and its subsequent cultivation. Consequently, this twofold approach of sudden awakening and gradual cultivation is the track followed by thousands of saints. Hence, of all the saints of old, there were none who did not first have an awakening, subsequently cultivate it, and finally, because of their cultivation, gain realization.

The so-called magic and miracles, you mentioned manifest because of the gradual permeation of cultivation based on an initial awakening; it should not be said that they appear simultaneous with the awakening. As it is said in the sutras, "The noumenon is awakened to suddenly, and is forged in accordance with this awakening. Phenomena cannot be removed suddenly; they are brought to an end step by step." For this reason, Kuei-feng, in a profound explanation of the meaning of initial awakening/subsequent cultivation, said,

> Although we know that a frozen pond is entirely water, the sun's heat is necessary to melt it. Although we awaken to the fact that an ordinary man is Buddha, the power of dharma is necessary to make it permeate our cultivation. When that pond has melted, the water flows freely and can be used for irrigation and cleaning. When falsity is extinguished, the mind will be numinous and dynamic and then its function of penetrating brightness will manifest.

These quotations should make it clear that the ability to perform magic and miracles in the phenomenal sphere cannot be perfected in a day; it will manifest only after gradual permeation.

Moreover, in the case of accomplished men, phenomenal spiritual powers are like an eerie apparition; they are only a minor concern of the saints. Although they might perform them, they do not give them undue emphasis. Nowadays, deluded and ignorant people wrongly assume that in the one moment of awakening, incalculable sublime functions, as well as magic and miracles, manifest in tandem. This is the sort of understanding I was referring to when I said that you did not know the proper sequence of practice and did not distinguish the root from the branches. To seek the path of Buddhahood while not knowing the proper sequence of practice or the root and the branches is like trying to put a square peg into a round hole. Can this be anything but a grave mistake? Because such people do not know of any expedients, they hesitate as if they were facing a steep precipice and end up backsliding. Alas, many have broken their ties with the spiritual family of the Buddha in this manner. Since they neither understand for themselves nor believe that others have had an understanding-awakening, when they see someone without spiritual powers they act insolently, ridiculing the sages and insulting the saints. This is really quite pitiful!

Question: You have said that this twofold approach of sudden awakening/gradual cultivation is the track followed by thousands of saints. But if awakening is really sudden awakening, what need is there for gradual cultivation? And if cultivation means gradual cultivation, how can you speak of sudden awakening? We hope that you will expound further on these two ideas of sudden and gradual and resolve our remaining doubts.

Chinul: First let us take sudden awakening. When the ordinary man is deluded, he assumes that the four great elements are his body and the false thoughts are his mind. He does not know that his own nature is the true dharma-body; he does not know that his own numinous awareness is the true Buddha. He looks for the Buddha outside his mind. While he is thus wandering aimlessly, the entrance to the road might by chance be pointed out by a wise advisor. If in one thought he then follows back the light (of his mind to its source) and sees his original nature, he will discover that the ground of this nature is innately free of defilement, and that he himself is originally endowed with the non-outflow wisdom-nature which is not a hair's breadth different from that of all the Buddhas. Hence it is called sudden awakening.

Next let us consider gradual cultivation. Although he has awakened to the fact that his original nature is no different from that of the Buddhas, the beginningless habit-energies are extremely difficult to remove suddenly and so he must continue to cultivate while relying on his awakening. Through this gradual permeation, his endeavors reach completion. He constantly nurtures the sacred embryo, and after a long time he becomes a saint. Hence it is called gradual cultivation.

This process can be compared to the maturation of a child. From the day of its birth, a baby is endowed with all the sense organs like everyone else, but its strength is not yet fully developed. It is only after many months and years that it will finally become an adult.

Question: Through what expedients is it possible to trace back the radiance of one's sense-faculties in one thought and awaken to the self-nature?

Chinul: The self-nature is just your own mind. What other expedients do you need? If you ask for expedients to seek understanding, you are like a person who, because he does not see his own eyes, assumes that he has no eyes and decides to find some way to see. But since he does have eyes, how else is he supposed to see? If he realizes that in fact he has never lost his eyes, this is the same as seeing his eyes, and no longer would he waste his time trying to find a way to see. How then could he have any thoughts that he could not see? Your own numinous awareness is exactly the same. Since this awareness is your own mind, how else are you going to understand? If you seek some other way to understand, you will never understand. Simply by knowing that there is no other way to understand, you are seeing the nature.

Question: When the superior man hears the dharma, he understands easily. Average and inferior men, however, are not without doubt and confusion. Could you describe some expedients so that the deluded too can enter into enlightenment?

Chinul: The path is not related to knowing or not knowing. You should get rid of the mind which clings to its delusion and looks forward to enlightenment, and listen to me.

Since all dharmas are like dreams or phantoms, deluded thoughts are originally calm and the sense-spheres are originally void. At the point where all dharmas are void, the numinous awareness is not obscured. That is to say, this mind of void and calm, numinous awareness is your original face. It is also the dharma-seal transmitted without a break by all the Buddhas of the three time periods, the successive generations of patriarchs, and the wise advisors of the world. If you awaken to this mind, then this is truly what is called not following the rungs of a ladder: you climb straight to the stage of Buddhahood, and each step transcends the triple world. Returning home, your doubts will be instantly resolved and you will become the teacher of men and gods. Endowed with compassion and wisdom and complete in the twofold benefit, you will be worthly of receiving the offerings of men and gods. Day after day you can use ten thousand taels of gold without incurring debt. If you can do this, you will be truly a great man who has indeed finished the task of this life.

Question: In our case, what is this mind of void and calm, numinous awareness?

Chinul: What has just asked me this question is precisely your mind of void and calm, numinous awareness. Why not trace back its radiance rather than search for it outside? For your benefit I will now point straight to your original mind so that you can awaken to it.

Clear your minds and listen to my words:

From morning to evening, throughout the 12 periods of the day, during all your actions and activities—whether seeing, hearing, laughing, talking, whether angry or happy, whether doing good or evil - ultimately who is it that is able to perform all these actions? Speak! If you say that it is the physical body which is acting, then at the moment when a man's life comes to an end, even though the body has not yet decayed, how is it that the eyes cannot see, the ears cannot hear, the nose cannot smell, the tongue cannot talk, the body cannot move, the hands cannot grasp, and the feet cannot run? You should know that what is capable of seeing, hearing, moving, and acting has to be your original mind; it is not your physical body. Furthermore, the four elements which make up the physical body are by nature void; they are like images in a mirror or the moon's reflection in water. How can they be clear and constantly aware, always bright and never obscured - and, upon activation, be able to put into operation sublime functions are numerous as sands of the Ganges? For this reason, it is said, "Drawing water and carrying firewood are spiritual powers and sublime functions."

There are many points at which to enter the numenon. I will indicate one approach which will allow you to return to the source. Do you hear the sounds of that crow cawing and the magpie calling?

Student: Yes.

Chinul: Trace them back and listen to your hearing-nature. Do you hear any sounds?

Student: At that place, sounds and discriminations do not obtain.

Chinul: Marvelous! Marvelous! This is Avalokitesvara's method for entering the noumenon. Let me ask you again. You said that sounds and discriminations do not obtain at that place. But since they do not obtain, isn't the hearing-nature just empty space at such a time?

Student: Originally it is not empty. It is always bright and never obscured.

Chinul: What is this essence which is not empty?

Student: As it has no former shape, words cannot describe it.

Chinul: This is the life force of all the Buddhas and patriarchs - have no further doubts about that. Since it has no former shape, how can it be large or small? Since it cannot be large or small, how can it have limitations? Since it has no limitations, it cannot have inside or outside. Since there is inside or outside, there is no far or near. As there is no far or near, there is no here or there. As there is no here or there, there is no coming or going. As there is no coming or going, there is no birth or death. As there is no birth or death, there is no past or present. As there is no past or present, there is no delusion or awakening. As there is no delusion or awakening, there is no ordinary man or saint. As there is no ordinary man or saint, there is no purity or impurity. Since there is no impurity or purity, there is no right or wrong. Since there is no right or wrong, names and words do not apply to it. Since none of these concepts apply, all sense-bases and sense-objects, all deluded thoughts, even forms and shapes and names and words are all inapplicable. Hence how can it be anything but originally void and calm and originally no-thing?

Nevertheless, at that point where all dharmas are empty, the numinous awareness is not obscured. It is not the same as insentience, for its nature is spiritually deft. This is your pure mind-essence of void and calm, numinous awareness. This pure, void, and calm mind is that mind of outstanding purity and brilliance of all the Buddhas of the three time periods; it is that enlightened nature which is the original source of all sentient beings. One who awakens to it and safeguards that awakening will then abide in the unitary, "such" and unmoving liberation. One who is deluded and turns his back on it passes between the six destinies, wandering in *samsara* for vast number of kalpas. As it is said, "One who is confused about the one mind and passes between the six destinies, goes and take action. But one who awakens to the *dharmadhatu* and returns to the one mind, arrives and is still." Although there is this distinction between delusion and awakening, in their basic source they are one. As it is said, "The word *dharma* means the mind of the sentient being." But as there is neither more of this void and calm mind in the saint, nor less of it in the ordinary man, it is also said, "In the wisdom of the saint, it is no brighter; hidden in the mind of the ordinary man it is no darker." Since there is neither more of it in the saint nor less of it in the ordinary man, how are the Buddhas and patriarchs any different from other men? The only thing that makes them different is that they can protect their minds and thoughts-nothing more.

If you believe me to the point where you can suddenly extinguish your doubt, show the will of a great man and give rise to authentic vision and understanding, if you know its taste for yourself, arrive at the stage of self-affirmation and gain understanding of your true nature, then this is the understanding-awakening achieved by those who have cultivated the mind. Since no further steps are involved, it is called sudden. Therefore it is said, "When in the cause of faith one meshes without the slightest degree of error with all the qualities of the fruition of Buddhahood, faith is achieved."

Question: Once the noumenon is awakened to, no further steps are involved. Why then do you posit subsequent cultivation, gradual permeation, and gradual perfection?

Chinul: Earlier the meaning of gradual cultivation subsequent to awakening was fully explained. But since your feeling of doubt persists, it seems that I will have to explain it again. Clear your minds and listen carefully!

For innumerable kalpas without beginning, up to the present time, ordinary men have passed between the five destinies, coming and going between birth and death. They obstinately cling to "self" and, over a long period of time, their natures have become thoroughly permeated by false thoughts, inverted views, ignorance, and the habit-energies. Although, coming into this life, they might suddenly awaken to the fact that their self-nature is originally void and calm and no different from that of the Buddhas, these old habits are difficult to eliminate completely. Consequently, when they come into contact with either favorable or adverse objects, then anger and happiness or propriety or impropriety blaze forth: their adventitious defilements are no different from before. If they do not increase their efforts and apply their power through the help of *prajña*, how will they ever be able to counteract ignorance and reach the place of great rest and repose? As it is said, "Although the person who has suddenly awakened is the same as the Buddhas, the habit-energies which have built up over many lives are deep-rooted. The wind ceases, but the waves still surge; the noumenon manifests, but thoughts still invade." Son Master Ta-hui Tsung-kao said:

Often gifted people can break through this affair and achieve sudden awakening without expending a lot of strength. Then they relax and do not try to counteract the habit-energies and deluded thoughts. Finally, after the passage of many days and months, they simply wander on as before and are unable to avoid *samsara*.

So how could you neglect subsequent cultivation simply because of one moment of awakening? After awakening, you must be constantly on your guard. If deluded thoughts suddenly appear, do not follow after them—reduce them and reduce them again until you reach the unconditioned. Then and only then will your practice reach completion. This is the practice of herding the ox which all wise advisors in the world have practiced after awakening.

Nevertheless, although you must cultivate further, you have already awakened suddenly to the fact that deluded thoughts are originally void and the mind-nature is originally pure. Thus you eliminate evil, but you eliminate without actually eliminating anything; you cultivate the wholesome, but you cultivate without really cultivating anything either. This is true cultivation and true elimination. For this reason it is said, "Although one prepares to cultivate the manifold supplementary practices, thoughtlessness is the origin of them all." Kuei-feng summed up the distinction between the ideas of initial awakening and subsequent cultivation when he said:

He has the sudden awakening to the fact that his nature is originally free of defilement and he is originally in full possessio of the non-outflow wisdom-nature which is no different from that of the Buddhas. To cultivate while relying on this awakening is called supreme vehicle Son, or the pure Son of the *tathagatas*. If thought-moment after thought-moment he continues to develop his training, then naturally he will gradually attain to hundreds of thousands of *samadhis*. This is the Son which has been transmitted successively in the school of Bodhidharma."

Hence sudden awakening and gradual cultivation are like the two wheels of a cart: neither one can be missing.

Some people do not realize that the nature of good and evil is void; they sit rigidly without moving and, like a rock crushing grass, repress both body and mind. To regard this as cultivation of the mind is a great delusion. For this reason it is said, "Sravakas cut off delusion thought after thought, but the thought which does this cutting is a brigand." If they could see that killing, stealing, sexual misconduct, and lying all arise from the nature, then their arising would be the same as their non-arising. At their source they are calm, why must they be cut off? As it is said, "Do not fear the arising of thoughts: only be concerned lest your awareness of them be tardy." It is also said, "If we are aware of a thought at the moment it arises, then through that awareness it will vanish."

In the case of a person who has had an awakening, although he still has adventitious defilements, these have all been purified into cream. If he merely reflects on the fact that confusion is without basis, then all the flowers in the sky of this triple-world are like smoke swirling in the wind and the six phantom sense-objects are like ice melting in hot water. If thought-moment after thought-moment he continues to train in this manner, does not neglect his training, and keeps *samadhi* and *prajña* equally balanced, then lust and hatred will naturally fade away and compassion and wisdom will naturally increase in brightness; unwholesome actions will naturally decrease and meritorious practices will naturally multiply. When the defilements are exhausted, birth and death cease. When the subtle streams of defilements are forever cut off, the great wisdom of complete enlightenment exists brilliantly of itself. Then he will be able to manifest billions of transformation-bodies in all the worlds of the ten directions following his inspiration and responding to the faculties of sentient beings. Like the moon in the nine empyrean which reflects in ten thousand pools of water, there is no limit to his responsiveness. He will be able to ferry across all sentient beings with whom he has affinities. He will be happy and free of worry. Such a person is called a Great Enlightened World Honored One.

Question: In the approach of subsequent cultivation, we really do not yet understand the meaning of maintaining *samadhi* and *prajña* equally. Could you expound on this point in detail, so that we can free ourselves of our delusion? Please lead us through the entrance to liberation.

Chinul: Suppose we consider these two dharmas and their attributes. Of the thousands of approaches to enter the noumenon there are none which do not involve *samadhi* and *prajña*. Taking only the essential outline into account, from the standpoint of the self-nature they are characterized as essence and function—what I have called the void and the calm, numinous awareness. *Samadhi* is the essence; *prajña* is the function. Since *prajña* is the functioning of the essence, it is not separate from *samadhi*. Since *samadhi* is the essence of the function, it is not separate from *prajña*. Since in samadhi there is prajña, *samadhi* is calm yet constantly aware. Since in *prajña* there is *samadhi*, *prajña* is aware yet constantly calm. As Ts'ao-ch'i [the Sixth Patriarch Hui-neng] said, "The mind-ground which is without disturbance is the *samadhi* of the self-nature. The mind-ground which is without delusion is the *prajña*, of the self-nature." If you have this sort of understanding, you can be calm and aware naturally in all situations. When enveloping and reflecting the characterstics of *samadhi* and *prajña* respectively—are not two, this is the sudden school's cultivation of *samadhi* and *prajña* as a pair.

The practice of samadhi and *prajña* intended for those of inferior faculties in the gradual school initially controls the thinking processes with calmness and subsequently controls dullness with alertness; finally, these initial and subsequent counteracting techniques subdue both the dull and the agitated mind in order to enter into stillness. Although this approach also holds that alertness and calmness should be maintained equally, its practice cannot avoid clinging to stillness. Hence how will it allow those who would understand the matter of birth and death never to leave the fundamental calm and fundamental awareness and cultivate *samadhi* and *prajña* as a pair naturally in all situations? As Ts'ao-ch'i said, "The practice of self-awakening has nothing to do with arguing. If you argue about first and last, you are deluded."

For an accomplished man, maintaining *samadhi* and *prajña* equally does not involve endeavor, for he is always spontaneous and unconcerned about time or place. When seeing forms or hearing sounds, he is "just so." When wearing clothes or eating food, he is "just so." When defecating or urinating, he is "just so." When talking with people, he is "just so." At all times, whether speaking or keeping silent, whether joyful or angry, he is "just so." Like an empty boat riding on the waves which follows the crests and troughs, or like a torrent flowing the mountains which follows the bends and straights, in his mind he is without intellection. Today, he is at peace naturally in all conditions without destruction or hindrance. Tomorrow, in all situations, he is naturally at peace. He follows all conditions without destruction or hindrance. He neither eliminates the unwholesome nor cultivates the wholesome. His character is straightforward and without deception. His seeing and hearing return to normal and there are no sense-objects to come in contact with (which could cause new defilements to arise). Why should he have to bother with efforts at effacement? Since he has not a single thought which creates passion, he need not make an effort to forget all conditioning.

But hindrances are formidable and habits are deeply ingrained. Contemplation is weak and the mind drifts. The power of ignorance is great, but the power of prajña is small. He still cannot avoid being alternately unmoved and upset when he comes in contact with wholesome and unwholesome sense-objects. When the mind is not tranquil and content, he cannot but work both at forgetting all conditioning and at effacement. As it is said, When the six sense-bases absorb the sense-spheres and the mind no longer responds to environment, this is called samadhi. When the mind and the sense-spheres are both void and the mirror of the mind shines without obscuration, this is called *prajña*. Even though this is the relative approach to *samadhi* and *prajña* which adapts to signs as practiced by those of inferior faculties in the gradual school, it cannot be neglected as a counteractive technique. If restlessness and agitation are blazing forth, then first, through *samadhi*, use the noumenon to absorb the distraction. For when the mind does not respond to the environment it will be in conformity with original calmness. If dullness and torpor are especially heavy, use *prajña* to investigate dharmas critically and contemplate their voidness, and allow the mirror of the mind to shine without disturbance in conformition with the original awareness. Control distracting thoughts with *samadhi*. Control blankness with *prajña*.

When both activity and stillness disappear, the effort to counteract them is no longer necessary. Then, even though there is contact with sense-objects, thought after thought returns to the source; regardless of the conditions he meets, every mental state is in conformity with the path. Naturally *samadhi* and *prajña* are cultivated as a pair in all situations until finally the student becomes a person with no concerns. When this is so, one is truly maintaining *samadhi* and *prajña* equally. One has clearly seen the Buddha-nature.

Question: According to your assessment, there are two types of *samadhi* and *prajña* which are maintained equally during cultivation after awakening: first, the *samadhi* and *prajña* or the self-nature; second, the relative *samadhi* and *prajña* which adapts to signs.

The self-nature type means to be calm yet aware in all circumstances. Since the person who has awakened to the self-nature is always spontaneous and free from attachment to objects, why does he need to trouble with effacing the defilements? Since there is not even one thought which creates passion, there is no need to make vain efforts at forgetting all conditioning. Your assessment was that this approach is the sudden school's equal maintenance of *samadhi* and *prajña* which never leaves the self-nature.

The relative type which follows signs means either to absorb distraction by according with the noumenon or to investigate dharmas critically and contemplate their voidness. One controls both dullness and agitation and thereby enters the unconditioned. But your assessment was that this practice is for those of inferior faculties in the gradual school. We are not yet free of doubt about the *samadhi* and *prajña* of these two different approaches. Would you say that one should first rely on the self-nature type and then, after cultivating *samadhi* and *prajña* concurrently, make further use of the countermeasures of the relative approach? Or should one first rely on the relative type so that after controlling dullness and agitation, he can enter into the self-nature type? If, after initially using the *samadhi* and *prajña* of the self-nature, he is able to remain calm and aware naturally in all situations, thus rendering the counteractive measures unnecessary, why would he subsequently have to apply the relative type of *samadhi* and *prajña*? It is like a piece of white jade; if it is engraved, its natural quality will be destroyed. On the other hand, after the initial application of the relative type of *samadhi* and *prajña*, if the work of counteraction is brought to a close and he then progresses to the self-nature type, this would be merely gradual development prior to awakening as practiced by those of inferior faculties in the gradual school. Then how would you be able to say that the sudden school's approach of initial awakening and subsequent cultivation makes use of the effortless effort?

If these two types can both be practiced in the one time that has no past or future (via sudden awakening/sudden cultivation), there would have to be a difference between the respective suddenness and gradualness of these two types of *samadhi* and *prajña*—so how could they both be cultivated at once? The sudden school adept relies on the self-nature type and eschews effort by remaining natural in all situations. Students of inferior capacity in the gradual school tend toward the relative type and exert themselves applying countermeasures. The suddenness and gradualness of these two types of practices are not indentical; their respective superiority and inferiority is obvious. So, in the approach of initial awakening and subsequent cultivation, why is it explained that there are two ways to maintain *samadhi* and *prajña* equally? Could you help us to understand this and eliminate our doubts?

Chinul: The explanation is obvious. Your doubts only come from yourselves! If you try to understand by merely following the words, you will, on the contrary, only give rise to doubt and confusion. It is best to forget the words; do not bother with detailed scrutiny of them. Now let us go on to my assessment of the cultivation of these two types of practice.

Cultivation of the *samadhi* and *prajña* of the self-nature involves the use of the sudden school's effortless effort in which both are put into practice and both are calmed; oneself cultivates the self-nature, and oneself completes the path to Buddhahood. Cultivation of the relative *samadhi* and *prajña* which adapts to signs involves the use of counteractive measures which are cultivated prior to awakening by those of inferior faculties in the gradual school. Thought-moment after thought-moment, confusion is eliminated; it is a practice which clings to stillness. These two types are different: one is sudden and the other gradual; they should not be combined haphazardly.

Although the approach involving cultivation after awakening does discuss the counteractive measures of the relative approach which adapts to signs, it does not employ the practices of those of inferior faculties in the gradual school in their entirety. It uses its expedients, but only as a temporary measure. And why is this? In the sudden school too there are those whose faculties are superior and those whose faculties are inferior; their "baggage" (their backgrounds and abilities) cannot be weighed according to the same standard.

If a person's defilements are weak and insipid, and his body and mind are light and at ease; if in the good he leaves the good and in the bad, he leaves the bad; if he is unmoving in the eight worldly winds; if the three types of feelings are calmed—then he can rely on the *samadhi* and *prajña* of the self-nature and cultivate them concurrently in all situations naturally. He is impeccable and passive; whether in action or at rest he is always absorbed in Son and perfects the natural noumenon. What need is there for him to borrow the relative approach's counteractive measures? If one is not sick, there is no need to look for medicine.

On the other hand, even though a person might initially have had a sudden awakening, if the defilements are engrossing and the habit-energies deeply ingrained; if the mind becomes passionate whenever it is in contact with sense-objects; if he is always involved in confrontations with the situations he meets; if he is always beset by dullness and agitation; or if he loses the constancy of calmness and awareness - then he should borrow the relative *samadhi* and *prajña* which adapts to signs and not forget the counteractive measures which control both dullness and agitation. Thereby he will enter the unconditioned: this is what is proper here. But even though he borrows the countermeasures in order to bring the habit-energies under temporary control, he has had a sudden awakening to the fact that the mind-nature is fundamentally pure and the defilements fundamentally empty. Hence he does not fall into the corrupt practice of those of inferior faculties in the gradual school. And why is this? Although during cultivation prior to awakening a person following the gradual approach does not forget to be diligent and thought-moment after thought-moment permeates his cultivation, he still gives rise to doubts everywhere and cannot free himself from obstacles. It is as if he had something stuck in his chest: he is always uncomfortable. After many days and months, as the work of counteraction matures, the adventitious defilements of body and mind might then appear to weaken. Although they seem lighter, the root of doubt is not yet severed. He is like a rock which is crushing grass: he still cannot be self-reliant in the realm of birth and death. Therefore, it is said, "Cultivation prior to awakening is not true cultivation."

In the case of a man who has awakend, although he employs expedients, moment to moment he is free of doubts and does not become polluted. After many days and months he naturally conforms with the impeccable, sublime nature. Naturally he is calm and aware in all situations. Moment by moment, as he becomes involved in sensory experience in all the sense-realms, thought after thought he severs defilements, for he never leaves the self-nature. By maintaining *samadhi* and *prajña* equally, he perfects supreme *bodhi* and is no longer different from those of superior faculties mentioned previously. Thus, although the relative *samadhi* and *prajña* is a practice for those of inferior faculties in the gradual school, for the man who has had an awakening it can be said that "iron has been transmuted into gold."

If you understand this, how can you have such doubts -doubts like the discriminative view that a sequence or progression is involved in the practice of these two types of *samadhi* and *prajña*? I hope that all cultivators of the path will study these words carefully; extinguish your doubts or you will end up backsliding. If you have the will of a great man and seek supreme *bodhi*, what will you do if you discard this approach? Do not grasp at the words, but try to understand the meaning directly. Stay focused on the definitive teaching, return to yourselves, and merge with the original guiding principle. Then the wisdom which cannot be obtained from any master will naturally manifest. The impeccable noumenon will be clear and unobscured. The perfection of wisdom-body does not come from any other awakening. And yet, although this sublime truth applies to everyone, unless the omniscient wisdom of *prajña*—the basis of the Mahayana—is started early, you will not be able to produce right faith in a single thought. And how can this merely result in a lack of faith? You will also end up slandering the three treasures and will finally invite punishment in the Interminable Hell. This happens frequently! But even though you are not yet able to accept this truth in faith, if it passes through your ears just once and you feel affinity with it for even a moment, the merit will be incalculable. As it says in *Secrets on Mind-Only*, "Hearing the dharma but not believing is still cause for the fruition of the seed of Buddhahood. Training on the Buddhist path but not completing it is still merit surpassing that of men and gods." But he who does not lose the right cause for the attainment of Buddhahood and who, morever, listens and believes, trains and completes his training, and guards his achievements without forgetting it, how can his merit be calculated?

If we consider our actions in our past wandering in *samsara*, we have no way of knowing for how many thousands of kalpas we have fallen into the darkness or entered the Interminable Hell and endured all kinds of suffering. Nor can we know how many times we have aspired to the path to Buddhahood but, because we did not meet with the wise advisors, remained submerged in the sea of birth and death for long kalpas, dark and unenlightened, performing all sorts of evil actions. Though we may reflect on this once in a while, we cannot imagine the duration of our misery. How can we relax and suffer again the same calamities as before? Furthermore, what allowed us to be born this time as human beings - the guiding spirits of all the ten thousand things—who are clear about the right road to cultivation? Truly, a human birth is difficult to ensure as "a blind turtle putting its head through a hole in a piece of wood floating on the ocean" or "a mustard seed falling onto the point of a needle." How can we possibly express how fortunate we are?

Whenever we become discouraged or indolent, we should always look to the future. In one instant we might happen to lose our lives and fall back into the evil bourns where we would have to undergo unspeakable suffering and pain. At that time, although we might want to hear one phrase of the Buddha-dharma, and would be willing to receive and keep it with faithful devotion to ease our misfortune, how would we ever encounter it there? On the point of death, remorse is of no use whatsoever. I hope that all of you who are cultivating the path will not be heedless and will not indulge in greed and lust. Do not forget to reflect upon this as if you were trying to save your head from burning. Death is fast closing in. The body is like the morning dew. Life is like the twilight in the west. Although we are alive today, there is no assurance about tomorrow. Bear this in mind! You must bear this in mind!

By relying on worldly conditioned, wholesome actions we will avoid the suffering of *samsara* in the three evil bourns. We will obtain the favorable karmic reward of rebirth among gods or men where we will receive abundant joy and happiness. But if we give rise to faith in this most profound approach to dharma of the supreme vehicle for only a moment, no metaphor can describe even the smallest portion of the merit we will achieve. As it is said in the sutras:

If one takes all the seven jewels in all the world systems of this trichiliocosm and offers them to all the sentient beings of those worlds until they are completely satisfied; or, furthermore, if one instructs all the sentient beings of those worlds and causes them to realize the four fruitions, the merit so gained will be immeasurable and boundless. But it is not as great as the merit gained from the first recollection of this dharma for the period of one meal.

Therefore, we should know that our approach to dharma is the holiest and most precious of all; its merit is incomparable. As the sutras say:

One thought of purity of mind is *bodhimandala*,

And is better than building seven-jeweled stupas as numerous as the sands of the Ganges.

Those jeweled stupas will finally be reduced to dust,

But one thought of purity of mind produces right enlightenment.

I hope that all of you who are cultivating the path will study these words carefully and keep them always in mind. If this body is not ferried across to the other shore in this lifetime, then for which life are you going to wait? If you do not cultivate now, you will go off in the wrong direction for ten thousand kalpas. But if you practice assiduously now, practices which are difficult to cultivate will gradually become easier until, finally, meritorious practice will advance of itself.

Alas! When starving people are given princely delicacies nowadays, they do not even know enough to put them in their mouths. When they are sick they meet the king of doctors but do not even know enough to take the medicine. If no one says, "What shall I do?" then what shall I do for them?

Although the character of mundane, conditioned activities can be seen and its effect experienced, if a person succeeds in one affair, everyone praises the rarity of it. The source of our minds has neither shape to be observed nor form to be seen; the way of words and speech is cut off there. Since the activities of mind are ended, *maras* and heretics have no way to revile us. Even the praises of Indra, Brahma, and all the gods will not reach it; so how can the mind be fathomed by the shallow understanding of ordinary men? How pitiful! How can a frog in a well know the vastness of the sea? How can a fox roar like a lion?

Hence we know that in this degenerate dharma age, a person who is able to hear this approach to dharma, realize its rarity, and receive and keep it with faithful devotion has for innumerable kalpas served all the saints, planted all the roots of goodness, and fully formed the right cause of *prajñā*—he has the most proficiency. As the *Diamond Sutra* says, "If there is a person who can have faith in these words, it should be known that this man has planted all the roots of goodness in front of incalculable numbers of Buddhas." It also says, "This is spoken in order to produce the great vehicle; this is spoken in order to produce the supreme vehicle." I hope that those of you who are aspiring to the path will not be cowardly. You must display your ardor. Good causes made in past kalpas cannot be known. If you do not believe in your superiority and, complacently resigning yourself to being inferior, you decide that you will not practice now because it is too difficult, then even though you might have good roots from past lives, you sever them now. The difficulty will keep growing and you will move farther from the goal. Since you have now arrived at the treasure house, how can you return empty-handed? Once you lose a human body, for ten thousand kalpas it will be difficult to recover. Be careful. Knowing that there is a treasure house, how can a wise person turn back and not look for it—and yet continue to resent bitterly his destitution and poverty? If you want the treasure you must throw away this skin-bag.[36]

CHAPTER EIGHT

Taego Pou & the Unification of Zen Schools

Chinul's writings and the work of his successors at the Samadhi and Prajña Community at Suson-sa went a long way in healing the rift between the Son and Kyo schools, a schism that had been going on for four centuries. Harmony was not restored overnight, to be sure, but the tone of dialogue between the two approaches was now one of accommodation rather than confrontation. One of the roadblocks in the way of greater harmony lay in the fact that all the schools of Son and Kyo were autonomous. There was no mechanism for these disparate schools to come together to resolve their differences.

The way out of this morass came through two unifications: one in 1356, and the other in 1424. The first saw all the nine mountain schools of Zen brought together in a single school, the Chogye School. This was accomplished through the efforts and initiative of Zen Master Taego Pou (1301-1382).

Taego was initiated as a monk at the age of 13 at Hwa-om temple by Zen Master Kwangjo. In his teens he visited a number of contemporary Zen masters and, at the age of 19, was given the famous kong-an for study: "Ten thousands things return to one; where does the one return to?" Taego worked diligently on his kong-an and at the age of 33 when he was residing at Kamno-sa temple in Kaesong, the Koryo capital, he had an awakening. To mark his enlightenment, he wrote a poem which concluded with this stanza:

> I drank up all the Buddhas and Patriarchs;
> All the mountains and rivers,
> Without my mouth.

After this breakthourgh, he started working on the *Mu* koan. At the age of 37, he attained final awakening and wrote:

> After I break through a solid gate,
> Clear wind blows from time immemorial.

At the age of 41, Taego settled down at Chunghung-sa temple on Samgak Mountain, near Seoul. He attracted a large number of students and another temple had to be built nearby to accommodate all of them. It was called the Taego Monastery after the name of the master.

In 1347 he traveled to Yuan China. What the motivation or circumstances behind this decision were are not known. In China, he met Ch'an master Shih-wu, an 18th-generation successor of Lin-chi I-hsuan. Shih-wu recognized Taego's enlightenment and gave him Inka. For a while Taego resided at Yen-king temple in Yenking, the capital of Yuan China and gave a series of public lectures which were attended by overflowing crowds. Hearing of his fame, the emperor, Shun-tsung sent him a gift but instructed the messenger to first test him by asking him the following question:

> Please accept this as a slight token of His Majesty's gratitude. But His Majesty attached this condition: that you receive it without using your hands.
>
> Without any hesitation, Taego replied, "Of course I will accept the gift without using my hands if you hand it to me without using your hands!"

The messenger realized here was a genuine Zen Master and of-fered his obeisance to Taego.[37]

Taego returned to Korea in 1353 at the age of 52 and was ap-pointed an official monk at the court of King Kongmin. While re-siding at the court, he presented a petition to the king, part of which read:

> Oh, what a pity that the nine Zen schools are only engaged in fac-tional wrangling! Originally Zen had only one gate, but now by each opening his own gate the number has become plural. So each school is given over to petty squabbles. This cannot be the equal and non-ego way of the Buddha. At this juncture, if the nine schools are unified into one, Buddhism will be greatly developed.[38]

The king was impressed by Taego's arguments for the need of unification of the Zen schools. In 1356, he set up an office charged with the responsibility of bringing about this unification. Taego was appointed the head of this office and under his direc-tion, one unified school of Zen, the Chogye School, appeared in Korea.

Taego left the royal court in 1358, apparently against the king's wishes, and retired into the mountains. After he left the court, his jealous rivals spread malicious gossip against Taego and poisoned king's ears. The king ordered Taego to be put under house-arrest at Songni-sa temple on Songni mountain. Years later, the king re-gretted his decision and invited Taego to come back to the royal court. In 1371, Taego returned to the court as an official monk and stayed at Hyongwon-sa temple on Sosol Mountain. He passed away on December 24, 1382 at the age of 81.

Today, Taego is revered as the founder of the Chogye Zen sect. His contribution in merging the nine disparate Zen schools into one single school is a milestone in Korean Buddhist history. It greatly helped the Zen sangha of his time to regain a sense of harmony and strength. That strength was sorely needed in diffi-cult times to come. The unification of 1356 was the First Unifica-tion. There were now six Doctrinal schools (Chong-am, Ch'ontae,

Hwaom, Chaun, Chungsin, and Sihung schools) and one Zen school (Chogye).

The Second Unification took place in 1424. Sejong (r.1418-1450), the fourth king of the Yi dynasty (1392-1910) is considered by Koreans to have been their greatest ruler. Sejong was a master-administrator and is best known for commissioning the invention of an indigenous system of writing which the Koreans called *Hangul* (created in 1443). The writing system is still in use today and has been responsible for almost universal literacy in the country. Sejong reorganized almost every aspect of the Korean people's lives—in religion, politics, culture, economy, language, national defense. Buddhism did not escape his attention.

In 1424, by a royal decree, the not-so-old Chogye school of Zen merged with two of the Doctrinal schools (Ch'ontae and Chong-am) to form the new *Sonjong* (Son School). The remaining four Doctrinal schools (Hwaom, Chaun, Chungsin and Sihung) were merged into one to form the *Kyojong* (Doctrinal School).

It should be noted that both the first and the second "unifications" were primarily administrative endeavors. They did not by any means resolve the basic ideological differences between the two approaches of Zen and Doctrinal schools. The resolution of those difference, to whatever extent it took place, came through Chinul's pioneering efforts and writings two centuries earlier, which continued to be the only frame of reference for all harmonizing efforts.

ZEN MASTER MUHAK AND HIS LINEAGE

About 150 miles southwest of Seoul, Korea's coast is dotted with small, indistinct islands. One of them is Ganwol-do Island. Not much bigger than an average suburban American house, this island contains just the two very tiny buildings which comprise Ganwol-do temple. The island is surrounded on three sides by water and is connected tenuously on the fourth side with the nearest fishing village. Until 1984, the only way for an outsider to approach the island was on a fishing boat. The strategic importance of these islands, however, prompted the Korean government to connect most of them with the mainland by dirt-roads built on landfill. It is now possible to drive to the fishing village nearest to Ganwol-do and from there walk the short distance to the island-temple. On the seaward side of the temple, which sits on a promontory, a primitive wall keeps the temple buildings from being overwhelmed when an angry sea lashes the island with tidal waves. The massive boulders below the wall, rust-colored through aeons of existence, duplicate pictures of a stark lunar landscape. All in all, it is as secluded and forbidding a place as one can hope to find for a monastic retreat. The Ganwol-do temple is a classical example of the remote, isolated spots discovered by Korean monks throughout the ages to give themselves up to their meditation in seclusion. Most of these spots are deep in the mountains in this extremely rugged, mountainous peninsula.

Ganwol-do temple was established around 1376 by Muhak Chacho (1317-1405), one of the greatest Zen masters in Korean Buddhist history. A younger contemporary of Zen Master Taego Pou, he lived during the last years of the Koryo dynasty and the first years of the new Yi dynasty. Both his teacher Naong Hyegun (1320-1376) and his successor Hamho Tuktong (1376-1433) were distinguished Zen masters in their own right.

Naong Hyegum, Muhak's teacher, is credited, along with Taego Pou, with introducing the kong-an oriented Lin-chi Zen from China into Korea, although Chinul had already made use of Ta-hui's methods of the Lin-chi school, as we noted earlier. But it would appear that the use of these methods was either localized at Songgwang-sa or did not gain wide currency in the rest of the Zen schools after Chinul's death. When Naong was 20 years old, he saw a neighbor die and asked an old man in the village, "Where does a person go after death?" Nobody could answer this question for him. Obviously important for him, he went to a temple on Kongdok Mountain and applied to become a monk under the resident Zen Master Yoyon (dates unknown).

According to Naong's story, Yoyon asked him, "Why do you want to become a monk?" Naong replied, "I wish to transcend the Triple World (of suffering) and save mankind. Please teach me how to do so." Yoyon asked again, "What kind of Thing has come here?" Naong answered, "Only that which can speak and hear comes here. I don't know how to do ascetic practices, please teach me the secret way of doing so." Yoyon said, "I don't know either. Go to another Zen master and ask him!"[39] So Naong went to Hwaom temple and practiced constantly day and night. Some time later, he went to China where he met Ch'an master Chih-k'ung (d.1363) at the Fa-yuan temple. Chih-k'ung had just returned from India. Naong stayed with him for a few years and received Inka from him. Later, he went to Ch'ing-hui temple and met Ch'an Master P'ing-shan, a 19th-generation successor of Lin-chi I-hsuan.

On meeting P'ing-shan, who was seated in meditation, Naong took several steps eastwards and several steps westward before his seated figure.

The master asked him, "Where do you come from?"

"I have come from Fa-yuan temple."

"Whom have you seen before?"

"I met Master Chih-kung who had come from India."

"What was Chih-kung doing?"

"He was using a Thousand Swords every day."

"Aside from a Thousand Swords of Chih-k'ung, bring me your one sword."

Naong hit him with a seat cushion. Master P'ing-shan cried, "This thief is going to kill me," and tumbled down from his meditation cushion. Naong lifted him to his feet and said, "My sword can kill a man and can also bring him back to life."[40]

At this reply, the master burst out laughing and invited Naong into his room. After a stay of several months, Naong received Inka from P'ing-shan.

Muhak Chacho (1317-1405), Naong's most famous disciple, left home at the age of 18. He was initiated as a monk by one Master Soji who was a chief disciple of the National Teacher Haegam of the Songgwang-sa temple, probably the fourteenth-generation successor of Chinul. (No dates are available either for Soji or Haegam.) Muhak studied sutras under a certain master Hyemyong (no dates) and Zen under Naong. He attained enlightenment and received transmission from Naong. One day, Naong asked Muhak,

"Chao-chou was once looking at a stone bridge, accompanied by a wandering monk. He asked the monk, 'Who made this bridge?' The monk said, 'Mr. Li Ying made it.' Chao-chou further asked, 'Where did Mr. Li begin to build the bridge?' The wandering monk could not answer. Now, if I ask you the same question, what can you say?"

Without saying anything, Muhak formed a stepping stone with both of his hands.

Naong said, "Today I found out that you have not been cheated by the kong-an." He then gave Inka to Muhak.[41]

After receiving his Inka, Muhak went deep into Solbong Mountain where he lived in an isolated cave and made his clothes out of grass and hemp. For his food he ate pine bark and pine blossoms, grass-roots and wild fruits. In this cave and under these conditions, he practiced Zen for nine years. Later, when he came out of the mountains, people remarked that in his daily life, Muhak was like a "great mountain," quiet in words and noble in manner. He never seemed to be perturbed about all the happenings around him. A story is told that once when he was at Pudo temple, seated in meditation, a fire broke out. Everyone was in an uproar and a state of confusion, but Muhak continued to sit in his meditation posture, completely unaffected by all the chaotic hustle and bustle around him.

Muhak converted King Taejo (r.1392-1398), the founder of the Yi dynasty, to Buddhism. He helped the king select a new site for his capital, the present-day city of Seoul. A close and warm relationship grew between the king and the monk and in the first year of Taejo's reign, Muhak was appointed a monk at the royal court. A story concerning the give-and-take between the king and his monk has come down to us:

> One day the king came to visit Muhak at the Hoeryong-sa temple. The king dismissed all his attendants and said to Muhak, "Due to my preoccupation with the affairs of state, I cannot even laugh as I please. Today we shall have a private conversation where we

can dispense with all formalities and talk to each other freely. Just enjoy each other's company." Muhak said, "You had better first break the ice by making a joke, your Highness." The king said, "O.K. Muhak, you look like a hungry pig looking for dung." Muhak bowed to him and said, "Your Highness looks like Shakyamuni Buddha on the Vulture Peak." The king was dissatisfied with such an answer and said, "While I compared you to a pig, why do you compare me to the Buddha?" Muhak replied, "It is because a pig can only see a pig and a Buddha only sees Buddha." The king burst into laughter. Then he said, "You are smarter than I am by one degree. But your reply is a kind of Zen teaching and not a joke!"[42]

When Muhak became ill in his old age, his attendant brought him some medicine which he refused, saying, "An old man of 80 needs no medicine." Just before his death, a monk asked him, "When the four elements—earth, water, fire and air—which constitute the physical body, separate from each other, where does the man go?" Muhak answered, "The six senses are originally empty. When the four elements separate from each other, it is like a dream. There is no such thing as coming and going." The monk asked again, "Is there anything in you that is not sick, though you are sick now?" Without speaking, Muhak pointed to a monk sitting beside him. The monk persisted, "The body is composed of these four elements which are perishable. What is True Body?" Spreading his arms, Muhak said, "This is Oneness." Immediately after uttering these words, he passed away.[43]

Although Muhak's Dharma successor, Hamho Tuktong (1376-1433), left a number of writings behind him, very little is known about his life. His importance derives chiefly from the fact that his writings considerably influenced Sosan Taesa (1520-1604), the most important monk during Korea's Yi dynasty. The work for which Hamho is best known is called *Comments of Five Masters on the Diamond Sutra* . It has been pointed out that the preface combines elements from the *Awakening of Faith* (one of the seminal texts of Mahayana Buddhism attributed to Ashvaghosa, the

12th Patriarch of Indian Buddhism and a noted philosopher) and from Lin-chi's teaching:

> There is "One Thing" that has neither name nor form, that penetrates both the past and the future, that lies hidden in one single particle of dust but embraces six directions of the universe. It contains all mysteries, it adapts to all circumstances. It presides over the three entities (heaven, earth, humanity), and prevails over all beings. It is wider and higher than anything else. Whether we look upwards or downwards, it appears clear. However we hear it, it sounds clear. What a mysterious and divine thing it is! It began earlier than the universe; it has no beginning. It ends later than the universe; it has no ending. What a profound thing it is! What shall I call it? Emptiness or form? I don't know how to name it. It is indescribable.[44]

"The creative side of the preface is that this first aspect (*The Awakening of Faith* postulates two aspects or orders—the transcendental and the phenomenal, the universal and the particular, the infinite and the finite, the static and the dynamic) is equated to the Zen concept of truth as inexpressible.'[45] In his *Handbook for Zen Students*, Sosan Taesa later adopted this synthesis directly from Hamho.

Other works authored by Hamho are the three volumes of *Commentary on the Perfect Enlightenment Sutra* and *Hamho's Zen Records*. Hamho is said to have written the following poem minutes before he died:

> It is clear like emptiness and quietness.
> Originally there is "One Thing."
> Spiritual light brightens all over,
> It is full in all directions.
> No more body and mind,
> No more birth and death.
> In coming and going, living and dying,
> There are no obstacles for me.[46]

CHAPTER NINE

Buddhism Under the Yi Dynasty

We have seen earlier how the military and the lower-echelon bureaucrats, the so-called Neo-Confucianists, had begun to resent the economic and political influence of the Buddhist establishment during the early and middle years of the decadent Koryo dynasty. During the last years of the dynasty, this resentment had become a tidal wave. Yi Taejo (r.1392-1398), the founder of the new dynasty, came to power with the help of these dissatisfied elements of governmental infrastructure. Although personally a Buddhist (having been converted to Buddhism by Muhak Taesa, whom he had made the "National Teacher") he owed his power to the Neo-Confucianists. The Neo-Confucianists, all militantly anti-Buddhist, were divided into two camps—those who advocated the reduction of Buddhist power and wealth, and those who called for a complete abolition of Buddhism. The latter view became increasingly popular among the lower-echelon bureaucrats who were excluded from real power and were usually unpaid by the bankrupt Koryo government.

Taejo himself, while he recognized the need for an economic reform of Buddhism, was resistant to large-scale social change. The reforms which he initiated were, therefore, aimed at curtailing the competition of Buddhist temples with the state for land, taxes, serfs and citizens who were subject to corvee labor and military service. One of the first measures of the new regime was to make donating land to Buddhist temples illegal. In addition, the lands of many temples were confiscated and turned over to the military. The monk licensing system was made stricter, and the monks were required to pay a licensing fee to the government in order to receive their ordination. All in all, Taejo did not feel that Buddhism and Confucianism were mutually exclusive, as some of the more militant Neo-Confucianists were advocating. Rather, he saw Buddhism as a religion and Confucianism as a social-administrative system. As a result, the measures against Buddhist establishment were primarily economic, and were neither too severe nor too abrupt.

This changed under the third king of the Yi dynasty, T'aejong (r.1400-1418) who was a younger son of Taejo. T'aejong moved steadily to reduce the economic, political and social influence of Buddhism. The number of temples allowed to exist was reduced first to 242 and then even further to 88. The rest were confiscated by the government. Most temples lost their tax-exempt status, and the number of attendants and the temple land-holdings were strictly limited. The positions of "National Teacher" and "Royal Teacher" (positions through which Buddhists had been able to exercise political influence) were abolished. Buddhist rites and rituals which had completely dominated the Koryo society were now replaced by Confucian rites, at least in the upper levels of the society.

Sejong (r.1418-1450) continued the policy of curtailing Buddhism. The number of monks allowed to pass the monk examination was now limited to 60 every three years. In 1424, as we have seen earlier, he reorganized the competing Buddhist schools into two major sects—Sonjong and Kyojong.

Buddhism got a slight respite during the reign of Sejong's son Sejo (r.1455-1468) who was a Buddhist and sought to protect Buddhism socially and economically. He guaranteed the rights of monks accused of crimes (which had been denied them under the earlier Yi dynasty kings) and exempted them from corvee labor. He devoted his energies to publication of Buddhist texts and generally encouraged Buddhist arts and culture.

The tide turned for the worse during the reign of Sonjong (r.1469-1494) who succeeded Sejo; and it became a tempest during the reigns of two subsequent kings, Yonsang'un (r.1494-1506) and Chungjong (r.1506-1544) when persecution of Buddhism reached its nadir. Under Yonsang'un, the delicate relationship between Buddhism and the state through laws recognizing the existence of Buddhism was destroyed. The two headquarter-temples of the Zen and the Doctrinal schools in the capital were disbanded. Monks were forbidden entry into the capital city and in some cases the temples were turned into stables or into *kiaseng* (Korean version of geisha houses) quarters. Monks and nuns were discouraged from becoming ordained; monk examinations were discontinued and all monk ranks within the sects were abolished. As a result many, if not most, monks returned to lay status. The distinction between Zen and Doctrinal monks became tenuous since the monk-examination system had been, in the past, the only mechanism to distinguish one from the other.

Under Chungjong, the destruction and appropriation of Buddhist property increased and the social status of the monks sank even lower. The monks became objects of contempt and maltreatment, especially by the *yangban* youth. There are many recorded instances of Confucian scholars encouraging these youths to plunder and burn Buddhist sutras as well as temple buildings. The great bells at the former headquarter-temples of the Zen and Doctrinal schools—Hungch'onsa and Hungdoksa—were melted down and turned into weapons. Temples were torn down and the timber was used for housing construction. In 1535, a system of monk-identification cards was initiated so that, whenever necessary, monks could be mobilized for corvee labor.

In view of all these harsh measures, it is nothing short of a miracle that Buddhism survived at all in Korea. Two factors seem to have been responsible. Primary was the tenacity of the hermit-monks who kept the teachings and practice alive deep in the mountains. We have very little information about these monks but it seems reasonable to imagine that they must have been remarkable people with extraordinary faith and perserverance to continue practicing under such harsh conditions, and against such overwhelming odds. The second factor which came to Buddhism's rescue was the support by women in the royal palace—the queens and the concubines who continued to have faith in Buddhism as a protector of their families. It would have been comic, were it not so grim, to see these women pray to Buddha for the safety and prosperity of their house and menfolk while at the same time these very men were destroying Buddhist temples.

In any case, the regency of Queen Munjong (r.1545-1565) came as a succor to Buddhism during the darkest days of its repression. Queen Munjong began the work of reviving Buddhism against the opposition of her ministers and court officials. In 1550, she restored the monk examination system and re-established two headquarter-temples for Zen and Doctrinal sects. Pongun-sa in Kwangju City became the headquarters for the Zen sect and Pongson-sa in Yangju City the headquarters for the Doctrinal school. She appointed the monk Houng Pou (1515-1565) as the Abbot of Pongun-sa and head of the Zen Sect; the monk Sunjin (no dates available) was appointed as the head of the Doctrinal school.

It was against this background that Sosan Taesa (1520-1604) was born. Sosan is the most important monk during Yi dynasty (1392-1911) and was responsible for reviving, however briefly, Korean Zen during its darkest days. But before we look at Sosan's life and achievement, we need to take a brief look at his lineage.

THE LINEAGE FROM TAEGO TO SOSAN

Zen Masters Naong Hyegun (1320-1376) and Taego Pou (1301-1382) are credited with formally introducing the teachings of Lin-chi Zen into Korea. Naong's lineage was short-lived, but Taego's line continued relatively unbroken and is the one to which all the Zen monks in Korea today trace their origins.

Taego's Dharma successor was his senior disciple, Hwanam Honsu (1320-1392) who became a monk at the age of 19 when he witnessed the sudden death of a close friend and realized the transiency of life. He went into the Diamond Mountains and spent the rest of his life there. He is said to have left behind 33 disciples.

Hwanam's Dharma successor was his senior disciple, Kwigok Kagun (dates unknown). All the records concerning his life were probably destroyed as a result of the anti-Buddhist activities of the time. The only thing we know about him is that he was the author of *Sonmun Yomsong Sorhwa* (Commentary on the Interpretation of Zen Gate), an important text used by later generations of Korean Zen monks.

Kiwgok Kagun was succeeded by Pyokke Chongsim. This particular succession may very well have been a fabrication; for, according to one story, Pyokke claimed Kiwgok Kagun to be his teacher only at his deathbed, and that too at the behest of his students asking to make the line of succession continuous. We have no way of verifying this story one way or another.

Pyokke Chongsim's dates are unknown but he seems to have lived at least until 1492. It is said that early in his life he went to Ming China (1368-1644) where he studied Zen and made pilgrimages to famous temples. On his return to Korea, he found the persecution against Buddhism at its height. One story has it that he was forced to give up his robe and return to lay status. Another story claims that still later he was forced to live in hiding on Hwangak Mountain with his wife and children. The only fact about Pyokke Chongsim on which the scholars seem to agree is that he transmitted Zen to Pyoksong Chiom (1464-1534) and Kyo (Doctrinal) to Chongyon Popchun (dates unknown). Today almost all Korean monks trace their lineage back to Pyokke Chongsim (and hence to Taego.) This may be, as some have speculated, due to Sosan Taesa's greatness. On the other hand, scholars have also speculated that Sosan's students may have fabricated the whole line of succession from Taego to Pyokke Chongsim in order to identify their own line with the Lin-chi sect. In any case, the significant fact is that both Taego and Pyokke Chongsim were Lin-chi Zen masters, and the efforts of Sosan's students, if there indeed were such efforts, to identify with a Lin-chi lineage highlights the esteem in which Lin-chi was held at the time. It is quite possible that it may have been the only Zen sect to survive the persecution, through the efforts of hermit monks deep in the mountains.

Pyoksong Chiom, Pyokke's successor, was a military man who had served with distinction on the "Northern Expedition" of 1491 under General Ho-Jong. After he was decorated for valor, he wrote:

> What a pity it is that a man, once born into this world, could not find his own original mind, but only kept himself busy with combat after combat. I am honored by the military merit, but what ephemeral fame it is![47]

Soon after writing this, he went to Kyeryong Mountain and had his head shaved to become a monk. He was noted for sitting in deep samadhi for hours, even days. He received Inka from Zen master Pyokke Chongsim. After his certification, he wandered around for five years, roaming from hermitages on Diamond Mountain to Nungga Mountain.[48] Because of the raging persecution against Buddhism, he had to hide in his later years, on Chiri Mountain. At the time of his death, he was staying at Suguk hermitage on Chiri Mountain and reading the *Lotus Sutra*. When he came across a chapter on upaya (expedient means) in the sutra, he called his students and said to them,

> Being ignorant, man neglects his own light and continues transmigrating. So, Buddha, taking compassion on man, tried to save him by *upaya*. But it is only Upaya, not real truth. The real truth is something formless and empty, not expressible in words. If you believe in the real form of Buddha, then you must find your own mind. Only after you attain such enlightenment, can you open the secret-treasure and see the Buddha Land. Today I will show you the Nirvana-form. You should not seek outside but rather grope inside for your original mind.[49]

After this talk, Pyoksong asked his attendant to bring him a cup of tea. After drinking his tea, he retired to his cell and closed the door behind him. Days later, his disciples found him dead, still sitting in a cross-legged meditation posture.

Pyoksong Chiom transmitted his Zen dharma to Puyong Yong-gwan (1485-1567) who passed it on to Sosan. Pyoksong Chiom's other famous disciple, Kyongsong Ilson (1482-1568), was also a teacher of Sosan's.

CHAPTER TEN

Sosan Taesa

Sosan (1520-1604) is generally considered to be the greatest Zen Master and the most renowned monk during Korea's Yi dynasty (1392-1910). He has been called one of Korea's three most important Buddhist thinkers, along with Won Hyo (617-686) and Chinul (1158-1210). Sosan's role in the nation's defense during the Japanese invasion of 1592 enabled him to transcend the limited world of Buddhism and become a folk-hero in Korea's national history.

We have noted earlier the times of persecution and suppression of Buddhism prevailing when Sosan was born in 1520. He was born in the northern city of Pyongyang in a family of minor government officials. Both his parents were 47 years old when he was born, and they died within a year of each other when Sosan was nine years old. He had been a precocious child at a very early age; his father seems to have tutored him in the Chinese and Confucian educational system. After his parents' death, the local magistrate summoned the newly-orphaned Sosan for an interview. The magistrate, one Mr. Yi, tested him on his ability to compose verses in Chinese and was so impressed by his talent that he adopted him as his own son.

Soon Magistrate Yi made arrangements for Sosan to go to Seoul, the capital, and continue his Confucian education there at Song-gyun-gwan (Seoul Royal School). Sosan tried passing a preliminary civil service examination but failed (the average age for passing this exam was about 25.) While in Seoul, Sosan lived at the home of a Confucian scholar who served as his tutor. While Sosan was appearing for his exams, the tutor got his transfer-orders for a new job in southern province of Cholla-do. After the exams were over, Sosan and some of his fellow-students decided to go south themselves to continue their studies with their teacher. However, when they arrived they discovered that, due to a mix-up, their teacher had been called back to Seoul. The young students, rather than starting immediately on their long journey back, decided to wander in the mountains and visit the Buddhist temples in the area.

While in the mountains, Sosan made the acquaintance of an old monk, who said to him, "You do not have the look of an ordinary person. Why do you not turn your attention to passing the examination of the empty mind and cut off the mind which thinks of fame and fortune?"

"What is passing the empty mind examination?" Sosan asked.

The elderly monk blinked his eyes. "Do you understand?" he asked.

"I don't know," said Sosan.

"It's difficult to express in words," said the monk. He then gave Sosan a number of Buddhist scriptures to study (a treasure in those days). Whether Sosan found his own way or the monk so directed him, soon thereafter Sosan went to Sanggye-sa temple on Chiri Mountain. There he met the monk Sung-in (dates unknown) under whom he became a monk and studied sutras for three years. After those three years, when Sosan was 18 years old, Sung-in said to him, "You are now very much conversant in sutras and your learning can hardly be matched by anyone else. But you are a complete blank in Zen. So you had better begin to study Zen and try to seek after Mind and Emptiness."

Sosan asked, "To study Zen, to whom shall I look for guidance? Please tell me."

"At present, Zen Master Puyong is very famous for Zen. Go to him and ask for it."[50]

So Sosan made his way to Master Puyong and asked him, "Since early days, I have liked to learn, so I have already mastered all the Chinese classics of Confucianism including the Four Books and the Three Classics. After I became a monk I read all the Buddhist Sutras and am well-conversant in them. But I don't know anything about Zen. I can't understand the meaning of 'Buddha is Mind.' Would you tell me the meaning?"

"That is, as you say, the mind that you can't understand," said Puyong.

Sosan understood a little bit, but was not completely satisfied. So he asked again, "What is the meaning of Bodhidharma coming from the West?"

Master Puyong answered, "I am busy now. Come back again after a couple of days." As Sosan was leaving the room, the Master called out, "Sosan!" Surprised, Sosan turned back and answered, "Yes?"

"What is this? Tell me quick, tell me quick!"

Sosan could not answer, but from that day he began to practice earnestly with the kong-an "What is this?" While he tried to keep the Great Doubt, he always felt hindered by the knowledge he had gained from reading so many books. He went for advice to Master Puyong who told him,

> Zen practice is quite different from any worldly study. All the knowledge and learning that you received before should be discarded. You should give up thinking that you are doing something now. Your mind should be blank; you you should again be like a one-year old baby. Thus you should devote yourself more to ignorance than to knowledge. It is all right if you have a realization abruptly on hearing a Patriarch's kong-an, but it happens seldom. You cannot but have a doubt if there is anything you don't know. So if you devote yourself to ignorance that means you doubt. If you doubt, then the doubt will be broken at length.

To practice Zen well, you must break through the kong-an of Patriarchs and to realize the truth you must cut the thoughts away. Keep doubting without any words or thoughts.

Do it as if you had something in your throat that you cannot vomit or swallow; do it as if you were always thinking of paying off your debts; do it as if you were a hen hatching eggs; as if you were a cat watching a mouse-hole; as if you were a mosquito trying hard to pierce the back of an iron-horse...[51]

With this advice in mind, Sosan devoted himself even more strenuously to his Zen practice. One day he asked his teacher,

"What is it like when one seeks for Buddha?"

"It's like looking for an ox while riding on an ox."

"What is like after you know Buddha?"

"It is like coming home riding on an ox."

"How can I keep on practicing Zen if I attain realization?"

"You should keep on practicing Zen as a cowboy with a whip keeps his cow from trespassing in another's field."

Soon after this exchange with his teacher, Sosan heard a cuckoo crying in the garden and attained partial realization. He composed two verses to commemorate the occasion:

> Suddenly I hear a cuckoo singing outside the window.
> The spring mountains which fill my eyes are all my old home.

> Returning from drawing water, I turn my head.
> Blue mountains in white clouds without number.[52]

Sosan records that he received Inka from Puyong Yonggwan after his realization. He then went to visit another Zen Master Muk Taesa for further study and received Inka from him as well.

For the next eight years, Sosan lived a quiet and secluded life in various temples and retreat huts scattered all over the Chiri Mountain. One day, as he was on his way to visit a friend in a nearby village, he heard the cry of a rooster and had another awakening. He again composed two verses:

Although the hair is white, the mind is not white,
A man of old once divulged.
Now that I have heard the rooster's cry,
All that a man can do has been done.

On suddenly reaching my home, everything is just as it is.
The ten million [pages of the] *Tripitaka* are originally empty
paper.[53]

Soon thereafter, Sosan traveled to Odae Mountain in the north-
east where he stayed for six months, and then to the Maitreya
Peak in the Diamond Mountains further north. During this
period of his life (in his late 20's and early 30's) he composed a
number of poems and letters of instruction for students who
sought him out.

This was also the time when the Regent Queen Munjong began the task of reviving Buddhism with the help of monk Houng
Pou (1515-1565). In 1551, the first monk examination in nearly 50
years was held and 406 monks from the Zen sect alone passed. In
1552, in the advanced examination, 21 Zen monks and 12 Sutra
monks passed. Sosan was one of the monks who passed this latter
advanced examination. He was 32 years old at the time. The next
year he became the abbot of a temple whose name is not known.
He held this position for two years. He was also appointed head
of the "Association for the Transmission of Dharma." Three
months after this appointment, he was made head of the Doctrinal
Sect as well as Abbot of Pongsonsa, the head temple for that sect.
Only three months after that, he became head of the Zen sect
without giving up his position as head of the Doctrinal sect. He
was also given the title of *Todaesonsa*, the highest public office in
Buddhist hierarchy. Sosan held, simultaneously, his positions as
head of the Zen and Doctrinal schools for three years, until the
age of 38.

In 1557, he resigned from his posts and returned to the mountains. The historical significance of Sosan's tenure in office has
been described thus:

From Sosan on, the distinction between Son and Kyo which had already become tenuous after the abolition of the monk examination system, grew even more tenuous. He himself, although a Son master, became head of both the Son and Kyo Orders, which is an indication of the relative insignficance of the distinction on the one hand, and of the superior position of Son on the other hand by this time. Sosan signified the emergence of a new type of Buddhist leader in the following generation of Buddhist monks—one versed in both Kyo and Son but with definite identity as a Son master nonetheless. Thus Chinul's vision [of a combined study of Son and Kyo, with Kyo subordinate to Son] became reality in Korea at least from 17th century on.[54]

Thus, after his resignation, Sosan "took hold of his walking stick" and headed for the Diamond Mountains After six months there, he again went to Chiri mountain where he stayed for the next six years in various temples and retreat huts. After that he wandered far and wide over the mountains of Korea until his body was "light as a goose feather." Sometime in 1568, when he was 49 years old, Sosan decided to stay at Myohyang Mountain in the northwestern part of the country (now in North Korea). It is because of this mountain that he came to be known as *Sosan* (Western mountain). With only a few interruptions, he stayed on Myohyang mountain for the rest of his life.

His stay on Myohyang Mountain was a time of much teaching and writing. He met most of his important disciples—Samyong Yujong, Soyo T'aehung, Paegun Powan, Pyokchon Uichon, and others—during this period. It is said that during his lifetime he had more than a thousand students of whom 70 were outstanding. By 1564, he had begun working on *Handbook for Zen Students*, a tract which has exercised immense influence on the succeeding generations of Korean Zen monks. Samyong, his best known disciple, wrote a preface to it, and the book was published in 1579. Sosan also wrote instruction booklets for his most senior disciples, as well as biographies of his teachers, and he produced a large number of poems and letters. He became well-known as a poet, and his literary abilities were appreciated even by the Confucianists.

In 1589, a conspiracy to overthrow the government was uncovered. Some monks were involved and somehow both Sosan and Samyong were accused and imprisoned, but both were soon released by a special command of the king. When the king found that Sosan had never failed to offer prayers for the king, the country and its people, and had also written a verse of mourning upon the former king's death, he invited Sosan to the palace and presented him with a painting and a verse in his own hand.

In 1592, the Japanese invaded Korea in order to fulfill Hideyoshi's vision of conquering both Korea and China in the name of the Japanese emperor. In less than 20 days they marched from Pusan, on the southern tip of the peninsula, to Seoul, the capital, in the north. The king and the court, unprepared and unable to meet the Japanese challenge, fled the capital. In desperation, the king asked for help from Ming China and also tried to rally the Korean people behind him. Among those who responded to his call was Sosan. The king was reportedly moved to tears and said,

> Whereas some of my minsters and regular generals don't want to follow me, you, an ascetic monk, volunteers to fight for the country. What a laudable spirit you have! Your courage will be a great help in saving this country.[55]

Sosan was 73 years old at the time. The king appointed him the Supreme Commander of all the monk-soldiers. Sosan issued a manifesto to all the temples in the country:

> Every monk in the country should go to the battle front and fight for this country, except the old and the sick who should pray in earnest in their temples.[56]

With the help of his disciples, Sosan raised a militia of about 5,000 monks. Considering the persecution against them in the previous two centuries, that must have been every able-bodied monk in Korea. Sosan provided the moral leadership and inspiration to the monk-army while the active leadership was turned over to his disciples. The monks' militia assisted the Chinese Ming troops substantially and was especially instrumental in recapturing the important northern city of Pyongyang. Several monks fought heroically on the battlefield, including Samyong Taesa.

There is an oft-told story about a monk, a certain Yon'gyu of Kap-sa temple, an old priest who had the job of collecting firewood for the temple from the hillside. At some point, he had taken to carving pieces of wood into fighting sticks in his spare time and storing them in the temple. The head monk was understandably distressed and encouraged him to read sutras in his spare time instead, but the old monk continued in his ways for many years. One day word came that the Japanese armies were marching from the south and would probably be attacking the temple soon. Yon'gyu rallied the monks, gave them the weapons and rudimentary instructions in how to use them. When the Japanese soldiers arrived, the monks were ready for them. Yon'gyu, old though he was, led the charge and the Japanese army, caught unaware by the scale and intensity of resistance, was repulsed. Yon'gyu was mortally wounded in the battle and was brought back to the temple where he died. The enraged Japanese army regrouped and returned with larger forces. They overwhelmed the temple and burnt it to the ground. These heroes of Korean resistance were duly recognized by the government for their contribution to the war effort.

Korean Buddhism, however, paid a terrible price for their resistance against the Japanese invaders. With almost no exception, all the Buddhist temples were burnt to the ground by the Japanese. Temples which had stood for centuries, with their priceless works of art and religious relics, were reduced to heaps of ashes. The bitterness generated by the wanton destruction during the Hideyoshi invasions of 1592 and 1598 were only compounded by the Japanese occupation of Korea from 1911 to 1945 and their efforts to subvert Korean Buddhism during that period. That bitterness persists even to this day.

For his role in the nation's defense against the invaders, Sosan earned the everlasting gratitude of his countrymen. "He is widely known among non-Buddhists in Korea not so much because he revived Buddhism in an age of persecution or because he was an outstanding Zen master, but rather because of the concern for the nation and love of the people that he displayed during the invasion of 1592."[57]

Li Ju-sung, the Ming army commander who came to assist the Korean army against the Japanese, composed a poem in Sosan's honor:.

> Caring little about worldly fame,
> He had been immersed only in Zen.
> But on hearing of the nation in danger
> He came down from the mountain.[58]

Popular folk stories survive to this day which tell of Sosan and Samyong performing magical feats to bewilder the enemy or make their blood run cold (feats like creating illusory tigers or snakes in the path of the Japanese armies or creating storms when they were about to set forth in battle).

After the capital, Seoul, had been recaptured and the king returned to his palace, Sosan resigned from his post and turned over the responsibility of leading the monks' militia to his disciples Samyong Yujong and Noemuk Ch'oyong. The king bestowed an honorary title on Sosan: "First Zen Master in the Nation, Commander of Zen and Doctrine, Assister of the Sects, Establisher of Doctrine, Highest Sage Who Saves All."

Sosan returned to his mountain hermitage and resumed his quiet life of meditation and teaching. He did some wandering around on Chiri and Odae Mountains and composed verses like the following:

> A host told the dream to a guest
> The guest told the dream to the host.
> The two who have told the dream
> Are those who are in the dream.

And a poem of enlightenment:

> For ten years I have been meditating without coming out of
> the mountains;
> Though I walk across the forest the birds are not frightened.
> Last night there was a wind blowing around the pond under
> the pine tree;
> Today a fish has a crest, and the crane cried three times.

Another poem during his last days reads:

> Thousands of thoughts and ideas
> Are nothing but snow on a hot oven.
> A muddy ox wades on the water,
> And the earth and the sky break up.[59]

On January 23, 1604, Sosan washed himself, lit incense and
called together his disciples for a final Dharma speech. It is said
that after the speech, he wrote a verse on the back of a portrait of
himself:

> Eighty years before, this portrait [is said to be like] me;
> Eighty years later, I will be [said to be like] this portrait.[60]

Then he wrote letters to his disciples Damyong and Ch'ong who
were not there; and, sitting in meditation posture, Sosan closed
his eyes for the last time.

In his approach to Zen practice, Sosan was a direct spiritual
descendant of Chinul. Without drawing a sharp line between the
Zen and scholarly approaches, Chinul had made sutra studies and
meditation practice complimentary to each other. But, after everything had been said and done, Chinul remained a Zen master
and, to his way of thinking, sutra studies were subordinate to Zen
practice. Sosan followed Chinul's approach though he seems to
have been more outspoken about it. For one thing, by Sosan's time,
Lin-chi style of Zen had become predominant in Korea, and it is

with this school of Zen that Sosan and his disciples sought to identify themselves. Chinul did not face a similar situation. Indeed, Chinul only barely explored the "hwadu" method of Ta-hui (himself a patriarch of the Lin-chi school), no doubt because his information about Ta-hui's method was scanty. Sosan explored the method fully. Sosan did not write any specific text on the Sutras or lecture upon them, something which Chinul did quite often. In his *Handbook for Zen Students*, Sosan uses Chinul's thought to establish an introductory base, and proceeds to give elaborate instructions in the use of "hwat'ou" or "kong-an" method. Overall, while acknowledging the usefulness of doctrinal study, Sosan was not as interested in theoretical distinctions or doctrinal analysis as Chinul. Because of later historical developments, it is Sosan's approach to Zen, rather than Chinul's, that seems to have had a greater influence on Korean Zen down to the present day.

Due to Sosan's importance in the development of Zen thought in Korea, included here is his *Handbook for Zen Students*, the work for which he is best known and which has exercised the most influence on the training methods of Korean Zen monks.

SOSAN TAESA'S HANDBOOK FOR ZEN STUDENTS

The *Handbook* is Sosan's longest and most representative work. According to the translator, Rebecca Bernen, the selections which follow are based on the writings of Zen masters such as Chinul and Ta-hui. Thus, Sosan's Handbook is a direct development of the T'ang China Zen/Ta-hui/Chinul/native Korean Zen matrix. The *Handbook* was written between 1564 and 1579 and Sosan appended his own comments onto each selection. In some cases he also adds a concluding remark, and occasionally a commentary on the concluding remark as well. The following is a translation of the first third of the complete, original text.[61]

*Thanks to Rebecca Bernen for permission to reprint this translation.

Preface

Those who studied Buddhism in antiquity would not speak as the Buddha had not spoken or act as the Buddha had not acted. Thus they treasured only the sacred literature of the sutras and nothing else. But for those who study Buddhism today, that which they hand on and recite are the writings of government officials; that which they seek out and hold onto are the verses of these officials. Today's Buddhists even color their paper with red and green and decorate their buildings with fine silk. No matter how many verses they have, they are not satisfied; they consider these writings to be the greatest treasure. Alas! How can Buddhists of old and Buddhists today have such different values?

Although I am not worthy of the task, I am intent on the study of the ancient teachings and consider the sacred writings of the sutras to be a great treasure. But these writings are nonetheless numerous as leaves in thick foliage and the sea of the *Tripitaka* is vaster than the ocean, and it seemed that later others of the same intention would surely not be able to avoid the labor of picking through the leaves one by one, so from among the writings I selected several hundred maxims which are the most important and to the point and wrote them down in one place. The result can well be called concise yet complete in meaning. If one were to take these maxims as one's stern teacher, study thoroughly, and attain their true meaning, then there in each sentence would be a living Buddha. Do your best!

But as for a single statement which would go beyond words, an extraordinary treasure, it is not that I would not use it; it is just that I would rather reserve it for a special opportunity.

Handbook for Zen Students

1. There is one thing here. From the beginning it is clear and bright and divine. It has never appeared nor has it ever disappeared. Its name cannot be obtained nor can its shape be obtained.

Comment: What is this one thing?
A man of old composed an ode:.
Before the ancient Buddhas were born

Everything was one, circular and complete.
Since even Shakyamuni himself did not understand it
How could Mahakasyapa transmit it?
That is why this one thing has never appeared nor has it ever disappeared,
and it cannot be named or described.

The Sixth Patriarch once told the assembly, "I have one thing. It has no name or written symbol. Nonetheless, do any of you understand or not?"
Zen Master Shen-hui immediately stepped forward and said, "It is the original source of all the Buddhas; it is my own Buddha nature." This is the reason Shen-hui was not the Sixth Patriarch's true heir.

When Zen Master Huai-jang came from Mt. Sung, the Sixth Patriarch asked him, "What thing has thus come here?" Huai-jang did not know what to do. It was only eight years later that he had the self-confidence to say, "If you say it is a thing [lit. one thing], then you have already missed the point." This is the reason Huai-jang was the Sixth Patriarch's true heir.

Summation: The sages of the three teachings have all emerged from this statement. Whoever would try to explain this should be careful lest one lose one's eyebrows.

2. The Buddhas' and patriarchs' appearing in the world was the same as waves arising where there is no wind.
Comment: "The Buddhas and patriarchs" are those like the World Honored One and Mahakasyapa. "Appearing in the world" means that with great compassion as their essence they save all beings. But if one sees with the insight of the one thing, then each person's face is from the beginning completely perfect. Why then make use of others to add cosmetics and put on powder? This is why their appearing in the world is raising enormous waves.

The *Akasagarbha Sutra* says, "The written word is the doing of mara; name and form are the doing of mara; even the phrases spoken by the Buddha are the doing of mara. This is what [the quotation above] means.
This directly shows us our original share; the Buddhas and patriarchs have no particular ability.

Summation: Heaven and earth lose their colors; sun and moon are without light.

3. But since in Dharma there are many aspects and people have many different capacities, it does no harm to set forth [expedient teachings].

Comment: "Dharma" means the one thing. "People" means sentient beings. In Dharma there are the two aspects of immutability and changing-with-conditions. Among people, there are two kinds of capacities, some for sudden enlightenment, others for gradual cultivation. Thus there is no harm in setting forth written and spoken words. This is like the saying, "In an official position, even a needle is not admitted; privately, a horse and cart are allowed in."

Although I have called all beings "completely perfect", they are born without the eye of wisdom, and they submit themselves to samsara. Therefore, if not for the golden blades of [the Buddhas and patriarchs] appearance in the world, who would cut away the thick blinding membrance of ignorance? As for crossing the ocean of suffering and ascending the shore of happiness, this is all due to the great compassion of the Buddhas and patriarchs. Therefore, even with lifetimes numberless as the Ganges' sands, it is difficult to repay them even one part in ten thousand.

This means that since beneficial new influences have been widely shown [by them], one feels gratitude to the Buddhas and patriarchs for their deep kindness.

Summation: The king ascends the treasure palace; the common people break into song.

4. By force, all kinds of names have been set up, for instance "mind," "Buddha", or "sentient beings". But one must not hold on to names and give rise to explanations. Right here, just this as it is! If thoughts are stirred up, that is a mistake.

Comment: Forcing these three names onto the one thing is an inevitable part of the Doctrine. That it is not permissible to hold on to names and think up explanations is also an inevitable part of Zen. With one hand holding up, with the other pressing down, now setting up and now destroying all of this is the free activity of the King-of-Dharma's Dharma commands.

This completes what is said above and introduces what is said below; it explains why the expedient teachings [lit. doings and appearances] of the Buddhas and patriarchs are each different.

Summation: After a long drought, a wonderful rain falls. In a distant land, one meets an old friend.

5. The World Honored One's transmission of mind in three places constitutes the purpose of Zen; that which he said during his entire life constitutes the path of Doctrine.

Therefore it is said that Zen is the Buddha's mind and Doctrine is his words.

Comment: The three places of transmission are: first, when the Buddha shared his seat in front of the Many Children Pagoda; second, when he held up a flower in front of the assembly at Vulture Peak; and third, when under two trees he showed his two feet through his coffin. This is what is called the special transmission to Mahakasyapa of the Zen lamp.

"One lifetime" refers to the five types of Doctrine that the Buddha taught during forty-nine years [after his enlightenment]. The first is the doctrine of Earthly and Heavenly Rebirth. The second is the Hinayana doctrine. The third is Mahayana doctrine. The fourth is the Sudden doctrine. The fifth is the Perfect doctrine. That is what is called Ananda's starting the flow of the sea of Doctrine.

Thus the source of Zen and Doctrine is the World Honored One. The branching of Zen and Doctrine occurs with Mahakasyapa and Ananda. Using no words to reach the wordless state is Zen; using words to reach the wordless state is Doctrine. But mind is the Dharma of Zen; words are the Dharma of Doctrine. Thus, although Dharma has only one taste, views and explanations of it differ as widely as heaven and earth.

This section has distinguished the two paths of Zen and Doctrine.

Summation: You must not let this pass by and lie around in the weeds.

6. Therefore if one has lost it in words [lit. in one's mouth], then picking up a flower or smiling becomes merely the traces of Doctrine, but if one has attained it in one's mind, then even the coarse words and petty talk of the world become the purpose of Zen which has been specially transmitted outside of Doctrine.

Comment: Since Dharma has no name, words cannot reach it. Since Dharma has no form, mind cannot reach it. One who would sum it up in words has lost original Mind [lit. king of original Mind]. If one has lost one's original Mind, then even though the World Honored One picks up a flower and Mahakasyapa smiles, it all falls to the level of worn out words, and in the end it is a dead thing. For one who has attained it in one's mind, not only common talk explains well the essentials of Dharma, but even the utterings of sparrows profoundly expresses the Truth.

Therefore when Zen Master Pao-chi heard the sound of wailing, he leapt with joy that filled body and mind. It was because of this also that when Zen Master Pao-shou saw a fist fight, [his mind] opened and he understood his [original] face.

This section has elucidated the depth of Zen and the shallowness of Doctrine.

Summation: A bright pearl is in the palm of the hand; roll it this way, roll it that way.

7. I have "one word". Cutting off thinking and forgetting karmic connections, sitting motionless with no occupations: when spring comes, the grass turns green by itself.

Comment: Cutting off thinking and forgetting karmic connections is attaining it in the mind. This is what is called "the person of the Way at ease." Ah! this is what kind of person he is: from the beginning without karmic connections or things to occupy him, when hunger comes he eats and when tiredness comes he sleeps. Among the blue streams and green-covered mountains he wanders as he pleases; in the fishing villages and wineshops he is at ease with no hindrances. Though he is completely unaware of the calendrical succession of years and months, when spring comes, the grass turns green by itself, as it always has.

This section sets apart those who wish to reflect inwards with concentrated thought [lit. one thought].

Summation: One was going to say there is no one; just then, there is someone.

8. The Doctrinal path only transmits the Dharma of One Mind, and the Zen path only transmits the Dharma of Seeing Nature.

Comment: Mind is like the substance of a mirror; nature is like the mirror's light. Nature is naturally pure and clear; in an instant of cutting through [and realizing it], one returns to and attains original mind.

This section shows the hidden importance of the one thought in which realization is attained.

Summation: Mountains and streams, layer upon layer; the pure and clean air surrounding the old home.

Comment: There are two kinds of mind. The first is original source mind; the second is the mind which ignorantly clings to forms. There are two kinds of nature. The first is original Dharma nature; the second is nature in which nature and form are in opposition. Therefore among Zen and Doctrine followers alike there are those who are deluded; they hold on to names and think up explanations. At times they take what is shallow to be deep; at other times, they what is deep to be shallow. They make insight and practice into a great illness. Therefore [Sosan] has here made clear the distinction.

9. But when the Buddhas expounded the sutras, they first distinguished the various principles of Dharma, and only later expounded Ultimate Emptiness. When the patriarchs make a statement, however, no traces remain in the intellectual realm and truth appears from the mind's source.

Comment: Since the Buddhas are the ones to be depended on throughout the ages, it is necessary for them to explain Truth in detail. Since the patriarchs save and liberate others in their own time, their objective is to cause profound realization.

"Traces" refers to the traces of the patriarch's words; "intellect" refers to the intellectual realm of the student.

Summation: Commenting at random; the arm does not bend outwards.

10. The way the Buddha expounded was like a bow; the way the patriarchs expound is like a bowstring. Even when the Buddha expounded unobstructed Dharma, it just barely returned to the one (essential) flavor. If one brushes away the traces of this one flavor, only then does the One Mind which the patriarchs show appear. Therefore it is said that the saying "The pine tree in front of the courtyard" does not exist in the Dragon Tripitaka.

Comment: "Expounded like a bow" refers to the fact that a bow is bent; "expounded like a bowstring" refers to the fact that a bowstring is straight. "Dragon Tripitaka" means the Tripitaka in the palace of the Dragon King.

A monk asked Chao-chou, "What is the meaning of the patriarch's coming to the West?" Chao-chou answered, "The pine tree in front of the courtyard." This is what is called the extra-ordinary purport of Zen.

Summation: Fish swim, the water is muddled; birds fly, feathers fall.

11. Therefore the student should first, in accordance with the true words of the Doctrine, clearly discern that the two principles of immutability and changing-with-conditions are (respectively) the (intrinsic) nature and (manifested) form of one's own mind, and that the two paths of sudden enlightenment and gradual cultivation are the beginning and the end of one's own practice. Only then should the student put aside (lit. put down) doctrinal principles, and only getting hold of the one thought that is appearing before one's own mind, carefully study the purport of Zen. Then surely one will have what is there is to be attained. This is called the way to get out, the road to life.

Comment: This restriction does not apply to those who have a superior capacity and great wisdom. But those of average or less than average capacities may not skip over any steps [of understanding Doctrine].

The Doctrinal principles of immutability and changing with conditions and sudden enlightenment and gradual cultivation contain [the distinction of] "before" and "after." But in Zen Dharma, in the midst of one moment of thought, immutability and changing-with-conditions nature and forms, and substance and function all fundamentally belong to one time. Abandoning identity, abandoning difference—this is the identity of difference and identity.

Therefore the great masters of the [Zen] sect, relying on Dharma and abandoning words, just directly point at one thought in order that one may see nature and become Buddha. It is in this way that Doctrinal principles are put aside [lit. put down].

Summation: In the bright clear daylight, clouds hide deep valleys; in a dense and deep secluded place, the sun shines in the clear sky.

12. In general, students [of Zen] should study live words and should not study dead words.

Comment: If one brings forth one's understanding from live words, then one is worthy of being a teacher of Buddhas and patriarchs. If one brings forth one's understanding from dead words, then no matter how one seeks to save oneself it cannot be done. Thus what follows specially holds up live words in order that one may become enlightened oneself and understand live words ([lit. enter into live words].

Summation: Anyone who wants to see Lin-chi surely must be made of iron.

Commentary: As for the "hua-t'ou," there are two paths to it: the path of words and the path of meaning. "Studying words" refers to the live words of the short-cut path which directly cuts through. Since no mental route or verbal route is laid out, there is no reason to grope or search. "Studying meaning" refers to the dead words of the path of Perfection and Suddenness. Since a logical route and a verbal route are laid out, one hears explanations and thinks about ideas.

13. Whenever one is studying a particular kung-an, then if one does one's work with sincerity of mind—like a hen brooding on her eggs, like a cat watching a mouse, like a hungry person thinking of food, like a thirsty person thinking of water, like a child longing for its mother—then surely there will be a time when one will penetrate and understand.

Comment: The "kung-an" of the patriarchs consist of 1,700 cases, such as "The dog has no Buddha nature," "The pine tree in front of the court-yard," "Three pounds of flax," and "A dry shit-stick."

When a hen broods on her eggs, the warmth continues without inter-ruption. When a cat watches a mouse, its mind and eyes are [one-pointedly] fixed [on their object]. As for a hungry person thinking of food, a thirsty person thinking of water, a child longing for its mother, all are done out of genuineness of mind. Since this is not an artificially constructed state of mind, it is called "sincere." In studying Zen, without this sincerity of mind there is no such thing as being able to break through and understand.

14. In studying Zen, one must have three things of essential importance. One is a foundation of great faith ([it. faculty of great faith]. The second is great zealous determination. The third is a great feeling of doubt. If even one of these is lacking, then it is like a tripod vessel with a broken foot; in the end it is useless.

Comment: The Buddha said, "In becoming Buddha, faith is the foundation." Yung-chia said, "In cultivating the Way, first of all one must have determination." Meng-shan said, "In studying Zen, if one does not have doubt about the meaning of what is said, then that is a great illness." He also said, "Out of great doubt is certain to come great enlightenment."

15. In one's everyday activities [lit. daily, as one responds to conditions], if one only raises the topic [hua-t'ou], "The dog has no Buddha nature," and raises it again and again, having doubt and doubting again, until one feels that there is no logical route, no theoretical route, and no flavor [of any kind], and one's mind has become hot and uncomfortable—just then, that is the point at which a person abandons body and life. This is also the original foundation of becoming a Buddha or being a patriarch.

Comment: A monk asked Chao-chou, "Does a dog have Buddha nature, or not?" Chao-chou said, "No." This one word is the gateway to our sect. It is also a weapon with which to crush the many kinds of bad knowledge and wrong understanding. It is also the [true] features of the Buddhas, and essential substance (lit. marrow] of the patriarchs. One must penetrate this gateway. Only then can one hope to become a Buddha or a patriarch.

> A man of old composed an ode:
> When Chao-chou shows his sword
> Its cold frosty light flashes.
> If you would question or discuss
> It will slice your body in two.

16. In raising the "hua-t'ou" one should not accept the first answer that comes to mind; one should not think and deliberate about it; also, one should not wait for enlightenment even as one holds to delusion. As one approaches the point where it is no longer possible to think and the thinking mind has no place to go, it is like a mouse who, having crawled into an ox's horn, cannot get out. Furthermore, ordinarily that which calaculates and arranges is consciousness-feeling; that which wanders following birth and death is consciousness feeling; that which gets scared by things and trembles with fright is [just] consciousness feeling. Nowadays people do not know that these are errors; they merely stay inside [the horn] and poke around [looking for a way out].

Comment: In practicing "hua-t'ou" there are ten kinds of errors. The first is deliberating of it with one's intellect; the second is getting stuck on (the Zen master's) raising of the eyebrows and blinking of the eyes; the third is finding the meaning of life in busying oneself in the verbal route; the fourth is citing evidence from what has been written; the fifth is, when giving rise to the "hua-t'ou" accepting the first thing that comes to mind; the sixth is busying oneself staying in a state where nothing happens; the seventh is understanding in terms of "existence" and "emptiness," the ninth is understanding in terms of "principles of the Way," the tenth is holding to delusion and awaiting enlightenment.

Abandoning these ten kinds of error means that when one only raises the "hua-t'ou," one really concentrates with all one's energies and only questions, "What is this?"

17. This matter is like a mosquito which lands on an iron ox without so much as asking how and in what manner [it is going to bite it]. When it cannot get is mouthpiece in, it forgets everything and, putting all its life into one effort, with its whole body it pierces in.

Comment: This again completes the meaning of what is said above so that those who are studying live words will not get discouraged and give up. An ancient said, "In studying Zen, one must penetrate the barrier [gateway] of the patriarchs; for profound enlightenment, one must cut off the mind route to the end."

18. The study [of Zen] is like the method for tuning a stringed instrument; one must find the median between taut and slack. If one makes too much of an effort at it, then one comes near to clinging [to things as real]; if one forgets about it, then one falls into ignorance. [Sometimes the notes come] slowly and distinctly; [sometimes they come] thick and fast.

Comment: Those who play stringed instruments say that only if the strings are neither too loose nor too taut is there is a clear sound throughout. The same thing is true of studying [Zen]. If one is too diligent, then one stirs up one's energies [lit. blood] so that they become disturbed; if one forgets about it, then one enters into a cave of ghosts. Neither slowly nor hastily—the key to it is between these two.

19. In one's study [of Zen], when one reaches the point where one walks without knowing that one is walking and sits without knowng that one is sitting, just at this time the 84,000-strong army of "mara" will be keeping watch at the gate of the six senses ([lit. six faculties] adapting themselves to whatever one's mind gives rise to. If one's mind does not give rise [to anything], then what can they do?

Comment: "Mara" is the name of demons who take delight in [the cycle of] birth and death. The "84,000-strong army of mara" is none other than the 84,000 mental afflictions of the multitude of beings. Demons originally have no existence of their own. When those who are cultivating [Buddhist] practice lose their concentration, it is due to this deviation [lit. branching off] that demons originate.

The multitude of beings comply with their circumstances, thus demons comply with them. A person of the Way resists his circumstances, thus demons resist him. Therefore it is said, "The higher the Way, the more demons flourish."

If in the midst of Zen meditation one sees a filial son and stabs one's [own] thigh or sees a pig and grabs one's ([own] nose, both are visions arising from one's own mind, [but] one projects them as demons outside [oneself]. If one's mind does not give rise [to anything] then all the skillful devices [of the demons] amount to no more than cutting water or blowing on a beam of light. An ancient said, "If a wall has a crack in it, the draft comes in. If one's mind has a slight opening, demons slip in."

20. Giving rise to mind is the "deva mara;" not giving rise to mind is the "mara of the five skandhas;" sometimes giving rise to mind and sometimes not giving rise to mind is the "mara of the passions." But in our correct Dharma there is no such thing.

Comment: In general, being at peace with the world [lit. forgetting schemes] is the Buddhist Way; discriminating is the "mara realm." But the "mara realm" is a thing in a dream. Why bother to discuss it?

21. In studying [Zen)] if one is "fused into one whole" then, even though in this lifetime one is unable to penetrate, when one is on the point of death one will not be pulled [into a bad rebirth] by one's evil karma.

Comment: Karma is ignorance. Zen is prajña [wisdom]. It is a natural principle that light and darkness are not an equal match.

SOSAN'S SUCCESSORS

Sosan left behind some outstanding successor-monks. The most notable among them was Samyong Yujong (1543-1610) whose reputation we have already noted. Like Sosan, Samyong lost his parents at an early age and in 1556, at the age of 13, became a monk. In 1561, he passed the monk examination, presumably the preliminary examination. Little is known about his activities after this period, but it is recorded that in 1575 he was offered the position of Abbot of Pongun-sa, the head temple of the Zen sect. This was the same position that Sosan had held earlier. But Samyong refused the offer and, in the same year, started his Zen studies with Sosan. It will be remembered that Sosan had moved to Myohyang Mountain in 1568 and had started to attract large numbers of students. Samyong soon became one of his outstanding disciples.

When the Japanese invaded Korea in 1592, Sosan and his senior disciples gathered a 5,000-strong monks' militia. Sosan was the rallying point, the moral inspiration for the monks' army, while Samyong was its field commander. He was given the title "General of Monk Forces." Samyong's forces joined with the Chinese Ming army and recaptured Pyongyang. It is said that in 1594, he visited the camp of a Japanese general as a negotiator and took stock of enemy strength. Acts like these and his continued association with the monks' militia enabled him to take an active part in the fighting against the Japanese when they invaded a second time in 1598. In 1604, he was part of a "Peace Embassy" to Japan and carried a letter from the Korean king. He successfully concluded a peace settlement and brought home 3,500 Korean prisoners-of-war.

A kind of personality cult has grown in Korean folk tradition around Sosan and Samyong. Both are represented as master-practitioners of magic. Stories claim that they created snakes and tigers in the path of enemy forces to confuse and frighten them. In Korean folk tradition, all Zen masters are assumed to have magical powers. The origins of these beliefs are hard to pinpoint but it is likely that it is a holdover from the strong shamanistic element in popular Korean imagination.

In one story, Sosan and Samyong were taking a walk through the mountains, and Sosan was slightly ahead. Samyong took an appraising look at his teacher, a short, frail man of ungainly appearance. Samyong, by contrast, was a giant of a man—handsome, with a powerful presence. Struck by the contrast, Samyong could not help speculating why this physically unimpressive man should be his teacher. Soon they came to a waterfall. To his utter amazement, Samyong saw that the water of the fall was flowing upwards rather than coming down. He cried out to Sosan, "Look, this waterfall is upside down. So unnatural!". Sosan mildly replied, "Yes, just like your mind." Samyong instantly understood that Sosan had been cognizant all along of what was going through his mind and had used his magical powers to teach him. He bowed to Sosan and apologized profusely to his teacher. Sosan "released" the waterfall and the water began to come down naturally!

Still another story says that when Samyong was in Japan during the peace mission of 1604, the Japanese, who had no doubt learned of his and Sosan's nefarious activities against them, locked him up in a room at night. They then heated the room from underneath to a temperature high enough to roast him alive. The Japanese opened the door in the morning, expecting to see Samyong dead and roasted. To their amazement, they saw Samyong seated calmly in a meditation posture with icicles hanging from his beard.

Samyong did not leave behind many written texts since "his life was spent amid the wind and dust of troops and horses."[62] But he is known to have been a gifted poet and calligrapher. Samyong is one of the four great disciples of Sosan to have left strong lineages behind him. Samyong spent his last years at Hae-in sa temple and died in 1610. The sub-temple where he stayed in his last days is today a beautifully restored temple for Zen meditation.

Another of Sosan's students to initiate a strong lineage is Zen Master Pyonyang Ongi (1581-1644). Like most Korean monks, he became an orphan at an early age. This happened to Pyonyang in the midst of Japanese invasion, when he was 11 years old. At that tender age, he left for the Diamond Mountains and went around as a beggar to different Zen temples. He was initiated as a monk at Pyohun temple and there he studied the sutras until he was 18. The following year he started his Zen studies with Sosan at the Mahayon temple. He soon attained enlightenment and received

Inka from Sosan. No dates are available for this event but it must have been during the last one or two years of Sosan's life.

After Sosan's death, Pyonyang left the monastery and wandered around the countryside. He lived a life of complete freedom, even to the extent of discarding his monk's robes. By turns he was a beggar, a shepherd, a water-seller, a charcoal-seller and engaged in other unusual (for a monk) occupations. It would appear that he spent his whole life as a wandering ascetic. But every place he went he taught Zen through his words and actions. There are several stories concerning him in the Korean oral tradition:

> One day when Pyonyang was still a student at Sosan's temple, he was late in returning to the temple. Sosan asked him where he had been. Pyonyang said he had climbed the Piro-bong peak to pick up wild mushrooms, so he was late. Sosan asked him if he had seen any mountain lions up on the peak. Pyonyang didn't say anything but suddenly he roared loudly and leaped at Sosan and bit him. Sosan instantly grabbed his Zen stick with his free hand and struck out at him. But Pyonyang jumped away clear and stood aside. Sosan laughed loudly and said, "Wonderful, wonderful! Today I have been beaten."
>
> Next day, Sosan gathered all his students in the lecture hall and said, "On Diamond Mountain there is a ferocious mountain lion. All of you be careful, or you will be attacked by him. Already yesterday, I myself was bitten." Then he pounded his Zen stick on the podium once and left the lecture hall.

Later he called Pyonyang to his room and gave him Inka. Another story is of the time when Pyonyang worked as a shepherd:

> [During his wanderings] one day he saw several hundred sheep coming down from a mountain posture, and suddenly he thought, "My name "Pyonyang" means "Sheep Whip". Why did Master Sosan give me this name? Was he foretelling me that I would be a shepherd?" Thinking of this conjecture and also contemplating a quiet life in the mountains with only the sheep around him, he decided to become a shepherd. He took off his robes and found some rags to dress himself. He then went to the shepherd's house

and introduced himself as a Mr. Chang and asked for a job without salary, just enough food to live on. The shepherd was very happy to get his deal and put him to work.

Pyonyang took the several hundred sheep to their pasture every day and took good care of them. He felt the pasture was the best place to practice Zen meditation because there was no one to talk to him and he could remain silent. Even when he returned to the shepherd's home in the evening, he lived in a separate hut so that it was possible for him to meditate all night. He felt very peaceful. Nobody knew him, nobody visited him and he could continue his Zen practice day and night without disturbance. For two years, he drove the sheep to the mountain pasture with the cry, "*Moo-ut-ko, moo-ut-ko,*" which means "Who am I? Who am I? Except for this cry, he didn't speak any other words for two years. All the people in the village came to call him Mr. Moo-ut-ko

One day, he suddenly felt the urge to leave. He left a short note for the shepherd which said, "I left your home this morning because my karmic relationship with your sheep is finished today."[63]

After leaving the shepherd's home, Pyonyang made his way to Pyongyang, then the largest city in northern part of Korea (today the capital of North Korea). He did not have any money, so feeding himself was a problem. He saw a number of a number of water-vendors selling water to households and thought it was an excellent way of make a living. Also, he wanted to test his Zen practice away from the quiet of a monastery or a mountain pasture. He acquired some bamboos and two buckets and made himself a water-carrying frame. He went to the Vendors' Union and got his license to sell water. Then he began to supply water to the households free of charge. The only thing he asked for was some food at mealtimes. All the housewives naturally liked him and asked for his name. "My name is 'Moo-ut-ko.'" Through a pronunciation misunderstanding, the housewives thought his name was "Mok-ko" which means "Mr. Eating!" The confusion came about partly because of the pronunciation of *moo-ut-ko* and partly because Pyonyang always refused money and only asked for something to eat. So he came to be known as Mok-ko Hara-boji which means "the eating grandfather."

Among the water-vendors, on the other hand, Pyonyang came to be known as a wise man; for he would talk to them about Zen practice without the jargon and usually crowds would gather around to listen to his words. Among the water-vendors, therefore, he came to be known as "The Runaway Monk."

After working as a water-vendor for some time, Pyonyang decided he would no longer walk around the city but would try sitting in one place and test his practice in still another way. He decided to become a charcoal-seller. He bought a piece of straw mat, spread out several buckets of charcoal on it and sat down with his legs crossed. This was in the busiest and noisiest part of the town. All day long he would sit there and, despite all the noise and commotion around him, would enter into deep samadhi. The marketplace became a Zen monastery for him! When the housewives who had known him recently as a water-seller, saw him, they said, "Look, there is the Eating Grandfather. He is just sitting there like a piece of stone. He must be mad!" And the water-vendors who had known him recently as a wise man came by, they too shouted, "Hey, there is the Runaway Monk. He is just sitting there. He must have gone crazy!" Finally one day a woman came to the marketplace who had visited him at his temple in the past. She recognized him and told everbody who he was—a famous Zen master and a successor to Sosan's Dharma. Everyone was very surprised.

Because his identity was now known and also because he had been able to test his Zen practice in a busy market-place to his own satisfaction, Pyonyang left the city and returned to his monastery on the Diamond Mountain.

CHAPTER ELEVEN

Kyong Ho and the Revival of Korean Zen

An eleventh-generation Dharma successor of Pyonyang Ongi was Zen Master Kyong Ho (1849-1912). As the monk most responsible for reviving Korean Zen from its doldrums and lethargy of 300 years, Kyong Ho is as significant a personality in Korean Zen history as Chinul and Sosan.

After the Japanese invasions of 1592 and 1598, and the role played by the Buddhist monks in the nation's defense, Buddhism revived for a brief period of time. But then the kingdom settled into lethargy, cut off from all international contacts or trade for the next three centuries or so. It was during this period of time that Korea earned its nickname of "The Hermit Kingdom." Sealed unto itself, Korea became a backwater country. The policy of repression and neglect of Buddhism was resumed by Yi dynasty, Confucian bureaucrats soon after peace treaties were signed with Japan. Only a handful of Doctrinal monks and temples remained in the cities. Almost without exception, Zen monks retreated into their mountain caves and somehow kept the tradition alive. The "Mind-Seal" of transmission continued to be handed down from successor to successor.

Buddhist temples seem to have been offered some mild form of protection during the reign of King Chongjo (r.1777-1800). After that, it was a time once again of benign neglect, if not of actual persecution. In the later years of 19th century, King Kojong (r.1864-1906) issued some significant government decrees which not only protected Buddhism but enabled it to regain some of its old profile. In 1865, for example, he decreed that henceforth monks would be exempt from forced corvee labor on public construction projects. In 1889, he made the temples tax-exempt as they had been during the Silla and Koryo dynasties.

Of far greater significance to Korean Zen was the emergence of a dynamic personality, the monk Kyong Ho. Like so many other monks, Kyong Ho had lost his father at an early age, when he was nine years old. His mother, unable to support herself and a son, went to live at Chongye temple in Kyongju, probably as a temple-attendant, and her son went with her. There he was initiated as a monk by one Master Kyeho.

At age fourteen, Kyong Ho started studying Confucianism under a Confucian scholar who was visiting the temple. He proved to be a brilliant student and had soon mastered all the basic Confucian texts. At this point, his teacher, Kyeho, gave up his robe and moved to Seoul to return to secular life. Left without a teacher, Kyong Ho made his way to Tonghak-sa temple on Kyeryong Mountain to study Buddhism under the well-known Zen Master, Manhwa. At Tonghak-sa, he also studied Taoism in addition to Buddhism. Soon he became well-versed in the three streams of East Asia's spirituality and humanism—Confucianism, Taoism and Buddhism.

At the age of 23, he was appointed a lecturer in Buddhist sutras at Tonghak-sa. It was a singular honor for someone so young to be appointed to such a prestigious position. (Today, Tonghak-sa is the largest Buddhist college for nuns in the country and has about 200 nun-students in residence.) Kyong Ho was a gifted and charismatic lecturer and large crowds came to hear him speak.

In 1879, when he was 30 years old, Kyong Ho decided to visit his old teacher, Kyeho, whom he had not seen in a long time and for whom he retained a great deal of affection. So he started walking on his journey to Seoul. On his way, he passed a small village. There were no people in the streets. Immediately he knew something was wrong and he began to feel an overwhelm- ing sense of disaster. He knocked on the door of a house and, finding no answer, opened the door. There were five corpses on the floor, in various stages of decomposition. He opened the door of the next house, and there were more corpses rotting on the floor. As he walked through the main street, dazed and terrified, he noticed a sign. "Danger: Cholera. If you value your life, go away."

The sign struck Kyong Ho like a hammer. He recognized his own fear and thought, "I am supposed to be a great sutra master; I already understand all of the Buddha's teachings. Why am I so afraid? Even though I understand that all things are transient, that life and death are aspects of the one reality, I am very attached to my body. So life is a hindrance, and death is a hindrance. What can I do?"

Rather than continue on his way to Seoul, he turned back and returned to his temple. He summoned all his students and said, "You have all come here to study the sutras, and I have been teaching you. But I know now that the sutras are only Buddha's words. They are not Buddha's mind. As many sutras as I have mastered, I still haven't attained true understanding. I can't teach you any more. If you wish to continue your studies, there are many qualified sutra masters who will be glad to teach you. But I have decided to understand my true self, and I will not teach again un- til I attain enlightenment."

Kyong Ho locked himself into his room. Once a day, a student brought him food, leaving the platter outside the closed door. All day long, Kyong Ho sat or did lying-down Zen. He meditated on a kong-an which he had seen in a Zen book: "Zen Master Yong Un said, 'Before the donkey leaves, the horse has already arrived.' What does this mean?" "I am already as good as dead," he thought; "if I can't get beyond life and death, I vow never to leave this room." Every time he began to feel sleepy, he would take an awl and plunge it into his thigh.

Three months passed. During this time, Kyong Ho didn't sleep even for a moment. When his mind grew dim, he would place his jaw on a sharp-edged sword to jolt himself back into the kong-an. He struggled day and night to break through.

One day the student who was attending him went to the nearby town. There he happened to meet a certain Mr. Lee, who was a close friend of Kyong Ho's. Mr. Lee asked, "How's your master doing nowadays?"

The student narrated Kyong Ho's great vow. "He is doing hard training. He only eats, sits, and lies down."

"If he just eats, sits, and lies down, he will be reborn as a cow."

The student got very angry. "How can you say that? My teacher is the greatest scholar in Korea! I'am postive that he will go to heaven after he dies!"

Mr. Lee said, "That's no way to answer me."

"Why not? How should I have answered?"

"I would have said, 'If my teacher is reborn as a cow, he will be a cow with no nostrils.'"

"A cow with no nostrils? What does that mean?"

"Go ask your teacher."

When he returned to the temple, the student knocked on Kyong Ho's door and told him of his conversation with Mr. Lee. As soon as he had finished, to his amazement, Kyong Ho kicked open the door and came running out. "That's it! The cow with no nostrils!" Kyong Ho shouted and started dancing cheerfully. The student was amazed and thought his teacher had gone crazy. But this was the moment when Kyong Ho had broken through his kong-an. The day was October 15, 1879. Kyong Ho had attained the great enlightenment. He wrote this poem to mark the occasion:

> I heard about the cow with no nostrils,
> And suddenly the whole universe is my home.
> Yon am mountain lies flat under the road,
> A farmer, at the end of his work, is singing.[64]

Soon afterward, he went to Zen Master Manhwa for an interview. Manhwa recognized his awakening and gave him Transmission. He also received from Manhwa the dharma name Kyong Ho which means "Empty Mirror." He thus became the 75th patriarch in his line of succession.

In the spring of 1880, he frequently visited his mother who was living at Ch'ongjang monastery on Yon am Mountain, near the town of Sosan. Around this time, he composed a long poem, "Song of Enlightenment:"

> I look around in all directions,
> but cannot find anyone to whom I may transmit my kasa and
>   bowl.
> O, I can find no one!
> In spring, flowers are in full bloom in the mountain.
> In autumn the moon is bright and the wind is cool.
> I sing a song of no birth,
> But who will ever listen to my song?
> My life and fate, what shall I do?
> The color of the mountain is the eye of
> Avalokitesvara Bodhisattva
> The sound of the river is the ear of
> Manjusri Bodhisattva
> Mr. Chang and Mrs. Lee are Vairochana Buddha.
> Sentient beings call on Buddha or Patriarch, Zen or Kyo,
> But in origin all of them are one.
> The stone man blows the flute and the wooden man sleeps,
> But the common man does not realize his own mind,
> And they like to call it a holy land!
> What nonsense!
> What a pity!
> They are nothing but the trash of hell.
> Looking back on my former life,
> I find numerous births and deaths and transmigrations,
> In long, long, countless kalpas.
> Now I see it vividly before my eyes, Oh, what a sight it is!

I was fortunate enough to be born a man and attain the realization.

Hearing someone say "A cow without nostrils,"
I realized the true mind,
Where there is no name nor form.
I radiate great light in all directions.
The single bright light on the forehead is the Pure Land.
The divine form around the head is God's world.
Four skandhas are pure body;
Paradise is the hell of boiling cauldron and the hell of cold water;
Heavenly world is the hell of sword-trees and sword-mountains;
Buddha Land is a heap of dried dung;
Triple World is an ant hill;
Trikaya is emptiness.
Wherever you touch, there is the heavenly truth.
Oh, how wonderful! How miraculous!
The wind is cool through the pine trees, everywhere is blue mountain.
The moon is bright in autumn, the sky is like water.
Yellow flower and green bamboos, canary-song and swallow-sound,
In all these, there is Great Function.
The golden crown of a worldly king is but the thorny crown of a prisoner;
The Diamond Seal of a heavenly king is but an eyeball of a skull.
Countless Buddhas are always manifest in grass, trees, stones;
The *Avatamsaka* and *Lotus Sutras* are but my walking, staying, sitting, and lying.
To say there is no Buddha and no Bodhisattva is no nonsense;,
To change hell into heaven,
That is in my power.
Thousands of sermons and thousands of secret meanings
Are realized on waking up from sleep and they are in full bloom before my eyes.
Where can I find time and space?
The great light is full in all directions.
In a word, I am the very great Dharma king.

There is nothing right, wrong, good or bad;
The ignorant, hearing this, call me a liar and do not believe me;
But the enlightened believe me and do not doubt,
And they will attain Nirvana.
I warn men in the dust of this world,
That if once they lose the human body,
They will hardly get again in thousands of kalpas.
The blind donkey relies only on his own legs,
Not knowing of safety and danger;
Everybody is like this.
But why doesn't he try to learn from me, I wonder?
If he learns from me, he will be a great man,
In the heavenly or in the human form.
Therefore, I tell you in earnest,
That I pity those wanderers because I was once one of them.
To whom shall I transmit my Kasa and bowl?
I can't find anyone in any direction.[65]

Kyong Ho also received Inka from Yongam who was the resident Zen Master at Ch'ongjang monastery (where his mother was staying). In 1881, the age of 32, he succeeded Yongam as the Head priest at that temple. (Yongam was an 11th-generation successor of Zen Master Sosan.)

Sometime in his 40's, Kyong Ho set out on a missionary journey around Korea. We have no record of the circumstances or motivations which prompted him to undertake this journey, but it was a turning point in Korean Buddhism for these missionary activities led to the revival of Korean Zen and Buddhism after three centuries of dormancy. Kyong Ho taught at some of the famous temples as Pomo-sa, in Pusan; Sangwon-sa on Odae Mountain, Sokwang-sa on Unbong Mountain, and many others. At the age of 52, he settled in residence at Haein-sa and supervised the publication of *Tripitaka Koreana* (the Buddhist Canon) from woodblocks which had been carved in the Koryo dynasty. Such was the state of affairs that no printed copy was in existence at that time. He also initiated the construction of a Zen-training monastery at Haein-sa temple. He was now the premier monk in Korea and aspirants gathered around him in large numbers. He encouraged them to go out and establish temples in cities and towns. All these activities made him stand out as the most influential and renowned Zen monk of his time. In addition to his priestly contributions, Kyong Ho was also a gifted poet and calligrapher. His talent as a calligrapher is said to have been unmatched by any Korean monk in modern times. Also, under the pen-name Nanju, he composed popular songs and poems.

In 1903, Kyong Ho disappeared from public view and from the official Buddhist world. He settled in a remote fishing village in the rugged region of Hamyong province (now in North Korea).where he wore secular clothes and let his hair grow. He taught letters to illiterate village children and even worked as a hired hand on small village farms. He would join villagers in their groups and talk about the state of affairs in the outside world. Before his death, on April 25, 1912, he summoned two of his disciples, Zen Masters Mang Gong and Su Wol to his bedside to hear his will and last testament. He wrote the following poem:

> Light from the moon of clear mind
> drinks up everything in the world.
> When mind and light both disappear,
> What.....is.......this?[66]

Moments after finishing the poem, he was dead.

Kyong Ho left behind some illustrious disciples—Zen Masters Mang Gong (1872-1946), Han Am (1876-1951), Hye Wol (1861-1937), Su Wol (1855-1928) and Yong Song (1864-1940). It would not be an exaggeration to say that whatever strength Korean Zen has today, is solely due to Kyong Ho and his dharma heirs. Together they provided the inspiration and energy for a revitalization of Korean Zen tradition in the 20th century.

After Kyong Ho's death, his disciple, Zen Master Mang Gong, collected his teacher's works scattered in various temples around the country. These *Collected Works of Kyong Ho* were published in 1942 and include his sermons, correspondence, biographies of ancient Korean monks, poems and assorted writings. One essay, "How to practice (monastic) austerity," has exerted tremendous influence on Zen monks in Korea since Kyong Ho's time. Part of this essay reads:

> To practice [austerity] is no easy task. It [priestly vocation] is not designed to allow the eating of good food or wearing good clothes, but to the becoming of a Buddha; thus to transcend life and death. To become a Buddha one should search one's own mind. To search one's own mind one should consider that one's flesh is but a corpse and consider that all earthly affairs are but a dream regardless of whether they are right or wrong, that life is short and transitory, and that upon death man suffers the eternal pains of hell or is reincarnated a beast or a ghost. Therefore one should constantly search one's own mind, forgetting all worldly affairs.[67]

From the oral tradition of Korean Zen, some exchanges between Kyong Ho and his students.have been passed down. In their spontaneity, some of them are reminiscent of Ch'an repartees during the golden age in T'ang China:

One evening, Kyong Ho and his student Mang Gong were returning to their temple after their begging trip. It had been a good day for them; the bag was full of rice. But now it was late in the afternoon and the bag was getting heavier and heavier to carry. They took turns carrying it but still the monastery.was far away Since Mang Gong was the student, it was only proper that he carry the bag most of the time. Kyong Ho, however, kept walking fast and Mang Gong could barely keep up with him. This brought a number of protests from Mang Gong about the heaviness of the bag.

Soon they passed through a village. As they turned a corner, they saw a lovely, young woman come out of a doorway, carrying a full jar of water on her head As Kyong Ho was a few steps ahead, he saw the girl first. All of a sudden, just as their paths were about to cross, he reached out, grabbed the girl and kissed her full on the mouth. She cried out in alarm and fright, and her jar fell down to the ground and broke. Bewildered and afraid, she ran back into her house and soon there were loud voices inside the house. Out of the house they came, brothers and aunts, armed with sticks and clubs, screaming bloody murder. Soon the whole village was in an uproar.

Kyong Ho and Mang Gong ran for their lives, Mang Gong with the heavy rice bag on his back. It was every man for himself. Never had the villagers seen two men run so fast. After a short while, they gave up the chase as the monks were now outside their village. Kyong Ho and Mang Gong stood bent over, huffing and wheezing. Mang Gong's indignation was still to overcome his terror and relief at having escaped from this bizarre situation. Just then Kyong Ho asked, with a faint smile on his lips, "Was that rice bag heavy, sunim?"

"What heavy? I didn't even realize it was on my back, and we ran so far!"

"Well," Kyong Ho said, "Aren't you lucky to be my student! During that little episode back there, you no longer had 'heavy' in your mind and you managed to travel miles, almost all the way home, in a single breath!" And looking back at the village in the distance Kyong Ho burst out laughing.

Another story tells of the occasion when Kyong Ho was staying for a short time at Pusok-sa temple. There a layman came to see him.

The layman asked Kyong Ho, "Why did Bodhidharma come to China from India?"

Kyong Ho hit him with his stick.

The layman said, "You may hit me as much as you please, but you have missed giving me the answer by 180,000 miles."

Kyong Ho said, "I ask you in turn, 'What is the reason of Bodhidharma's coming to China from India?'"

Now the layman hit Kyong Ho with the staff.

Kyong Ho said, "A stupid dog runs after the stone, but a fierce lion bites the man."

The layman understood and bowed in gratitude. Kyong Ho smiled and went into his room.

Once when Mang Gong was a young student, he was sitting with Kyong Ho outside. Out of the need to say something, he said, "My nostrils are itching."

Kyong Ho asked, "Why is that?"

"There are bees, bees flying in and out of my nose!" Mang Gong answered.

"If there were really bees going in and out of your nose, your nostrils wouldn't itch!" retorted Kyong Ho.

Caught between his own remorse at having spoken to his teacher idly, and Kyong Ho's straightforward comment, Mang Gong's mind opened.

On another occasion, Mang Gong and Kyong Ho were walking through a forest and got caught in a sudden downpour. They took shelter in a kind of cave built with large rocks. No sooner were they out of rain when Kyong Ho started glancing upward at the large rock over their head again and again. This made Mang Gong little uneasy. He asked "Sunim, why do you keep looking up at that rock?"

"I'm afraid the rock might fall down on us."

How is that big rock going to fall? asked Mang Gong with surprise. Kyong Ho said, "The safest place is the most dangerous."

Some of Kyong Ho's sayings have found a prominent place in the Korean Zen lore. Zen teachers since his time have used these sayings to point the way to their own students and help them deepen their awareness:

> 1. Don't wish for perfect health. In perfect health there is greed and wanting. So an ancient said, "Make good medicine from the suffering of sickness."
>
> 2. Don't hope for a life without problems. An easy life results in a judgmental and lazy mind. So an ancient once said, "Accept the anxieties and difficulties of this life."
>
> 3. Don't expect your practice to be always clear of obstacles. Without hindrances the mind that seeks enlightenment may be

burnt out. So an ancient once said, "Attain deliverance in distur-
bances."

4. Don't expect to practice hard and not experience the weird.
Hard practice that evades the unknown makes for a weak commitment. So an ancient once said, "Help hard practice by befriend-
ing every demon."

5. Don't expect to finish doing something easily. If you happen
to acquire something easily the will is made weaker. So an ancient
once said, "Try again and again to complete what you're doing."

6. Make friends, but don't expect any benefit for yourself.
Friendship only for oneself harms trust. So an ancient once said,
"Have an enduring friendship with purity in heart."

7. Don't expect others to follow your direction. When it happens that others go along with you, it results in pride. So an ancient once said, "Use your will to bring peace between people."

8. Expect no reward for an act of charity. Expecting something
in return leads to a scheming mind. So an ancient once said,
"Throw false spirituality away like a pair of old shoes."

9. Don't seek profit over and above what your work is worth.
Acquiring false profit makes a fool [of oneself]. So an ancient once
said, "Be rich in honesty."

10. Don't try to make clarity of mind with severe practice. Every
mind comes to hate severity, and where is clarity in mortification?
So an ancient once said, "Clear a passageway through severe practice."

11. Be equal to every hindrance. Buddha attained Supreme Enlightenment without hindrance. Seekers after truth are schooled in
adversity. When they are confronted by a hindrance, they can't be
overcome. Then, cutting free, their treasure is great.

Along with Chinul and Sosan, Kyong Ho stands out as one of
the towering figures in Korean Zen history. Some modern scholars have gone so far as to assert that whatever understanding
monks and laymen have today of Buddhism in Korea, it is due
solely to Kyong Ho's efforts. Certainly his role in the revival of
Zen and giving it the kind of prestige he did cannot be over-
stated. In Kyong Ho, we find the same combination of scholarly

brilliance and dedication to Zen practice as we do in Chinul and Sosan.

He also shares with Sosan the distinction of being a gifted artist and thus coming across as a multi-dimensional personality. Again he is closer to Sosan than to Chinul in that he was oriented more towards the kong-an method of Zen practice and placed less emphasis of cultivation of learning, i.e. sutra studies. His poetry, calligraphy and scholarship establish him as one of the most learned and artistically-gifted monks in Korean Buddhist history. In choosing to live the last years of his life in anonymous, secular surroundings, he displayed an originality which is so very rare in the Korean monastic sangha. On the one hand, he did not wish to be a prisoner of his fame and, on the other, he seemed to be making a statement that an enlightened person ought to function equally well under any circumstances without depending on a monastic support-system.

KOREAN BUDDHISM
AT THE BEGINNING OF THE 20TH CENTURY

Before we look at the lives of Kyong Ho's dharma heirs, it would be instructive to examine the conditions under which Korean Buddhism labored during the last years of the 19th century and the early years of the 20th century.

After the Sino-Japanese war of 1894-95 in which the Japanese handily defeated the Chinese, the Japanese began to add a military presence in Korea and include it in their "sphere of influence" just as the Chinese had for centuries. In the wake of efforts for political control came efforts by the Japanese Buddhists to bring Korean Buddhism under their own sphere of influence. In 1895, a Japanese priest, Zenrei Sano of the Nichiren sect, came to Seoul and requested the Korean government to repeal the ban on monk's entry into the capital city. The ban was duly lifted in April 1895 after having been in force for 272 years, since 1623. King Kojong further allowed, whether on his own or under Japanese pressure, the monks to live and build their temples in the capital. It is ironic that these measures of "liberation" should have come about through the effort of those who themselves intended to subjugate Korean Buddhism.

Japanese Buddhists started arriving in Korea in greater numbers. In 1896, there was a conference in Seoul of all Japanese and Korean Buddhists, in which it was formally agreed that Japanese Buddhism had a right to propagate its brand of Buddhism in Korea. In 1899, a new temple, Wonhung-sa, was built in Seoul to serve as the general headquarters of all Buddhist temples. As a corollary to this construction, a governmental department was created in 1902 to set policies for Korean Buddhism. Sixteen regional temples were selected as "Head Temples" and were charged with the responsibility of supervising all the sub-temples within their region. All regional and head temples were eventually under the control of general headquarters at Wonhung-sa, which in turn had its policies decided by the government's Department of Buddhist Affairs.

In 1904, the government took a monumental step. It turned over the control of Buddhist affairs to Buddhists themselves. So, belatedly, for the first time in their history, the Korean Buddhists were, in theory, masters of their own destiny. But, more important, it meant revocation of all persecutory policies that may still have existed on paper. The shadow of Japanese Buddhist presence in Korea, however, loomed large. Two conferences were held in 1908 and 1910 to effect the transition from government control to self-control. At the latter conference, a new temple, Kakwang-sa, was authorized to be built in Seoul to serve as the new headquarters of Korean Buddhism. Also, an Archbishop in the person of Yi Hae-kwang, was elected to serve as the head of Korean Buddhism. We must keep in mind that during all this time, the Zen and Sutra schools were still separate sects, having been "created" in 1424 with different identities, but both had agreed to work together for the sake of greater unity.

Things moved quickly at this point. Towards the end of 1910, the Japanese military was beginning to occupy Korea. At the same time, the Archbishop of Korean Buddhism, Yi Hae-kwang, secretly visited Japan to meet with the officials of the Soto sect. Out of this secret meeting came a document listing seven points of cooperation between the Soto sect and Korean Buddhism. This secret agreement brought about a storm of protest in Korea. Under the leadership of Man Hae, one of the greatest monk-poets of modern Korea and a prominent participant in Korea's independence movement, a meeting was called to discuss this document. Most of the monks present felt that the agreement would undermine the traditional features of Korean Buddhism and just at a time when Korean Buddhism was beginning to come into its own after suffering 500 years of persecution under the Yi dynasty. Those who opposed the policies of Yi Hae-kwang broke away from the headquarters and established their own alternative headquarters at Songgwang-sa in the south. They elected Kim Kyong-woon as their Archbishop, with Man Hae as his proxy. This headquarters was later moved to Pomo-sa near Pusa. All this infighting turned out to be a bad dream for shortly thereafter, on July 8, 1911, the occupying Japanese put into effect a series of laws that brought Korean Buddhism and its administration strictly under the control of the Japanese governor. This was no different from the situation under the Yi dynasty. The election of an Archbishop and the Abbots of regional head-temples as well as sub-temples was subject to confirmation by the Japanese governor. All temple property, including land, relics and treasures, were to be listed with the government and could not be sold or transfered without its permission. Once a year the Abbots of all 31 regional head temples had to meet with the Japanese governor to get their cue about policies and direction for the Korean Buddhist world.

As a result of these suppressive measures by the Japanese authorities came an urgent need within the Korean Buddhist sangha for greater unity and harmony. A preliminary meeting was held on November 30, 1928, between the representatives of the Zen and Sutra schools to explore this theme of unity. At a second meeting on January 3, 1929, they drew up a document outlining 31 points of agreement between the two schools. In 1935, finally, the two schools of Sonjong (Zen) and Kyojong (Doctrinal) were merged into one single sect, the Chogyejong.

This was a monumental step in the history of Korean Buddhism. There were to be no more ideological differences or administrative structures to govern the two different approaches. Henceforth all the temples in Korea, whether they had been formerly Son or Kyo, were now Chogye temples within which either of the practices could be undertaken without any sense of conflict. A new temple was built in Seoul to serve as the headquarters of the newly-formed Chogye Order. Chogye-sa continues to serve that function today.

Following the 1935 unification, Korean Buddhism earnestly began to put its house into order. Kyong Ho's dharma heirs provided the inspiration for this renewal and it was largely due to their efforts that Korean Buddhism was able to retain vestiges of its traditional form and spirit in the face of the onslaught by Japanese Buddhism. For example, it is reported that in 1945, at the time of the end of Japanese colonial rule, of the estimated 7,000 Korean monks, only 600 were traditional, celibate monks of the Chogye Order. The rest had chosen to get married, Japanese-style, under various inducements and pressures from the Japanese authorities. Of these 600 monks, about 250 to 300 were at Su Dok-sa and other temples on Duk Sahn Mountain under the leadership of Mang Gong; about 50 were at Sangwon-sa on Odae-san Mountain under Zen Master Han Am's direction, and the rest were scattered throughout the country. The monks who chose to get married wore different robes, got preferential treatment from the Japanese authorities and were appointed to important position at large temples.

After the liberation from the Japanese colonial rule in 1945, the dislike between the Chogye monks and the "Japanese-style" monks became quite intense. The president of the new Republic of Korea, Syng-man Rhee, was a devout Buddhist and fiercely anti-Japanese. In 1954 he issued an ordinance asking all married monk-abbots to leave the temples because they had been traitors to the traditional Korean Buddhist system. Simultaneously, the Chogye Order undertook the task of reforming itself from within, setting up new administrative controls and policies in keeping with the changing times. This process goes on even today.

CHAPTER TWELVE

Kyong Ho's Dharma Successors: The Re-Emergence of Korean Zen

ZEN MASTER MANG GONG

Mang Gong (1872-1946) is as towering a figure in modern Korean Zen as his teacher, Kyong Ho. Indeed there are those who believe that in some areas his contributions outstrip those of Kyong Ho. This most charismatic and brilliant of Kyong Ho's disciples was born in 1872 and became a novice-monk as a young boy. We do not have any details about his family or boyhood, but it seems reasonable to speculate that he came to the temple as an orphan. For several years, he studied sutras at Tonghak-sa temple.

One day, when he was 13 years old, there was a ceremony to mark the end of a three-month retreat and the beginning of "free" time. Among those present was Kyong Ho who happened to be visiting the temple at the time. Kyong Ho, it will be remembered, was a former lecturer on sutras at this very temple and it was here that he attained his great enlightenment in 1879. As part of the ceremony, he gave a talk, saying:

You must all study very hard, learn Buddhism, and become like
great trees, from which temples are built, and like large bowls, able
to hold many good things. The sutra says, "Water becomes square
or round according to the shape of the container it is put in. In
the same way, people become good or bad according to the friends
they have." Always have the Buddha in mind and keep good company. Then you will become great trees and containers of Dharma.
This I sincerely wish.

Everyone was filled with admiration at his understanding of the
dharma. Kyong Ho was then asked to give a talk. He said:

All of you are monks. Monks are free of petty personal attachments
and live only to serve other people. Wanting to become a great tree
or a container of dharma will prevent you from becoming a true
teacher.

Great trees have great uses; small trees have small uses. Good and
bad can all be used in their own way. None are to be discarded.
Keep both good and bad friends. You mustn't reject anything. This
is true Buddhism. My only wish for you is that you free yourselves
from all conceptual thinking.

No one was more impressed by Kyong Ho's talk than the 13-
year-old Mang Gong. As Kyong Ho was walking out of the Dharma room, Mang Gong ran after him and pulled at his robes. Kyong
Ho turned around and asked, "What do you want?"

"I want to be your student. Please take me with you."

Kyong Ho tried to make him go away, but Mang Gong would
not leave. Finally, Kyong Ho said, "You are still only a child. You
are not capable of learning Buddhism yet."

Mang Gong said, "People may be young or old, but is there
youth or old age in Buddhism?"

"You bad boy!", exclaimed Kyong Ho. "You have killed and eaten
the Buddha! Come along now."

So, he took Mang Gong to Ch'onjong-sa temple and left him
there under the care of monk Taeho. He also gave Mang Gong a

kong-an to work on, "Ten thousand dharmas return to One;
where does the One return to?"

For the next five years, Mang Gong worked on his kong-an day
and night. At last when he was at Pongok-sa temple, he sat facing
the wall meditating on this kong-an for several days, forgetting
even to eat and sleep. Then one night when he opened his eyes,
a large hole appeared in the wall in front of him. He could see
the whole landscape! Grass, trees, clouds, and the blue sky appeared through the wall with total clarity. He touched the wall. It
was still there, but it was transparent like glass! He looked up, and
he could see right through the roof. At this Mang Gong was
filled with an inexpressible joy. Early the next morning, he went
to see the resident Zen Master. He rushed into the interview
room and announced, "I have penetrated the nature of all things. I
have attained enlightenment."

"Oh, have you?" said the master. "Then what is the nature of all
things?"

Mang Gong said, "I can see right through the wall and the roof,
as if they weren't there."

The master said, "Is this the truth?"

"Yes. I have no hindrance at all."

The master took his Zen stick and gave Mang Gong a hard
whack on the head. "Is there any hindrance now?"

Mang Gong was astonished. His eyes bulged, his face flushed,
and the wall became solid again. The master said, "Where did
your truth go?"

"I don't know. Please teach me."

"What kong-an are you working on?"

"Where does the One return?"

"Do you understand One?"

"No."

"You must first understand One. What you saw was an illusion.
Don't be led astray by it. With more hard work on your kong-an,
you will soon understand."

Mang Gong came out of the interview room with renewed determination. For the next three years, he continually meditated on
his kong-an. Then one morning that was no different from other

mornings, he heard the words during the Morning Bell Chant, "If you wish to understand all Buddhas of the past, present and future, you must perceive that the whole universe is created by the Mind alone." Hearing these words, Mang Gong's mind opened up. He understood that all the Buddhas dwell in a single sound. He clapped his hands, laughed and sang the following verse of enlightenment:

> The true nature of empty mountain is beyond the millions of years and past and future.
> White cloud, cool wind, come and go by themselves endlessly.
> Why did Bodhidharma come to China?
> The rooster cries before dawn and then the sun rises over the horizon.

About a year later, there was an important ceremony at the temple. Kyong Ho was specially invited and was present. Mang Gong went to his room thinking, "This Zen Master and I are the same. We have both attained enlightenment. He is Buddha, so am I. But since he was my first teacher I will bow to him, just an ordinary monk will do."

After Mang Gong had bowed, Kyong Ho said, "Welcome. It's been a long time since I've seen you. I heard that you have attained enlightenment. Is that true?"

Mang Gong said, "Yes, Master."

"Wonderful. Now let me ask you a question." Kyong Ho picked up a fan and a writing brush and put them in front of Mang Gong. "Are these the same or different?"

Without hesitation, Mang Gong said, "The fan is the brush; the brush is the fan."

For the next hour, with grandmotherly compassion, Kyong Ho tried to teach Mang Gong his mistake. But Mang Gong wouldn't listen. Finally, Kyong Ho said, "I have one more question for you. In the burial ceremony, there is a verse that says, 'The statue has eyes, and its tears silently drip down.' What does this mean?"

Mang Gong was stunned. He could find nothing to say. Suddenly, Kyong Ho shouted at him, "If you don't understand this, why do you say that the fan and the brush are the same?"

In great despair, Mang Gong bowed and said, "Forgive me."

"Do you understand your mistake?"

"Yes, Master. What can I do?"

"Long ago, when Zen Master Jo-ju (C: Chao-chou) was asked if a dog has Buddha-nature, he said, 'No!' What does this mean?"

"I don't know."

Kyong Ho said, "Always keep this mind that doesn't know and you will soon attain enlightenment."

So, for the next three years, Mang Gong did very hard training. One day, he heard the great temple bell ring and understood Jo-ju's answer. He returned to Kyong Ho, bowed, and said, "Now I know why the Bodhisattva faces away: because sugar is sweet and salt is salty."[68]

Mang Gong became a famous Zen Master after he received Transmission from Kyong Ho. He came to Duk Sahn Mountain in 1905 and built a small hermitage there. Soon he became the Zen Master at Sudok-sa, a small but ancient monastery on Duk Sahn Mountain. His fame spread and soon several thousand practitioners gathered to learn from him.

Mang Gong became a pioneer in teaching Zen Buddhism to lay people and to nuns. There was a constant stream of visitors to his mountain temple. Since all these people could not be accomodated in the temples around Sudok-sa, Mang Gong built a temple called Jeung-hae sa (Samadhi and Prajña temple) further up on the mountain for the training of his senior students. During his lifetime, Sudok-sa became a magnetic center for Korean Zen monks and it is said that there was hardly a Zen monk in Korea who did not come to pay his respects to Mang Gong.

Mang Gong built a nunnery, called Kyonsong-am, on Duk Sahn Mountain for his student-nuns. Here hundreds of nuns came to train under him. Today, Kyonsong-am has a new building on the same site and is the largest training center for Zen nuns in Korea. Four of Mang Gong's 25 Dharma heirs were nuns. Of these the best known was the nun Ilyop (1896-1971), a long-time abbot of

Kyonsong-am. Other notable nun-heirs were Pophui and Man-song (dates unknown).[69]

Mang Gong won everlasting fame, not only among Korean Buddhists, but amongst Koreans in general, when he challenged the authority of the Japanese government for its interference in the affairs of Korean Buddhism. On March 11, 1937, Mang Gong and 30 other abbots of Korean Buddhist regional temples met with the Japanese governor, Minami Jiro, for his annual pep talk. For the past 25 years or so, there had been a steady infiltration and subversion of Korean Buddhism by the Japanese Buddhists with the active co-operation of the occupying Japanese government. With the formation of the Chogye Order in 1935 merging the two competing schools of Doctrinal and Zen, the Japanese government felt more threatened than ever before in its ability to make inroads into making Korean Buddhists disband their traditional, celibate sangha and allow their member-monks to marry in the Japanese-style.

At the 1937 meeting, it seems, the subtle pressures of the past became more explicit. A statement was made by the governor which said, "Korean Buddhism would do much better to follow Japanese Buddhism and co-operate with it." Suddenly, Mang Gong got up from his seat and strode over to where the governor was. With his fist, he struck the governor's table and gave out a deafening Zen shout, "Katz!" Then he said, "The universe of the Ultimate Truth was originally clear and empty. Where did the mountains, rivers and earth come from?" Mang Gong continued to speak to the shocked governor and the abbots, "For what reason should Korean Buddhism follow Japanese Buddhism? Any person who forces the monks to break their precepts will go straight to hell."[70]

This outburst seems to have put an end to Japanese effort to have the Chogye Order disbanded. To many observers, it was the turning point in the self-renewal of Korean Zen and Buddhism.

In his later years, Mang Gong built a small hut on Duk Sahn Mountain, near Jeung-hae sa and lived there alone with an attendant to take care of his needs. The name of the hut was "Hut for Turning the Disk of the Moon." Today, there is a beautiful pagoda on the way up the mountain from Sudok-sa to Jeung-hae sa in Mang Gong's memory. The calligraphy on the pagoda reads, "The whole world is a single flower."

On the last day of his life, it is said, he washed himself and sat on his meditation cushion. Looking in the mirror, he pointed at himself and said, "Well, the time has come when I have to take leave of you!" Saying this, he roared with laughter and breathed his last.

In keeping with the Zen tradition, the exchanges between Mang Gong and his students have exercised considerable influence in Korean Zen monks as a teaching vehicle. Some of them are recorded here:

> One evening, Mang Gong's attendant turned on the lamplight. The lamplight was reflected in the window. Seeing this, Mang Gong asked the attendant, first pointing to the lamp, "Is this lamplight correct?" then pointing to the reflection, "Is that lamplight correct?"
>
> The attendant immediately turned off the lamplight and asked, "Old teacher, what will you do?"
>
> Without speaking, Mang Gong turned on the lamplight and lifted it to its stand.
>
> Once a scholar came to visit Mang Gong and asked, "What is the teaching of Buddha?"
>
> Mang Gong said, "It's in front of your eyes."
>
> The scholar asked, "If it's in front of me, why can't I see it?"
>
> Mang Gong said, "Because you have you. So you cannot see."
>
> The scholar asked, "Do *you* see?"
>
> Mang Gong answered, "There is only you. But you cannot see. Besides that, there is me. So it's even more difficult to see."
>
> Then the scholar asked, "If there is no you, and there is no me, then who can see?"
>
> Mang Gong said, "No you, no me...Then who wants to see?"
>
> The scholar remarked, "No matter how valuable the gold dust is, it will still hurt when it gets into your eyes."

One day, Mang Gong and Su Wol (also a Dharma successor of Kyong Ho) were sitting together and having a conversation. Just then, Su Wol picked up a bowl containing burnt rice (a Korean delicacy and a favorite snack) and said, "Don't say this is a bowl of burnt rice. Don't say this is not a bowl of burnt rice. Just give me one word."

Mang Gong reached over, took the bowl from Su Wol and threw it out of the window.

Su Wol was very pleased, "Very good. That's wonderful."

Once Mang Gong received a letter from a lay practitioner asking, "Respectfully, I ask you, teacher: I don't understand what Buddha attained when he saw a star on the night of April 8 (traditionally celebrated as the day of Buddha's Enlightenment). What is the meaning of his experiencing spiritual awakening?

Mang Gong commented, "Sand fell down into the eyes."

A monk once made a circle in the air and asked Mang Gong, "Why is it that all the monks of the world between the sky and the ground cannot get into the middle of this circle?

Mang Gong also made a circle and said, "Why is it that all the monks cannot go out from the middle of this circle?"

Mang Gong once said, "People live with the hope that good things will come to them, but they don't know that when you get a good thing you get a bad thing. As you study the Way, give up [the idea] of being human. Become deaf, deformed and blind, and stay away from all other [external] things. Then Big I will be naturally realized."

The following two exchanges have been used since Mang Gong's time as kong-ans:

One afternoon, Mang Gong was eating watermelon with a group of other monks. Suddenly, he heard the shrill chirrup of a cicada - "mei-mei-mei-mei-mei...." from the trees and said loudly, "Anybody who can catch this cicada and bring it to me will not have to pay the price of a piece of watermelon. If you cannot catch it, then you have to pay me three coins. Everybody say something, now!"

Someone pretended to catch the cicada, someone made the shrill chirrup of the cicada, someone shouted KATZ, someone hit Mang Gong on the back and said, "I caught the cicada!"

Mang Gong did not accept any of these answers and said, "Everybody give me three coins."

Just then, the monk Kum Bong drew a circle in the air and said, "There is no Buddha in this circle. There is no circle in the Buddha."

Mang Gong said, "Kum Bong! You too. Give me three coins."

If you were there, what could you have done?

Once, at the end of a summer retreat, Mang Gong slowly came into the Dharma room, looked around at those gathered and said, "Today is the last day of the summer retreat. Everybody did very well. But I alone was without work. So I set a fishing trap, and today one fish has been caught in the net. Come, speak. How will you save the fish?"

A participant stood up and moved his mouth [like a fish].

Mang Gong, seeing this, slapped his own knee and shouted,

"That's correct! Caught one fish!"

Then another participant tried to say something. Immediately Mang Gong hit his knee and said, "Right! I have caught one more fish."

To any answer, Mang Gong gave the same response.[71]

ZEN MASTER HAN AM

Another great disciple of Kyong Ho was Zen Master Han Am (1876- 1951). He became a monk at the age of 19. We are told that before his ordination, he was employed as a farm hand where one day he witnessed the merciless beating to death of a farm laborer by his master. This incident brought to him the anguish and suffering of all human existence and he decided to abandon the world. He entered Chang-an temple on Diamond Mountain and was initiated there by one priest Kumwol. He studied the sutras until he was 24 and then moved south to Haein-sa temple to study Zen under Kyong Ho who was living there at that time. One day, during a sermon, Kyong Ho quoted the following words from the *Diamond Sutra*: "If one sees all forms as non-form, then can one directly see the *Tathagata*." Upon hearing these words, Han Am suddenly attained enlightenment and wrote the following poem:

> Blue mountain under foot, mountain peak on my head;
> There is originally no inside, outside, or middle.
> The lame walk, the blind see,
> The north mountain without words answers south mountain.[72]

Han Am received Inka from Kyong Ho and became a famous Zen master. In the spring of 1926, he moved to Sangwon-sa temple on Odae Mountain where several hundred practitioners gathered under him. For the next t25 years, until his death, he never left the mountain. With the outbreak of the Korean War, in the summer of 1950, Odae Mountain became a favored conduit for the North Koreans to smuggle spies into South Korea. In January 1951, for tactical reasons, a South Korean army corps, stationed in the area, decided to burn down both Sangwon-sa and Woljong-sa temples, both on Odae Mountain. All the monks living in these two temples were ordered to evacuate immediately

However much his students would plead with him to leave the temple, Han Am remained adamant on staying. He said that when he came to the temple 25 years earlier, he had vowed never to leave and he was not going to change his mind now. Ultimately everyone evacuated and Han Am was left alone. When the Communist soldiers came to the temple they did not bother him for they knew him by reputation and had great respect for him. Han Am started fasting and after many days of fasting died on March 22, 1951 while seated in a meditation posture.

According to one scholar of Korean Zen, Han Am is often compared to Mang Gong by both Son scholars and practitioners, calling the former a towering summit in the north and the latter a peak rising in the south. Since the Silla period, Odae Mountain, where his Sangwon temple was located, Sorak and other mountains in the Kangwon region had been called the "northern" mountains—henceforth the doctrine of Han Am which flourished in the northern part was called the "Northern School." Mang Gong, who resided in Jeunghae temple in Yesan, South Ch'ungch'ong province, and who exerted a far-reaching influence on the southern district, was regarded as leader of the "Southern School."

> The atmosphere at Han Am's Sangwon temple was candid and tranquil and the master preached Son Buddhism with a high regard for Scriptural Buddhism, never neglecting all the precepts required of a Buddhist. Han Am may be compared to an icy brook running through a wintery valley or to buds sprouting from a withered branch, while Mang Gong's Jeunghae temple was noisy with the whisperings of secular visitors. The latter was elegant and refined in his outward appearance while equipped with the courage and dignity of a fierce beast."[73]

ZEN MASTER YONG SONG

Another of Kyong Ho's disciples to attain great fame both as a Zen teacher and a revitalizer of Korean Buddhism was Yong Song (1864-1940). At the age of 14, Yong Song became a monk at Haein-sa temple and studied sutras. The records are not clear but it seems most likely that he started studying Zen with Kyong Ho when the latter became the resident Zen master at Haein-sa and seems to have been given the following kong-an by Kyong Ho: "Mountains, rivers and earth all have their original root. What is the root of human beings?" Yong Song locked his door and continued meditating on this kong-an day and night. He took only one meal a day. After 17 days, early one morning, he was suddenly enlightened and wrote the following poem to celebrate the occasion:

The man who looks for the bull in the Five Skandas Mountains, sits alone in the empty room in a single wheel of light. Who can say there are squares, round, long, short? One ring of fire burns up the many thousand worlds.[74]

When the Japanese occupied Korea and tried to subvert Korean Buddhism, Zen masters Mang Gong and Yong Song became the leading Buddhist personages calling for strengthening the traditional Korean Buddhist spirit. They also encouraged a spirit of nationalism through their teaching. Yong Song became an active participant in the struggle against Japanese colonialism, On March 1, 1919, in the now-famous nationwide demonstration against the Japanese occupation, Yong Song, along with another prominent Buddhist monk Man Hae (Han Yong-won) represented Korean Buddhism in a group of 33 leaders of different organizations. They were both put into prison for their role.

Yong Song advocated that Zen practice and farming should go hand in hand. To put his theory into practice, he reclaimed farm land in Manchuria and also made many orchards and farms on Paegun Mountain in South Cholla province.

In the early part of 1911, Yong Song initiated a 10,000-day meditation retreat in which participants took turns for various lengths of time at Chilbul-sa temple on Chiri Mountain. He also established Taegak-sa temple in the heart of Seoul where he created an office for the translation of Buddhist texts from Chinese into Hangul, the native alphabet. This was called the Buddhist Scriptural Translation and under its auspices the *Avatamsaka Sutra*, the *Perfect Enlightenment Sutra, Diamond Sutra* and many other sutras were translated into the Korean language for the first time.

Yong Song left behind a rich legacy of Zen texts: *Kwiwon Chongjong* (Stream returning to Source), *Kak-hae Ilyun* (Sun Wheel of Enlightened Ocean), *Susimnon* (Thesis on Cultivating the Mind), *Ch'onggong Wolnil* (Round Sun in the Clear Sky), *Yong Song's Zen Records*, and other writings.

ZEN MASTER HYE WOL

Another famous disciple of Kyong Ho was Hye Wol Haemyong
(1861-1937). He was born in Yesan, the town nearest to Sudok-sa
temple and the Duk Sahn Mountain. At the age of 11, Hye Wol
was initiated as a novice monk by a priest An Sujwa at Jeung Hae-
sa temple on Duk Sahn Mountain. At the age of 24, he visited
Kyong Ho and began his Zen studies under that renowned Zen
teacher. One day he listened to a talk by Kyong Ho on Chinul's
work *Susimkyol* (Secrets on Cultivating the Mind). In his lecture,
Kyong Ho said,

> The four elements, or, in other words, the physical body, can nei-
> ther preach the Dharma nor hear the Dharma. Only One Thing
> within you, without form but singularly bright, can preach the
> Dharma and hear the Dharma. What is the One Thing which is
> without form and singularly bright? This is the nature of all Bud-
> dhas, and also your original Mind.[75]

Upon hearing these words, Hye Wol clapped his hands and
cried out, "That's it. That's just it!" He danced around happily,
laughing loudly. He had attained awakening on hearing Kyong
Ho's words.

Hye Wol continued his studies with Kyong Ho and eventually
received Inka from him. After this he became famous and traveled
to many Zen monasteries to teach the students there. There are
numerous stories in the oral tradition about Hye Wol; for he was
an unusual Zen master. He never learned to read or write (in this
respect, he was quite typical of a majority of Korean Zen monks of
his time who disdained book learning and never learned to read
or study the sutras) and never studied the scriptures. Instead, at
every monastery where he stayed, he liked to go out with his students and clear away the forest to reclaim farming land for the
temple's use. It is said that he was always completely spontaneous,
like a child, in his activities and there was nothing artificial or
studied about him.

One time when Hye Wol was a resident teacher at Naewon-sa Zen monastery, he bought a large bull. Whenever he and his students would clear the forest, Hye Wol would use the bull to plow the newly-reclaimed land. He used to say to his students, "If the Zen practitioner eats too much or too well, he cannot study properly." Consequently, at the monastery, only barley and vegetables were served and the students regularly complained about the poor quality of food. One day Hye Wol had to go away from the monastery for a few days. While he gone, his students (including the future Zen Masters Ko Bong, Pak Kumbong and Chong Unbong) took the bull to the market and sold it. They then bought lots of rice, cakes, fruits, and candy. They took the food back to the monastery and ate extremely well for several days. When Hye Wol returned he did not see the bull and asked, "Where is my bull?" Everybody said they didn't know. Hye Wol gave an ultimatum, "Bring back my bull, otherwise I will punish all of you."

Since the students had sold the bull, they didn't know what to do. Finally Ko Bong took off all his clothes and entered the master's room, walking on all fours, going around the room and mooing loudly. "Here I have brought your bull," he said. Hye Wol hit Ko Bong on the ass and said, "My bull is a large golden one, not a small calf like this. Get out of here at once!" Then he went to the meditation hall and and said to the students, "Pak Ko Bong paid back the money from the sale of my bull." After that he never mentioned the bull again!

Another Hye Wol story is about the time when a farmer brought some rice as a gift to Hye Wol's monastery. As it was raining, the farmer, his horse and the rice were all wet. Hye Wol decided to test his students and asked them to write a Chinese character "which never gets wet even when it gets rained on." Some students wrote the character for Mind, others for Human Nature, others for wind and so forth. But Hye Wol shook his head each time and said no to each one of them. Finally Ko Bong wrote the character for "rain" and showed it to Hye Wol. They both looked at each other and smiled. Soon after this, Ko Bong received Inka from Hye Wol.

Still another story about Hye Wol goes like this: Whenever Hye
Wol gave a talk on Zen, he would say, "I have two swords. One is
the sword which kills men, and the other is the sword which
brings men back to life. Do you understand what kind of swords
are these, and when will I use them? Be careful, for when you
meet my swords, you will lose your life." A Japanese general, who
did not like Korean monks in principle, heard about this and
came to Hye Wol's monastery. He took out his long sword and
said to Hye Wol, "I have heard you claim you have a man-killing
sword and a sword which brings men back to life. How can you
have a sword when you are a monk? If you really have such a
sword, show it to me now, or I will kill you with my sword."

Hye Wol smiled gently and said, "I will show you my sword
now if you would really like to see it." "Show it to me now," said
the general. Then Hye Wol said, "Look behind you, it's there!" As
soon as the general turned his head to look at the "sword." Hye
Wol took a step and struck the general on the neck with his fist,
saying, "This is my sword. You are already dead." The general was
so surprised that he fell down. On getting up, he recognized Hye
Wol's courage and spiritual power and showed proper respect for
him.[76]

At the age of 61, Hye Wol moved to Sonam-sa temple, just outside Pusan. There he never paid any attention to the busy life of
the metropolis around him. Instead he devoted himself to
reclaiming the wasteland around the temple and converting it
into a farm land. "He treated everyone with benevolence and
made no distinction between those with whom he had been ac-
quainted for a long time and those whom he met for the first
time."[77] A certain monk Hyonch'ik Dongch'o (d.1959) visited Hye
Wol during his Sonam-sa years and recorded his impressions in
his *Mountain Diary*:

> When we [Hyonch'ik was accompanied by another monk] entered
> Anyang Hut [where Hye Wol later died], a shabbily clothed old man
> followed us into the guest chamber. As we bowed before him, he
> returned our greetings and asked us, even before we could sit
> down, "Do you know what can be seen harmoniously and what

can be heard harmoniously?" My companion answered in the negative and the aged priest said nothing more.

The following morning, as I was reading a newspaper, the old man came to me and again asked, "Do you know the meaning of....?" I replied that all was alike, while drawing a rectangle on the newspaper with my finger and another rectangle in the reverse way. He again passed no remark.

That day we stayed at Haejo hut for the night and then called on the priest at his hut again the following morning. On our way we had bought a few pears which we now peeled for the old man and which he ate gratefully. When I asked him whether his *ondol* floor was warm enough, he replied that when heated it got warm! I again asked him if he had enough bedclothing. He replied, "Namu Chongsung Kuwang Taesin." [This term which Hye Wol used frequently in answer to questions put to him has no particular meaning.] I presume he utilized the term as a a mean of expelling discernment and thinking. It is likely that he meant to urge me to stop my nonsensical chatter.

Staying with him for a few days, I tried to fathom his daily life and manners. I noticed that he received a stranger and a disciple who had studied under him for years in exactly the same way. It was as if I saw in him for the first time a man who had completely overcome all feelings of intimacy. I once read a discourse calling for the negation of distinction between intimate and remote and wondered how man could possibly reach the state in which he is free from all feelings of intimacy. However, as I observed the daily life of this great priest, I instantly realized that this task was within the reach of every man if he diligently attended to his religious practices. Now I keenly feel the necessity of learning directly from such a great master, Although it would be impossible for my dull vision to pierce to the depths of this great priest's mind, I felt that I had now liberated myself from all prejudice, concepts, discernment and narrow knowledge. To me his every act was a precious sermon."[78]

Hye Wol died at Anyang Hut in 1937 at the age of 77.

ZEN MASTER SU WOL

As we noted earlier, Kyong Ho left behind five Dharma heirs. The oldest of these was Su Wol (1855-1928). Su Wol's life-story is perhaps the most unusual of all of Kyong Ho's successors. He came from a poverty-stricken serf family, so poor that not only could he not read or write, he was not even able to get married. This was most unusual in a society where a boy was usually married in his teens irrespective of his station in life. At the age of 29, Su Wol applied to become a novice monk at Ch'onjang-sa temple in Sosan county. The head priest was naturally not enthusiastic about admitting this illerate, aged country boy. Moreover, Su Wol did not seem very eager to learn the sutras or to engage in Zen practice. In other words, he was a drifter. He was reluctantly admitted to the temple and ordained a priest in due course; however he was still given the menial chore of collecting firewood for the temple. The head priest at the temple assigned him a sutra and asked him to repeat the sutra to himself while collecting firewood. Su Wol had a pure heart and while he did not understand the meaning of the sutra, he devoted himself completely to the task of reciting it every waking moment of his life, no matter what task he was engaged in. Through his complete absorption in the recitation of the sutra, one day he attained great samadhi even though he was not aiming for it.

A few years later, Su Wol succeeded Priest Taeho as the Head Monk at Ch'onjang-sa temple. Later he moved to Sangwon-sa on Odae Mountain where he studied with Hanam Zen Master who, it will be remembered, was one of the five Dharma heirs of Kyong Ho. In 1907, Su Wol went to Pohyon temple on Myohyang Mountain, where he stayed for three years. It was at this temple that he met Kyong Ho and engaged in Zen studies under him. Soon he received Inka from Kyong Ho and became well-known through the Korean Buddhist world.

In 1912, when Kyong Ho was about to die, he summoned both Su Wol and Mang Gong to his bedside to hear his last will and testament. After cremating his teacher, Su Wol traveled further north and crossed the Yalu River into Manchuria. There he lived for three years at a small farmhouse, tilling the land and raising farm animals. It has never been clear why Su Wol left Korea and moved to Manchuria, then (and now) a Chinese territory. Some have speculated that it may have been because of the 1911 Japanese occupation of Korea. Many Korean farmers had moved into Manchuria to escape the occupation and it is possible that Su Wol may have been asked by the migrating Koreans to help them in their religious practice. In Manchuria, Su Wol built a small house and called it Hwaom-sa temple but that seems to have been the extent of his contribution as a priest. In all other respects, he was a farmer just like any other and this was hardly an ideal life for a monk or a famous Zen Master. Su Wol did not accept any disciples and did not leave any lineage behind him. He died in July 1928 at the age of 74.

In his purity of heart, Su Wol was more like Hye Wol than any of the other great disciples of Kyong Ho. Both were illiterate and underprivileged. But both were also typical of the Buddhist monks who kept the tradition alive during the long dark years of Yi dynasty rule through their dedication, perseverance and even saintliness. Su Wol himself kept silence all day and did not speak unless he was spoken to. No one ever saw him sitting in formal meditation posture but it may be presumed that he never stopped his meditation in his simple daily life. He always took on menial jobs like collecting firewood or tilling the land and didn't have the slightest trace of pretension in him. If a temple did not have any job for him to do, he would simply move on to another temple where he could do the menial chores. In this respect he was the true Zen man, living a life without leaving any trace.

CHAPTER THIRTEEN

Buddhism in Korea Today

Today there are an estimated 8,000 monks in Korea's traditional, celibate Chogye Order, and 15,000 nuns. Apart from their number, nuns provide much of the vitality which Korean Buddhism has to offer today. Nuns in their temples are more accessible and more connected to the laity, for whom they perform services and chanting. Nuns generally lead a life of much greater devotion to the Vinaya rules and provide the bedrock of trust and faith for the average Korean Buddhist.

Due to the patriarchal nature of Korean society, ordination by women was frowned upon for a long time, and it was not until the 1920's that women began to ordain. This was largely through the inspiration and leadership provided by Mang Gong Sunim, who, as we noted, built Kyongsong-am, the largest training center for Zen nuns in Korea.

In October 1985, the nuns in Korea formed an independent national organization affiliated with the Chogye Order. At the founding meeting, for the first time in Korean history, a nun gave lectures on the Vinaya. An important undertaking of this new organization is to formulate the Vinaya rules for nuns in keeping with changing times and society. In May 1986, they adopted a constitution and by-laws.

So far we have looked at the dharma heirs of Kyong Ho who, along with their teacher, were most responsible for revitalizing the spirit of Korean Zen in the first half of this century. There were other Zen masters during the same period who were indirectly influenced by Kyong Ho and made notable contributions to Korean Zen. One of them was a very unusual Zen Master, Hyo Bong (1888-1966). He took a degree in law from Waseda University in Japan and was a judge at the High Court in Pyongyang for six years. In July 1925, when he was 37 years old, he had to pass a death sentence on a criminal whose case was being tried before him. Having passed this sentence, he was deeply struck by a sense of the impermanency of human life, and that very night he disappeared without a word to his wife or family. He went into the Diamond Mountains and was initiated as a monk under Zen Master Sokdu (dates unknown). For seven years, we are told, he never lay down but slept sitting up in a crossed-legged position. He had never told anyone about his personal background; and since it was so unusual for someone to become a monk at his age, everyone assumed that he had failed in business. He took only one meal a day and never left the monastery. Zen Master Mang Gong gave him a nickname when he said that Hyo Bong's mind was like a wheat-pounder, for he always sat strong and straight without sleeping, like a hard wooden wheat-pounder. So he came to be called "The Wheat-Pounder Monk."

One day in 1932, an old friend of Hyo Bong's from Pyongyang, a Japanese judge, visited the temple by chance and immediately recognized Hyo Bong. He was greatly surprised and told Hyo Bong that everyone back home had assumed that he was dead since he hadn't left a word with his family nor resigned from the court. They both laughed. Hyo Bong said he was sorry for putting his family through this. He requested the Japanese judge not tell anyone in the monastery about his background. But the story leaked out anyway and he came to be called "The Judge Monk."

At last, Hyo Bong attained enlightenment, became a famous Zen Master, and taught at several Zen monasteries. In 1958, Hyo Bong became the Archbishop of Korean Buddhism and held this position until his death in 1966. He proved to be a great inspiration to Korean Buddhism during his term of office. He died on May 14, 1966, at the age of 78, while seated in a meditation posture. Moments before, he picked up his brush and wrote the following poem:

> All the teaching of my life
> Was like a sixth finger on a hand.
> If anyone asks me about today's event,
> I will answer: The round moon leaves its imprint on a thousand rivers.

Putting down his brush, he quietly passed away.[79]

His most famous disciple was Zen Master Ku Sahn Sunim (1909-1983) whose energy and vision helped Songgwang-sa temple regain its former position as the main Zen temple in Korea. Ku Sahn Sunim worked as a barber until the age of 28, when he became a monk under Zen Master Hyo Bong. For the next seven years, Ku Sahn Sunim worked with the hwa-tou "What is this?" After seven years, he had his first awakening and received Inka from Hyo Bong. Four years later, in 1948, Hyo Bong gave the formal transmission of lineage to Ku Sahn Sunim. But Ku Sahn himself was not satisfied with the depth of his understanding, so he returned to his hermitage and undertook severe ascetic practices, such as never lying down to sleep, standing in one position for days on end, and sitting in meditation with a knife-embedded stick under his chin to prevent himself from dozing off. Finally, in 1959, at the age of 50, he attained final awakening.

During the 1950's, Ku Sahn Sunim was active at the administrative headquarters of the Chogye Order in reforming Korean Buddhism from within. After getting transmission from Hyo Bong, he continued to travel around Korea, speaking to lay groups. Before and during the Japanese occupation (1911-1945), Korean monks had confined themselves to the cloistered world of their monasteries. But after the Korean War and the truce with North Korea, it was clear, at least to younger Zen masters, that in order to revitalize Korean Zen, it was going to be necessary to focus their energy on the lay believers. Strong gains by an aggressive Christianity and internal disorder had dried up much of the support from the lay community that had traditionally been taken for granted. Now it was necessary to bring them back to the fold. As a result, Zen masters like Ku Sahn and Seung Sahn devoted most of their energies in teaching lay people.

Ku Sahn Sunim became the resident Zen master at Songgwang-sa in 1967. In 1972, he paid a brief first visit to America and returned to his monastery with one American student, who became a monk there. Other students soon followed and Songgwang-sa ("Vast Pines Monastery") became the first and only temple in Korea to have a western sangha. It was an enormous learning experience for both the western students and the Korean monks. The western monks and nuns had to learn Korean as well as classical Chinese in order to competently read scriptures. They had to adapt to a way of life, of living, eating, working and doing meditation that had been in force at Songgwang-sa for nearly a thousand years. On their part, the Korean monks came into contact with people of a culture which places prime value on individuality and initiative.

Ku Sahn Sunim returned to California in 1980 to inaugurate the Korea-sa temple in Los Angeles which had been established by one of his students. (Korea-sa became the second temple in Los Angeles after Zen Master Seung Sahn's Tahl Mah-sa temple where Korean lay people as well as American students could practice Korean style of Zen.) In October 1983, Ku Sahn Sunim's health began to decline and by December of that year, he knew his time had come. He gathered his disciples together and told them he was departing. He then recited the following verse:

> Samsara and Nirvana are originally not two;
> As the sun rises in the sky
> it illuminates the three thousand worlds.[80]

On December 16, 1983, at his request his disciples helped him to a sitting meditation position. In that position he closed his eyes for the last time and passed into Nirvana. Ku Sahn was succeeded by Zen Master Il Gak (b. 1929), another disciple of Zen Master Hyo Bong, as the resident Zen master of Songgwang-sa.

Another Korean monk who has made a significant contribution to the understanding of Korean Zen in North America is Samu Sunim. He came to Canada in 1968, and in 1972 he started a Zen meditation group in Toronto. This group is today known as the Zen Lotus Society, and has a branch temple in Ann Arbor, Michigan. The Zen Lotus Society's publication, *Spring Wind*, has contributed greatly to articulating and amplifying the Korean Zen tradition.

CHAPTER FOURTEEN

Zen Master Seung Sahn

The transplantation of Korean Zen to the West, and whatever shape and identity it has taken here, can be attributed largely to the efforts of Zen Master Seung Sahn (b. 1927). In his native country, he has been hailed as the "Korean Bodhidharma" for bringing Korean Zen to the West.

Seung Sahn Soen Sa ("Soen Sa" means Zen Master) was born Duk-In Lee in a village near Pyongyang (now the capital of North Korea). His parents were Protestant Christians—his father an architect. The family owned a large orchard and was considered one of the richest in the village. He attended a Middle School in Pyongyang and took courses in science and engineering. This was at the time when Japan was entering the Pacific war in full earnest and its occupation policies in Korea were beginning to tighten the noose around the Korean people more than ever. Koreans were not allowed to learn their own language in the schools, but had to learn Japanese, which was also the language of all official business. The teachers in schools were mostly Japanese, and children of Japanese origin were favored regardless of scholastic standing. The intention was to make Koreans second-class citizens in their own country and to obliterate all traces of Korean culture from Korea.

In 1944, Seung Sahn joined the underground Korean independence movement, making short-wave radios for spying on the movement of Japanese troops. Within a few months, he was caught by the police and was saved from a death-sentence or life-imprisonment through the goodwill of his school principal. After his release, he and two of his friends stole large sums of money from their parents and crossed the heavily-patrolled Manchurian border in an unsuccessful attempt to join the Free Korean Army in Manchuria.

After the surrender of the Japanese in 1945, Seung Sahn Soen Sa came to Seoul and enrolled at Dong Guk University. In the meantime, Russian and Allied forces occupied areas north and south of the 38th parallel and all communication and travel between north and south were cut off. Seung Sahn Soen Sa was cut off from his parents and was never to see them again. The years at the university were a time of much emotional turmoil for him and also a time for thinking about the future: how to help his country and his people? Earlier he had tried revolutionary activities against the Japanese. Then the enemy was well-defined. Now the situation was more fluid. Communist cells in South Korea were trying to recruit students in order to overthrow the government of Syng-man Rhee and bring both north and south under the control of the Communists. Now Koreans were fighting Koreans!

Seung Sahn Soen Sa decided he could not help his country through politicial activism or academic studies. He had read western philosophy and Confucian texts but none seemed adequate to help the situation in Korea. Then a friend gave him a copy of the *Diamond Sutra*. In it he read, "All things that appear in this world are transient. If you view all things that appear as never having appeared, then you will realize your true self." When he read these words, all the confusion and conflicting thoughts seem to have been erased from his mind. He decided to become a Buddhist monk.

He went to Magok-sa temple and was ordained there as a novice monk in October 1948. Soon after his ordination he went up into the mountains to begin a 100-day retreat on Won Gak Mountain. He recited the "Shinmyo Janggu Dae" Dharani for 20 hours a day. He ate only pine needles, dried and beaten into a powder. He slept only from 9:00 to 11:00 p.m. and from 3:00 to 5:00 a.m. Several times a day he took ice-cold baths to ward off hunger and sleep.

Soon he was assailed by doubts. Why was this retreat necessary? Why did he have to go to these extremes? Couldn't he go down to a small temple in a quiet valley, get married like a Japanese priest, and attain enlightenment gradually, in the midst of a happy family? One night, these thoughts became so powerful that he decided to leave in the morning and packed up all his belongings. But the next morning his mind was clearer, and he unpacked. A few days later the same thing happened. In the following weeks, he packed and unpacked nine times.

By now 50 days had passed and his body was very weak and exhausted. Every night he had terrifying visions. Tigers and demons would stand in front of him, bellowing. He was in a state of constant terror. After a month of this, the visions became visions of delight. Buddhas and Bodhisattvas would appear and tell him he would go to heaven. By the end of 80 days, his body was strong again, but his flesh had turned green from eating pine needles.

One day, a week before the retreat was to finish, Seung Sahn Soen Sa was walking outside, chanting and keeping rhythm with his *moktak*. Suddenly, two handsome boys in multi-colored robes appeared on either side of him and bowed. Where could these demons have come from? At that moment, he remembered and clearly understood the phrase, "Insight into the true aspect of all phenomena". On the 99th day, he was again outside chanting and hitting the *moktak*. Suddenly he heard the crows cawing. All at once his body disappeared. He was in infinite space. From far away he could hear the moktak beating, and the sound of his own voice. He remained in this state for some time. When he returned to his body, he understood the phrase, "Insight which sees that phenomena themselves are the Absolute." The rocks, the river, everything he could see, everything he could hear, all this was his true self. All things are exactly as they are. The truth is just like this. The next day, he wrote this enlightenment poem:

> The road at the bottom of Won Gak Mountain
> is not the present road.
> The man climbing with his backpack
> is not a man of the past.
> Tok, tok, tok - his footsteps
> transfix past and present.
> Crows out of a tree,
> Caw, caw, caw.

When Seung Sahn Soen Sa came down from the mountain, he wanted to go and study with Zen Master Han Am at Sangwon-sa. Han Am was then the most respected Zen Master in Korea (Mang Gong had already died in 1946) and had not left his monastery in 25 years. However, the head monk at Magok-sa told him that he and some laymen were planning to start a Zen meditation community at Magok-sa and were searching for a Zen master who could be their teacher. He persuaded Seung Sahn Soen Sa to stay at Magok-sa and put him to work in the kitchen.

The embyronic Zen community at Magok-sa was able to persuade Zen Master Ko Bong (1890-1961) to come and lead their group. Ko Bong was one of the most prominent of Mang Gong's 25 Dharma heirs and had the reputation of being a brilliant, if somewhat unorthodox, Zen master. For one thing, he was very fond of wine; for another, he taught only nuns and lay people. Monks, he said, were too lazy or too arrogant to be good Zen students.

Zen Master Ko Bong arrived at Magok-sa on March 3, 1949, and stayed for one week. Seung Sahn Soen Sa received his Buddhist name "Haeng Won" from him and learned to sit Zen with everyone else the night before Ko Bong's departure for Sudok-sa. Seung Sahn Soen Sa felt he had attained enlightenment, so he took a moktak and went to Ko Bong's room. He put the moktak before Ko Bong and asked him, "What is this?" When Ko Bong just hit the moktak, Seung Sahn Soen Sa understood "just like this." They talked about his practice. Ko Bong asked him, "Why do you do mantra practice?" Seung Sahn Soen Sa said, "I want to get universal energy and save all people." Ko Bong said, "If you do a mantra, you can make your karma disappear and get universal energy, but attaining final enlightenment is very difficult that way. If you are attached to the mantra, you cannot save all people. If you practice with a kong-an, you will make your karma disappear and also get final enlightenment. This is very important." Seung Sahn Soen Sa understood but had no training in Zen langugage or Dharma-combat. He asked, "How should I practice then?" Ko Bong said, "A monk once asked Zen Master Joju (C: Chao-chou), 'Why did Bodhidharma come to China?' Jo-ju answered, 'The pine tree in the front garden.' What does this mean?" Seung Sahn Soen Sa understood but didn't know how to answer. He said, "I don't know." Ko Bong said, "Only keep this don't-know mind. This is true Zen practice."

Next day, Ko Bong left for Sudok-sa and Seung Sahn Soen Sa and other students put away all the cooking pots and pans and spent that summer eating only raw food. In the fall, Seung Sahn Soen Sa went to Sudok-sa to take part in the three-month winter retreat which started on October 15. There he read Zen books, saw and heard monks and Zen masters engage each other in Dharma-combat, and mastered the language of Zen. After he learned the techniques of Zen interviews, he became a free person. Any kong-an was no problem.

There was one week in the middle of the retreat when everyone trained extra hard with no sleep at all througout the whole week. Only seven days of continuous sitting. However, Seung Sahn Soen Sa found that monks were dozing off during the night and were not practicing hard enough. One night, he took all the pots and pans out of the kitchen and arranged them in a circle in the front yard. The next night, he turned the Buddha on the altar toward the wall and took the incense-burner and hung it on a persimmon tree in the garden. By this time the whole monastery was in uproar. There was talk of demons walking around or gods coming down from the mountain to warn the monks to practice harder.

The third night he went to Kyong Sone-am, the nuns'
monastery, where he took 70 pairs of nuns' shoes and put them in
front of Zen Master Duk Sahn's room, displayed as in a shoe store.
But this time a nun woke up to go to the outhouse and, missing
her shoes, woke everyone up. Seung Sahn Soen Sa was caught
and next morning the great temple bell was rung to summon everyone from the nearby temples. Seung Sahn Soen Sa was brought
before an assembly of about 200 monks and nuns for a trial. Most
of the monks voted to give him another chance (since he had
been highly recommended by Ko Bong), but the nuns were
unanimously against him. In the end, he was not expelled from
the monastery but had to offer formal apologies to the assembly of
all the high monks.

First, he went to Zen Master Duk Sahn and bowed. Duk Sahn
said, "Keep up the good work."

Then he went to the Head nun. She said, "You've made a great
deal too much commotion in this monastery, young man." Seung
Sahn Soen Sa laughed and said, "The whole world is already full
of commotion. What can you do?" She couldn't answer.

Next was Zen Master Chun Song who was famous for his wild
actions and unrestrained language. Seung Sahn Soen Sa bowed to
him and said, "I killed all the Buddhas of past, present and future.
What can you do?"

Chun Song said, "Aha!" and looked deeply into Seung Sahn
Soen Sa's eyes. Then he asked, "What did you see?"

Seung Sahn Soen Sa said, "You already understand."

Chun Song asked, "Is that all?"

Seung Sahn Soen Sa said, "There's a cuckoo singing in the tree
outside the window." Chun Song laughed and said, "Aha!" He
asked several more questions which Seung Sahn Soen Sa answered without difficulty. Finally, Chun Song leaped up and
danced around Seung Sahn Soen Sa, shouting, "You are enlightened! You are enligtened!" The news spread quickly, and people
began to understand the events of the preceding days.

On January 14, the retreat ended and Seung Sahn Soen Sa left
to see Ko Bong. On his way to Seoul, he met Zen masters Keum
Bong and Keum Oh. He had dharma-combat with both of them

and they both gave him Inka, the seal of validation of a Zen student's great awakening. When Seung Sahn Soen Sa arrived at Ko Bong's temple, he was still wearing his old patched retreat clothes and carrying a knapsack. He bowed to Ko Bong and said, "All the Buddhas turned out to be bunch of corpses. How about a funeral service?"

Ko Bong said, "Prove it!"

Seung Sahn Soen Sa reached into his knapsack and took out a dried cuttlefish and a bottle of wine. "Here are the leftovers from the funeral party."

Ko Bong said, "In that case, pour me some wine."

Seung Sahn Soen Sa said, "Okay, give me your glass."

Ko Bong held out his palm. Seung Sahn Soen Sa slapped it with the bottle and said, "That's not a glass, it's your hand." He put the bottle on the floor. Ko Bong laughed and said, "Not bad. You're almost done. But I have a few questions for you." He then proceeded to ask Seung Sahn Soen Sa some of the most difficult of the 1,700 traditional Zen kong-an. Seung Sahn Soen Sa answered without hindrance.

Finally, Ko Bong said, "All right. One last question. The mouse eats cat food, but the cat bowl is broken. What does this mean?"

Seung Sahn Soen Sa said, "The sky is blue, the grass is green." Ko Bong shook his head and said, "No."

Seung Sahn Soen Sa was taken aback. He had never missed a Zen question before. His face began to grow red as he gave one "like this" answer after another. Ko Bong kept shaking his head. Finally, Seung Sahn Soen Sa exploded with anger and frustration. "Three Zen masters have given me Inka. Why do you say I'm wrong?"

Ko Bong said, "What does this mean? Tell me."

For the next 50 minutes, the two sat facing each other, hunched like tomcats. The silence was electric. Then, all of a sudden, Seung Sahn Soen Sa had the answer. When Ko Bong heard it, his eyes grew moist and his face was filled with joy. He embraced Seung Sahn Soen Sa and said, "Your flower has blossomed. I am the bee; I am flying, dancing in the sky."

On January 25, 1950, in a formal ceremony, Seung Sahn Soen Sa received Transmission of Dharma from Ko Bong, making him the 78th Patriarch in that particular line of succession. In his Transmission Poem, Ko Bong wrote:

> I can see it, Seung Sahn Soen Sa.
> All Dharmas do not appear,
> All Dharmas do not disappear.
> This is the Dharma of no-appearance and no-disappearance.
> Its name is Paramita.

Then he said, "Someday Korean Buddhism will spread to the whole world through you. We will meet again in 500 years."

This was the only Transmission Ko Bong ever gave. Seung Sahn Soen Sa was 22 years old. Ko Bong asked him to spend the next three years in silence to deepen his understanding.

Soon the Korean War broke out and, like all able-bodied monks, Seung Sahn Soen Sa was drafted into the army. Since he was a Buddhist monk, he served as a chaplain in the auxiliary units and rose to the position of a captain after five years of draft duty. When he came out of the army, he found he was a famous person within the Korean Buddhist world, A young man who had become enlightened the age of 21 and had received Transmission from none other than Ko Bong, also a university graduate and a captain in the army!

In 1954, Syng-man Rhee, the President of the Republic of Korea, had issued a decree asking all Abbots of the temples who were married to leave the temples as they had betrayed the Buddhist tradition and were not fit to be in a position of authority. Their places were to be taken over by the celibate monks of the Chogye Order. At this time, Ko Bong was quite sick. So Seung Sahn Soen Sa brought him to Hwa Gae-sa temple on the outskirts of Seoul, where the married abbot had been "exiled." Seung Sahn Soen Sa became the abbot of the temple and looked after his teacher until Ko Bong died there in 1961. During his years at Hwa Gae-sa, Seung Sahn Soen Sa founded the United Buddhism Association, a community of lay people to encourage them to participate more fully in the revival of Korean Buddhism. Today United Buddhism Association continues to be very strong and has a large membership. It continues the task of fostering the spirit of traditional Buddhism at grass-roots levels.

During these years, Seung Sahn Soen Sa was also on the Board of Directors of Chogye Order which, in the mid-50's and -60's, was struggling with reforming its own house, seeking to reverse the havoc brought about by Japanese domination of Buddhist affairs in Korea. For a time he was an instructor in Zen at the newly-established Zen meditation hall at Dong Guk University, his alma mater. He was also the visiting Zen master at five temples in Seoul, including the large nunnery Bo Mun-sa.

In 1962, Seung Sahn Soen sa went to Japan and established a temple in Tokyo to serve the needs of Korean-Japanese people who were without spiritual guidance and who were being continually harassed by the North Korean propaganda about the evils of religion and Buddhism. He also assisted in the establishment of a temple in Hong Kong.

By 1971, he felt he had finished his work in Japan and Hong Kong. He had heard about the great interest in America in the study of Zen and also heard that there were many wild-spirited hippies there. To him it sounded like a fertile ground for introduction of Korean Zen, so he took hold of his metaphorical walking stick and landed in America. He had no money, didn't speak English, and didn't know anyone. By sheer chance, he met a Korean man on the plane who lived in Providence, Rhode Island, who promised to give the Zen Master a job in his laundromat if he ever came to Providence After spending a few days in Los Angeles, Seung Sahn Soen Sa did indeed turn up in Providence and started working in the laundromat, repairing washing machines. He rented a small apartment in a run-down section of town and hung up a sign for a Zen meditation center. Some students from Brown University heard about him and started coming to the apartment to learn about Zen first-hand from a Zen Master. This was the nucleus of Providence Zen Center, which started in September, 1972. A professor from Brown helped by translating his talks from Japanese into English, and in no time at all, two students moved into the tiny apartment to start a residential Zen center. This was a period of much camraderie, hilarity and not a little bewilderment on both sides. As Seung Sahn Soen Sa struggled with English and gave Zen interviews to students, it must have been something like the early years of Kamakura Zen when Chinese Ch'an masters arrived in Japan to teach Zen without any knowledge of Japanese.

What Seung Sahn Soen Sa brought to America, besides his hitherto unknown tradition of Zen, was a lively, down-to-earth personality. He turned out to be a unique kind of Zen master, accessible to all and sundry. As a result soon residential Zen centers opened in Cambridge, New Haven, New York, Berkeley, Los Angeles and Toronto. This growth of his teaching-style within only four years of his arrival in America was phenomenal. As his English improved, Seung Sahn Soen Sa took to traveling all over the country, disseminating his particular style of Zen. He gave public lectures in libraries and churches and university auditoriums, talking about Zen in simple, accessible and humorous ways. His flair for showmanship and gifts as a raconteur made the Zen stories he had to tell come alive for his audiences. Every place he went he encouraged those serious about Zen practice to start a group and promised he would visit them to lead retreats and provide other guidance. Very soon he started traveling to Europe, and especially to Poland where his teaching found an enthusiastic reception.

One innovation of Seung Sahn Soen Sa was to encourage his students to write to him about their problems and practice. He was always on the move himself, and it was not always possible for his dispersed students to have personal meetings with him. The following letters from his students, and his answers to them, were collected into "kong-an books" much like the exchanges between Ch'an teachers and students in T'ang China. At all his residential Zen centers, part of morning and evening practice is to read aloud a letter from a student and Seung Sahn Soen Sa's reply. Some of these letters, along with public talks and anecdotes, have been published in the popular book, *Dropping Ashes on the Buddha*.

Seung Sahn Soen Sa hardly missed any situation in daily life to teach Zen. Once when the very large temple bell was being cast in Korea for the Providence Zen Center, he told his students,

> Originally this metal was ugly rocks. Then the rocks were heated for a long time over a very hot fire, until finally they became liquid. Now this liquid will be poured into a mold and will take the shape of a big, beautiful bell, and when it cools someone will strike the bell, and the beautiful sound will fill the whole universe.
>
> We are all like rocks. And when we practice hard, we heat up our hearts making a big, hot flame, which melts our condition, situation and opinion until we become like molten metal, ready to assume the shape of a great Bodhisattva who, when struck with the cry for help, makes a big, deep sound which resonates and fills the whole universe, and makes everybody happy.

Another time, when he was in the hospital for a heart condition, many students wrote him expressing their concern. To one woman he wrote:[81]

July 15, 1977

Dear Marge,

Thank you for your letter. How are you?

I have just returned from the hospital. You worry about my body; thank you. Now I am following the hospital's instructions, and I am just beginning to take insulin. I had taken diabetes pills for 15 years, but the doctor said that these pills damaged my heart, so I went to the hospital, took some heart medicine and now my heart is working correctly, so my body is no problem.

When I was in the hospital, many of the doctors were interested in meditation. My doctors suggested that I try meditation so that my heart would get better quickly, so I did. When I first went to the hospital my heart was not beating in a regular way. This problem usually takes two or three months to fix. But I meditated, so it took only one week to fix, and the doctors were very surprised and happy. They said that now many doctors like meditation because it can help to fix your body. Several doctors wanted to learn more about meditation, so they arranged to come to my room and I taught them a little about Zen.

I told them that "fixing your body" meditation is a kind of concentration yoga meditation, but it is not correct meditation. This kind of yoga meditation lets your body rest and become strong. Some yogis only sit in a quiet place, breathing in and breathing out, and sometimes they live for 100 years for 1,000 years. It is possible to keep your body this long, but eventually it will die.

Correct meditation means freedom from life and death. Our true self has no life and no death. I said that if you attain your true self, then if you die in one hour, in one day or in one month, it is no problem. If you only do "fixing your body" meditation, your concern will only be with your body. But some day, when it's time for you to die, this meditation will not help you, so you will not believe in it. This means it is not correct meditation. If you do correct meditation, being sick sometimes is OK; suffering sometimes is OK; dying some day is OK. The Buddha said, "If you keep a clear mind moment to moment, you will get happiness everywhere."

How much do you believe in yourself? How much do you help other people? These are most important questions. Correct meditation helps you find your true way.

I told them I had asked the man in the bed next to me, "What is the purpose of your life?" He had a good job, a good family, a good wife, but these things could not help him. So he said, "Nothing." He understood "nothing" but his understanding could not help him, so he was suffering. Zen means to attain this nothing-mind.

How do you attain nothing mind? First you must ask, "What am I? What is the purpose of my life?" If you answer with words, this is only thinking. Maybe you say, "I am a doctor." But if you are with a patient and you are thinking, "I am a great doctor," you cannot perceive your patient's situation—you are caught in your thinking. Thinking is only understanding; like the man in the hospital you will find that understanding cannot help you. Then what? If you don't know, you must go straight—don't know.

Don't know mind cuts through thinking. It is before thinking. Before thinking there is no doctor, no patient; also no God, no

Buddha, no "I", no words—nothing at all. Then you and the universe become one. We call this nothing-mind, or primary point. Some people say this is God, or universal energy, or bliss, or extinction. But these are only teaching words, Nothing-mind is before words.

Zen is attaining nothing-mind, and using nothing-mind. How can you use it? Making nothing-mind into big-love-mind. Nothing action-for-all-people mind. This is possible. Nothing-mind neither appears nor disappears. If you do correct meditation, nothing-mind becomes strong and you perceive your situation clearly: what you see, hear, smell, taste and touch are the truth, without thinking. So your lmind is like a mirror. Then moment to moment you can keep your correct situation. When a doctor is with his patients, if he drops I-my-me and becomes one with them, then helping them is possible. When a doctor goes home and he is with his family, if he keeps a 100% his-family-mind, then understanding what is best for them is clear. Just like this. The blue mountain does not move. The white clouds float back and forth.

So, the doctors like Zen. Maybe they will try practicing!

I hope you only go straight-don't know, attain nothing-mind, use nothing-mind and save all beings from suffering.

Yours in the Dharma,

S. S.

Wherever he visted, although using slightly different words according to the situation, he always pointed to the need for keeping a "don't know" mind. Nowhere was this teaching encapsulated more clearly than in his "Three letters to a beginner," reprinted in *Dropping Ashes on the Buddha*.[82]

Seung Sahn Soen Sa always encouraged those who wanted to practice Zen to live in a Zen center with other students. He called this "washing the potatoes" practice:

Together action is like washing potatoes. When people wash potatoes in Korea, instead of washing them one at a time, they put them all in a tub full of water. Then someone puts a stick in the tub and pushes it up and down, up and down. This makes the potatoes rub against each other; as they bump into each other, the hard crusty dirt falls off. If you was potatoes one at a time, it takes a long time to clean each one, and only one potato gets clean at a time. If they are all together, the potatoes clean each other.[83]

Once when one of his students expressed concern that many people said they like Zen but do not want to practice, Seung Sahn Soen Sa remarked:

Many people like honey better than water. I think water is better than honey. Honey tastes good, but if you only eat honey, it is not good for you. It is possible to take much water, but only a little honey. Zen is very clear, simple and necessary like water. Every day you need water, and every day you need Zen, but most people prefer honey. Zen is clear, but not interesting to them. Most people have many desires, and Zen is cutting off desires, so people don't like this. Their whole life is only desire. If you practice Zen, then your life is only clear like water, with no taste, like water.

To another student who felt conflict between his Christian upbringing and his Zen practice, Seung Sahn Soen Sa said,

If you keep Don't Know mind, there are no opposites, so no Western, no Eastern, no American, no Korean, no Taoism, no Christianity, no Zen, no life, no death, no good, no bad, no name, no form, no God, no Buddha. That name is Primary Point. Primary Point is absolute. Everything is from Primary Point and returns to Primary Point. Then what is Primary Point? Primary Point's name is Don't Know. Don't Know mind is to cut off thinking To cut off all thinking is before thinking, no speech, no words.

How is one to keep this Don't Know mind? When a mother sends her son to war, even though she works, eats, talks to her friends and watches television, she always keeps in her mind the question, "When will my son come home?" Keeping Don't Know mind is the same. While working, while eating, while playing, while walking and driving, always keep the question, "What am I?"

By the summer of 1979, Providence Zen Center had moved from downtown Providence to a country-site in northern Rhode Island, where, amidst 50 acres of woods and ponds, an old nursing home was transformed into a practicing Zen community. Two brand-new meditation halls were added to the existing structure and in 1983 work started on a traditional Korean-style monastery. The work on the monastery was completed in 1985, and it became home and training center for traditional monks under Seung Sahn Soen Sa's guidance. The Diamond Hill Zen Monastery became the first and only place outside Korea to hold two three-month long retreats in a year. In a way, traditional Korean Zen had come home to America at the new monastery. Also in 1983, Seung Sahn Soen Sa started a new school under the name of Kwan Um Zen School to administratively bring together all the residential Zen centers and affiliate groups under his guidance, now numbering more than 50.

In the meantime, he had given Inka, the seal of approval for teaching kong-an practice, to some of his American students and these Master Dharma Teachers started leading retreats at the centers of Kwan Um Zen School. As Seung Sahn Soen Sa became more and more involved in teaching abroad, now including Brazil and Paris, the teaching responsibilities devolved more and more on the American Master Dharma Teachers. That process continues.

NOTES

[1] Hoover, *The Zen Experience*, p. 78.

[2] Buswell, *The Korean Approach to Zen*, p. 1.

[3] Providence Zen Center, *Daily Chanting Book*.

[4] Dumoulin, *History of Zen Buddhism*, p. 60.

[5] Hoover, *op. cit.*, p. 20.

[6] *Ibid.*, p. 131. This is a quote from Chang, Chung-yuan, *Original Teachings of Ch'an Buddhism.*

[7] This story is adapted from Zen Master Seung Sahn, *Dropping Ashes on the Buddha*, Stephen Mitchell, ed. pp. 60-61.

[8] *Ibid.*, pp. 61-63.

[9] Rhi, Ki-yong, *Wonhyo and His Thought*, Korea Journal, Vol. II (1971), No. 1, p. 7.

[10] Buswell, *op. cit.*, p. 7.

[11] Rhi, *op. cit.*

[12] Rhi, *op. cit.*, p. 6.

[13] Hong Jung-shik, "The Thought and Life of Wonhyo," *Buddhist Culture in Korea*, p. 29.

[14] Buswell, *op. cit.*,

[15] Zen Master Seung Sahn and Bernen, Rebecca, private translation at the Providence Zen Center.

[16] Adapted from Seo, Kyung-bo, *A Study of Korean Zen Buddhism*, p. 93.

[17] *Ibid.*, p. 170.

[18] Adapted from *Ibid.* p. 174.

[19] *Ibid.*, p. 113.

[20] *Ibid.*, p. 123.

[21] *Ibid.*, p. 140.

[22] *Ibid.*, p. 146.

[23] These stories are adapted from *Ibid.*, pp. 151-52.

[24] Hoover, *op. cit.*, p. 133. This is a quote from Hu Shih, *Ch'an Buddhism in China.*

[25] Seo, Kyung-bo, *op. cit.*, p. 154.

[26] *Ibid.*, pp. 197-98.

[27] Lee, Ki-baik, *A New History of Korea*, p. 132.

[28] Buswell, *op. cit.*, p. 16.

[29] *Ibid.*, p. 21.

[30] *Ibid.*, p. 23.

[31] *Ibid.*, p. 24.

[32.] *Ibid.*, p. 25.

[33] *Ibid.*, p. 26-27.

[34] *Ibid.*, p. 28.

[35] *Ibid.*, p. 33.

[36] *Ibid.*, pp. 140-159.

[37] Seo, *op. cit.*, p. 329.

[38] *Ibid.*, p. 328.

[39] *Ibid.*, p. 100.

[40] *Ibid.*, p. 101.

[41] *Ibid.*, p. 126.

[42] *Ibid.*, p. 127.

[43] *Ibid.*, p. 128.

[44] *Ibid.*, p. 116.

[45] Bernen, *Sosan Taesa and His Handbook for Zen Students*, p. 40.

[46] Seo, *op. cit.*, p. 116.

[47] *Ibid...*, p. 129.

[48] *Ibid.*, p. 103.

[49] *Ibid.*, p. 130.

[50] *Ibid.*, p. 338.

[51] *Ibid.*, p. 340.

[52] Bernen, *op. cit.*, p. 15.

[53] *Ibid.*, p. 17.

[54] *Ibid.*, p. 20. This is a quote from Keel, Hee Sung, *Chinul, the Founder of Korean Son (Zen) Tradition.*

[55] Seo, *op. cit.*, p. 344.

[56] *Ibid.*, p. 345.

[57] Bernen, *op. cit.*, p. 24. This is a quote from Kim, *Yong-t'ae Han-guk munhwasa taegye.*

[58] Seo, *op. cit.*, p. 345.

[59] *Ibid.*, p. 347.

[60] Bernen, *op. cit.*, p.25.

[61] This translation is adapted from Rebecca Bernen's unpublished thesis at Harvard University, *op. cit.*, 1978. Reprinted by permission of the translator.

[62] *Ibid.*, p. 92. This is a quote from Yi Sang-baek, *Han'guk sa: kunse chon'gi p'yon.*

[63] These stories are adapted from Seo, *op. cit.*, pp. 352-53.

[64] This story is adapted from Seung Sahn, *Dropping Ashes on the Buddha*, Stephen Mitchell, ed., pp. 146-47.

[65] Seo, *op. cit.*, p. 365.

[66] Seung Sahn, *op. cit.*, p. 148.

[67] Sok Do-ryun, *Korea Journal*, February 1, 1965, p. 31.

[68] Chun, Myung-suk, Private translation at Providence Zen Center.

[69] The stories on these pages are adapted from Seung Sahn, *op. cit.*, pp. 163-66.

[70] *Spring Wind, Women and Buddhism*, Vol. 6, nos. 1-3, pp. 354-55.

[71] These stories have been translated privately at the Providence Zen Center.

[72] Seo, *op. cit.*, p. 399.

[73] Sok Do-ryun, *Korea Journal*, April 1, 1965, p. 20.

[74] Seo, *op. cit.*, p. 400.

[75] *Ibid.*, p. 371.

[76] The stories here are from *Ibid.*, pp. 372-74.

77 Sok Do-ryun, *Korea Journal*, April 1, 1965, p. 18.

78 *Ibid.*, pp. 18-19.

79 Seo, *op cit.*, p. 405.

80 Kusan Sunim, *The Way of Korean Zen*, Stephen Batchelor, ed., p. 50.

81 Seung Sahn, *Only Don't Know*, pp. 3-6.

82 Seung Sahn, *Dropping Ashes on the Buddha*, pp. 12-19.

83 Seung Sahn, *Only Don't Know*, pp. 126-128.

Glossary

Avatamsaka School: Known as the *Hua-yen* school in China, *Kegon* school in Japan, and *Hwa-om* school in Korea, it follows the *Avatamsaka (Flower Garland) Sutra* as its basic text. This sutra is a monumental work and is considered by scholars to be the greatest achievement of Mahayana Buddhist scholarship and cosmology.

Bodhisattva (Sanskrit): *Bodhi* means perfect wisdom or *prajña*, and *sattva* means a being whose actions promote unity or harmony. One who vows to postpone the still bliss of Enlightenment in order to help all sentient beings realize their own liberation; one who seeks Enlightenment not only for himself but for others. The Bodhisattva ideal is at the heart of Mahayana and Zen Buddhism.

Bone-rank (Korean: Kolp'um): A system of centralized aristocracy adopted by the ancient kingdom of Silla. This system conferred or withheld a variety of special privileges, ranging from political preferment to aspects of everyday life, in accordance with the degree of respect due a person's 'bone-rank' or bloodline. Based on maternal lineage and involving many layers, it specified, for instance, that only persons of the *True Bone rank*, which included members of the Kim royal house, could occupy the throne or top military positions in Silla.

Buddha-nature: That which all sentient beings share and manifest through their particular form. According to the Zen school of Buddhism, the Buddha said that all things have Buddha-nature and therefore have the innate potential to become Buddha.

Dharani (Sanskrit): A long, mystical chant supposed to have innate power to induce various kinds of insights or magical powers.

Dharma combat: A spontaneous exchange between two monks or a teacher and student to test the level of insight of the other. Most of the stories in the traditional kong-an collections, such as *Blue Cliff Record* and *Mu Mun Kwan*, are examples of a Dharma combat.

Dhyana (Sanskrit): Literally, "concentration" or "paying attention," a unified state of absorption. "Ch'an" is the Chinese transliteration, or pronunciation, of dhyana.

Five Precepts: To abstain from: (1) taking life; (2) taking what is not given; (3) misconduct done in lust; (4) lying; (5) intoxicants taken to induce heedlessness.

Geomancy: A system of "wind water geography." In the Korean and Chinese belief-system, all places, especially in the mountains, have their own energy—negative or positive. A good geomancer can determine the nature of the energy of a place in accordance with the lay of the land. In Korea this system was used for selecting sites for temples or a sumptuous residence. At times it degenerated into rites of divination by Buddhist priests.

Great Courage: In the Zen tradition, the effort to persist in one's practice in the face of all intellectual, emotional and physical difficulties.

Great Doubt: Not perplexity, but a spirit of inquiry or a sense of wonder about the full significance of the teachings of the Buddha and the Ancestors which one has not yet personally experienced.

Great Faith: A basic belief in Zen that the insight achieved by the Buddha and the Ancestors is universally valid and possible for everyone to achieve.

Hwadu (Korean), Hut-t'ou (Chinese): Literally, "head" or "apex" of speech. It is the essential point in a kong-an story and is used as a topic of meditation in the Korean Zen tradition. While the kong-an is a description of the entire situation, the *hwadu* is the central point of the exchange. (See *Im-oo-koo*, for example.)

Hwarang-do (Korean): Literally, "the Way of the Flower Knights." These were the elite military units formed during the Three Kingdoms period which supplied the future military and political leadership within each of the three kingdoms. Buddhism provided the ethical framework to guide the military and social conduct of these young warriors. An echo of the *Hwarang* may be found in the Samurai warriors in medieval Japan.

Im-oo-koo (Korean): Literally, "What is this?' This is the *hwadu* given most often to beginning Zen students in Korea. It comes from an exchange between Hui-neng (638-713), the Sixth Patriarch of Zen, and his future successor, Huai-jang (677-744). When the latter arrived at Hui-neng's temple, the Patriarch asked him where he came from. Huai-jang said he came from Sung shan mountain. Hui-neng asked him, "What is this thing that has come here?" Huai-jang said, "To say that it is a thing is to miss the point altogether." Hui-neng asked again, "Can it still be cultivated and verified?" Huai-jang replied, "I would not say that there is no more cultivation and verification; only it can never be contaminated." The patriarch was extremely delighted and exclaimed, "Just this non-contamination is what all the Buddhas have been careful to preserve. As it is for you, so it is for me."

Inka (Korean): A certification by a Zen teacher of a student's completion or breakthrough in his or her kong-an practice.

Karma (Sanskrit): Karma means "cause and effect," and the continuing process of action and reaction, accounting for the interpenetration of all phenomena. Thus our present thoughts, actions and situations are the result of what we have done in the past, and our future thoughts, actions and situations will be the result of what we are doing now. All individual karma results from this process.

Kido (Korean): Literally, "energy way;" a chanting retreat.

Kong-an (Korean), Kung-an (Chinese), Koan (Japanese): Literally, "a public notice issued by the government." In Zen practice, kong-ans are the recorded sayings, actions or dialogues of Zen masters with their students or with other Zen masters. They are the core of Zen teaching literature. As a teaching tool, they are used by the teacher to test the intuitive clarity of a student's mind or to bring a student to a state of realization. There are approximately 1,700 traditional kong-ans.

Kwan Seum Bosal (Korean), Avalokitesvara (Sanskrit), Kwan Yin (Chinese), Kwan Um (Korean), Kannon, Kanzeon (Japanese): Literally, "One Who Hears the Cries of the World" and responds with compassionate aid, the Bodhisattva of Compassion.

Mandala (Sanskrit): Literally, a "chart" of the universe. In abstract terms it refers to the overall order and interweaving pattern of the cosmos. In graphic terms, it is used by some Buddhist sects, especially the Tibetan schools, in the form of an intricately drawn chart or a painting as a visualization aid in meditation.

Mantra (Sanskrit): Sounds or words used in meditation to cut through discriminating thoughts so that the mind can become clear; in some practices, mantra is used to induce various kinds of insight.

Moktak (Korean), Mokugyo (Japanese): A hollow, fish-shaped wooden instrument used as a drum to maintain the rhythm during chanting.

Noumenon: The Unconditioned. The absolute state of undifferentiation and thoughtlessness reached in a state of deep *samadhi*.

Its characteristics are complete calmness, detachment, and an erasure of any distinction between subject and object.

Roshi (Japanese): "Venerable (spiritual) teacher", a Zen master.

Samadhi (Sanskrit): A state of intense concentration. See "noumenon."

Sarira (Sanskrit): Literally, a "body." In Korean Buddhism, it refers to small crystals of varying sizes and colors that are sometimes found among the cremated remains of monks and other meditation practitioners. They are said to be an indication of spiritual maturity and are often enshrined and worshipped as sacred relics.

Soen Sa Nim (Korean): "Honored" Zen teacher, a Zen master.

Sunim (Korean): "Venerable", a monk or a nun.

Transmission: In Zen tradition, the handing over of the "Mind Seal" or the imparting of "Mind-to-Mind" communication between a Zen master to a student, confirming the student's qualification to be a holder of that particular lineage. Usually there is a public ceremony to mark the occasion.

Zazen (Japanese): Refers both to the specific physical posture used by Zen students during sitting meditation as well as to remaining focused on one's practice even while engaged in all activities of everyday life. Zazen means "sitting zen," and is a derivative from Chinese Ch'an which in turn is derived from Sanskrit Dhyana.

Bibliography

Bernen, Rebecca, trans. *Sosan Taesa and his Handbook for Zen Students.* Unpublished Thesis, Harvard University, 1978.

Buddhist Culture in Korea. International Cultural Foundation, ed. Seoul: Si-sa-yong-sa Publishers, 1982.

Buswell, Robert E. Jr., trans. *The Korean Approach to Zen: The Collected Works of Chinul.* Honolulu: University of Hawaii Press, 1983.

Chang, Chung-yuan, trans. *Original Teachings of Ch'an Buddhism: Selected from the Transmission of the Lamp.* New York: Random House, 1969.

Cleary, Christopher, trans. *Swampland Flowers: The Letters and Lectures of Zen Master Ta Hui.* New York: Grove Press, 1977.

Dumoulin, Heinrich. *A History of Zen Buddhism.* Paul Peachy, trans. Boston: Beacon Press, 1969.

Hoover, Thomas. *The Zen Experience.* New York: New American Library, 1980.

Ko Ik-Chin. "Wonhyo and the foundation of Korean Buddhism." *Korea Journal.* Vol. 21 (1981) No. 8, pp. 4-13.

Kusan Sunim. *The Way of Korean Zen.* Martine Fages, trans. Stephen Batchelor, ed. New York: John Weatherhill, 1985.

Lee, Ki-baik. *A New History of Korea*. Edward W. Wagner and Edward J. Shultz, trans. Seoul: Ilchokak Publishers, 1984.

Rhi Ki-yong. "Wonhyo and his Thought." *Korea Journal*. Vol. 11 (1971) No. 1, pp. 4-9.

Samguk Yusa: Legends and History of the Three Kingdoms of Ancient Korea. Grafton K. Mintz and Tae-Hung Ha, trans. Seoul: Yonsei University Press, 1972.

Seo Kyung-bo. *A Study of Korean Zen Buddhism Approached through the Chodangjip*. Seoul: private publication, dates unknown.

Seung Sahn. *Dropping Ashes on the Buddha: The Teaching of Zen Master Seung Sahn*. Stephen Mitchell, ed. New York: Grove Press, 1976.

_____. *Only Don't Know: The Teaching Letters of Zen Master Seung Sahn*. San Francisco: Four Seasons Foundation, 1982.

Sim Chae-ryong. "Son Buddhist Tradition in Korea: as represented by Chinul's Pojo Son." *Korea Journal*. Vol. 21 (1981) No. 8, pp. 14-28.

Sok Do-ryun. "Modern Son Buddhism in Korea." 3 pts. *Korea Journal*. Vol. 5 (1965). Nos. 1, 2, and 4, pp. 26-30, 27-32, and 17-22.

"Women and Buddhism." *Spring Wind*. Vol. 6 (1986) Nos. 1, 2, and 3, Zen Lotus Society, Toronto, Canada.

Wu, John C. *The Golden Age of Zen*. Taipei: United Publishing Center, 1975.

INDEX

About the Author

Mu Soeng Sunim is the Abbot of the Diamond Hill Zen Monastery near Providence, Rhode Island. He is a long-time student of the Korean Zen tradition, ordained a monk by Zen Master Seung Sahn.

Parallax Press publishes books and tapes on Buddhism and related subjects to make them accessible and alive for contemporary readers. It is our hope that doing so can help alleviate suffering and create a more peaceful world. Recent titles include *Being Peace*, by Thich Nhat Hanh, *The Return of Lady Brace*, by Nancy Wilson Ross, and *The Path of Compassion: Contemporary Writings on Engaged Buddhism*, compiled by the Buddhist Peace Fellowship. For a catalogue or further information, please write to:

Parallax Press
P.O. Box 7355
Berkeley, California 94707

This book was designed and typeset on an Apple Macintosh computer, using Microsoft Word. The typeface is 10 point Goudy Old Style, adapted for the LaserWriter by Judith Sutcliffe.